WORLD TRADE AFTER THE URUGUAY ROUND

The completion of the Uruguay Round promised a new era in international trading relations. However, there remain a wide range of issues which could threaten international trading stability, including regionalisation and regionalism, increases in non-tariff forms of protection, and the proliferation of unilateral and bilateral trade deals.

This volume assesses both the immediate impact of the GATT deal and the future of the world trading system. It concludes with an assessment of the long-term possibilities for creating a mutually beneficial world economic system.

Harald Sander is Associate Professor of Economics at Maastricht School of Management and has been affiliated with the Institute for Development and Peace, University of Duisburg and the Institute for Development Theory and Development Policy, University of Bochum. His research and publications cover the international and macroeconomic aspects of global financial and trade developments with special reference to developing countries.

András Inotai is General Director of the Institute for World Economics in Budapest, Hungary. He has also worked for the World Bank's Trade Policy Division. Among his major fields of research are the issues of economic integration of Central and Eastern Europe into the European Union and the world economy, and the reform of the Hungarian economic policy.

The Development and Peace Foundation was set up in 1986, on the initiative of Willy Brandt, with the aim of highlighting the links between development and peace and of encouraging appropriate political initiatives. It seeks to foster understanding and equity between peoples and states, to facilitate cooperations and development, and to improve awareness of global interconnections in the developed world and beyond.

The Foundation regularly commissions authors to write books about issues which are in keeping with their objectives.

ROUTLEDGE STUDIES IN THE MODERN WORLD ECONOMY

WORLD TRADE AFTER THE URUGUAY ROUND

Prospects and policy options for the
twenty-first century

*Edited by Harald Sander
and András Inotai*

A Development and Peace
Foundation Book

London and New York

First published 1996
by Routledge
11 New Fetter Lane, London EC4P 4EE

Simultaneously published in the USA and Canada
by Routledge
29 West 35th Street, New York, NY 10001

Reprinted 1997, 1998

Typeset in Garamond by
Florencetype Ltd, Stoodleigh, Nr. Tiverton, Devon
Printed and bound in Great Britain by
Intype London Ltd

A project of the Development and Peace Foundation in cooperation
with the Institute for Development and Peace.

British Library Cataloguing in Publication Data
A catalogue record for this book is available from the British Library

Library of Congress Cataloguing in Publication Data
World trade after the Uruguay Round: prospects and policy options for
the twenty-first century / edited by Harald Sander and András Inotai.
p. cm. – (Routledge studies in the modern world economy.
ISSN 1359–7965: 2)
"A Development and Peace Foundation book."
Includes bibliographical references and index.
ISBN 0–415–13736–5 (alk. paper)
1. Uruguay Round (1987–)   2. Commercial policy.   3. International
trade.   4. International trade – Forecasting.   I. Sander, Harald.
II. Inotai, András.   III. Series.
HF1721.W6596   1996
382'.3 – dc20   95–37225
CIP

ISBN 0–415–13736–5

CONTENTS

CONTENTS

CONTRIBUTORS

Fritz Franzmeyer is Head of the Department for International Economics at the Deutsches Institut für Wirtschaftsforschung (DIW) in Berlin and specialises in international trade and trade policy issues. He regularly contributes the chapter on Trade to the Development and Peace Foundation's *Global Trends. The World Almanac of Development and Peace*.

Murray Gibbs is Chief of the Systemic Issues Section of UNCTAD. Most recently, he was responsible for the assessment of the outcome of the Uruguay Round contained in the UNCTAD *Trade and Development Report 1994* and its supporting papers, and for the execution of projects to assist China and Russia in their process of accession to the World Trade Organization (WTO).

Harald Grossmann is staff member of the Hamburg Institute for Economic Research (HWWA). He specialises in the field of international trade and competition. Among his recent publications are articles on social standards in international trade and the World Trade Organization in *Intereconomics*.

Arthur J. Hanson is President and CEO of the International Institute for Sustainable Development (IISD) in Winnipeg, Canada. He was Professor and Director of the School for Resource and Environmental Studies at Dalhousie University in Halifax, Canada. He was also member of the IISD International Working Group that developed the *Trade and Sustainable Development Principles* in 1994.

Adrian Hewitt is Deputy Director of the Overseas Development Institute, London, and Research Advisor to the All Party Parliamentary Group on Overseas Development in the British Parliament. His research work covers Europe's relations with developing countries as well as other areas and policies. He is also co-editor of *Developing Policy Review* and on the editorial board of the *Third World Quarterly*. His latest book is entitled *Crisis or Transition in Foreign Aid*.

TABLES

CONTRIBUTORS

András Inotai is General Director of the Institute for World Economics in Budapest, Hungary. He has also worked for the World Bank's Trade Policy Division. Among his major fields of research are the issues of economic integration of Central and Eastern Europe into the European Union and the world economy, and the reform of the Hungarian economic policy.

Judit Kiss is Senior Research Fellow at the Institute for World Economics and Research Director of the Centre for Development Studies, both in Budapest, Hungary. Her major fields of research are issues in economic development and agriculture. Recently she worked intensively on the world agricultural system and the Uruguay Round of the GATT.

Antonique Koning is Research Fellow working jointly for the Overseas Development Institute in London and the European Centre for Development Policy Management (ECDPM) in Maastricht, the Netherlands. Her research covers European development policy, including trade and aid relations between the European Union and developing countries. She is co-author of the book *Europe's Preferred Partners? The Lomé Countries in World Trade*.

Georg Koopmann is staff member of the Hamburg Institute for Economic Research (HWWA). He specialises in the field of international trade and competition. Among his recent publications are articles on social standards in international trade and the World Trade Organization in *Intereconomics*.

Harald Sander is Associate Professor of Economics at Maastricht School of Management and has been affiliated with the Institute for Development and Peace, University of Duisburg and the Institute for Development Theory and Development Policy, University of Bochum. His research and publications cover the international and macroeconomic aspects of global financial and trade developments with special reference to developing countries.

Jeffrey J. Schott is Senior Fellow at the Institute for International Economics in Washington DC. He has worked and published extensively on international trade and trade policy issues as well as on other areas. Among his most recent publications is *The Uruguay Round: An Assessment*.

Nevin Shaw is a former Canadian trade negotiator. He represented Canada in the negotiations which led to the Canada–US Free Trade Agreement, the North American Free Trade Agreement (NAFTA) and the World Trade Organization (WTO). He has also been involved in Canadian competition and foreign investment policies and negotiations. Most recently he has been associated with the International Institute for Sustainable Development, Winnipeg, Canada, as Executive Interchange Fellow.

Christopher Stevens is on the staff of the Institute of Development Studies (IDS) at the University of Sussex. His principal research interests are the impact of EU economic policies on the Third World and the external dimension of food security in developing countries. He has been a consultant to the World Bank, the EC Commission, UNCTAD and various other supranational institutions, and has written extensively on the impact on developing countries of the European single market, the GATT round and preferential trade agreements.

ACKNOWLEDGEMENTS

We wish to thank the United Nations Publications Board for permission to reproduce 'The Uruguay Round of Multilateral Trade Negotiations: A Preliminary Assessment of Results' by the UN Department of Economic and Social Information and Policy Analysis, taken from the *World Economic and Social Survey 1994*, and the Institute for International Economics for permission to reproduce extracts from *The Uruguay Round: An Assessment*, by Jeffrey J. Schott.

INTRODUCTION

Harald Sander and András Inotai

It took the Uruguay Round of the General Agreement on Tariffs and Trade (GATT) more than seven years to finish its ambitious agenda – at least in part. The Round started in September 1986 in Uruguay with the Punta del Este Ministerial Declaration and was terminated in December 1993, about three years behind schedule. It was the longest and most comprehensive round of those periodic multilateral trade negotiations required by the GATT after the first agreement was signed by twenty-three signatory states in 1947. In the Uruguay Round negotiations 117 countries participated of which 88 were developing countries. The agreement came into effect on 1 January 1995 and established the World Trade Organization (WTO) which succeeds on a more comprehensive base what was formerly known as the GATT.

The Uruguay Round (UR) agenda was indeed very ambitious. Next to the traditional goal of GATT-sponsored rounds – to improve market access by negotiating multilateral tariff reductions – it aimed at a roll-back of non-tariff barriers to trade which started mushrooming right after the completion of the preceding Tokyo Round (1973–9) and at strengthening a non-discriminatory world trading system by bringing a wider array of issues under effective multilateral disciplines. Formerly exempted sectors, like textiles, agriculture and services are now included in the new agreements. 'New issues', such as trade-related intellectual property rights (TRIPs) and trade-related investment measures (TRIMs) have also been brought under the umbrella of multilateral trade negotiations.

It is interesting to note how these often very detailed negotiations have attracted the attention not only of policy-makers, academics concerned and directly affected groups, but also received the interest of a broad public, including non-governmental organisations active in the fields of development and environmental protection, with the latter actively following the negotiations and often making strong lobbying efforts. Moreover, a number of self-styled trade experts raised their voices, either announcing the imminent breakdown and fragmentation of the world economic system because the GATT will ultimately die, or issuing dark prophecies that a successful completion of the UR will lead to a world of unconstrained profit seeking which

1

would finally destroy human and social achievements and lead to environmental disasters on a worldwide scale.

To be sure, there are threats to the multilateral system of the GATT, and there are potentially dangerous conflicts between human and ecological imperatives on the one hand and the world trading system on the other. But these problems cannot be addressed properly either by joining the choirs of those singing siren songs or by intoning the gospel of totally unregulated trade. This volume aims to add rationality to the debate and to provide some ideas for the future development of the world trading system in a direction that is capable of reconciling the imperative of economic efficiency with the needs and aspirations of the people for a just and sustainable development.

To this end, the Development and Peace Foundation invited internationally renowned experts to contribute to this book. Part I reviews the issues, results and consequences of the UR against the background of a changing world trading environment. Part II is devoted to an exploration of the perspectives and policy options for the world trading system such as the future role of the WTO, the issues of social and environmental standards in international trade, the integration of Eastern Europe into the world trading system, and the future representation of developing countries in the international system.

In Chapter 1, **Harald Sander** reviews the recent threats to multilateralism that have been decisive for the problems faced within the UR and which will most likely continue to constitute future challenges for the world trading system: the rise in non-tariff protectionism, the new regionalism and the challenges emanating from the globalisation of finance, trade and production. The new protectionism and the new regionalism – the latter visible in the proliferation of new trading blocs and the extension of existing ones – both threaten the principle of multilateralism which is based on the principle of non-discrimination. Non-tariff protectionist measures, such as, for example, voluntary export restraints, which have mushroomed since the early 1980s, are directly targeted at certain (successful) exporters whose activities are perceived as a threat to a particular domestic industry. They constitute a double challenge to the GATT system as they are inherently discriminatory by introducing differential treatment, and since they are violating the principle of a rule-based trading system. The new regionalism is equally discriminatory by nature, but the evaluation of its effects is more controversial. While regional free trade areas can contribute to a more rational division of labour, they also have the potential to discriminate against non-members of the regional club and can thereby lead to a fragmentation of the world economy with negative consequences for global economic efficiency. Whether or not regional blocs will act as building blocks or stumbling blocks for the multilateral trade system, however, depends to a large extent on their behaviour, which – according to the author – will ultimately be influenced by the willingness and ability of those blocs (and their member countries) to resolve their unemployment problems by means other than discriminatory trade policies. As the globalisation of finance, trade and production (e.g. the surge in international cross-border investments and the advent of an emerging international integrated production system) tends to increase perceived insecurity and vulnerability, it may contribute to a rise in protectionism and (reactive) regionalism. However, it is clear that for these particular reasons the multilateral system has to respond to the challenges emanating from globalisation and to address the new issues involved, like those of beyond-the-border, national and/or regional policies, measures to attract cross-border investments which entail the twofold risk of unhealthy competition for production locations and the subsequent exclusion of disadvantaged regions, the risk of another wave of a new protectionism in response to the adjustment costs arising from globalisation, probably in the form of alleged anti-dumping cases and a protectionist misuse of environmental and social provisions. In the author's view a combination of national/regional policies and multilateral approaches is needed for a rational reaction to the challenges of globalisation in order to reconcile the imperatives of economic efficiency and human development.

Chapter 2, provided by the **United Nations Department of Economic and Social Information and Policy Analysis**, gives the reader a short overview of the major results of the UR negotiations. It covers specifically the results in market access negotiations, in the sectoral agreements on textiles, agriculture and services, it reviews how the new issues like TRIPs and TRIMs have been integrated into the multilateral system, and it outlines how the major multilateral disciplines of the GATT have been altered. Furthermore, quantitative studies of the impact of the UR on world trade and income are inspected and some caution is raised about the validity of the numbers given, as they typically ignore whole sectors, like services, and do not examine dynamic adjustments taking place in response to changing trading conditions. Moreover, the positive aspects of increased confidence after the conclusion of the round are virtually non-quantifiable. Nevertheless, the quantification efforts have some value, especially with regard to the likely distribution of the benefits from multilateral liberalisation to countries and regions, issues which are discussed in more detail in Chapters 3, 4 and 5. While the overall assessment of the UR in Chapter 2 is positive, it raises some caution that unilateral actions by industrial countries may continue. Furthermore, it reasons that the temptation to react to competition from cheap-labour countries by coupling the issues of social and environmental standards with market access concessions for protectionist purposes is a matter of concern. Therefore, the chapter stresses the important fact that a 'GATT/WTO programme is drawn up including items on trade, labour standards, competition policies, investment rules, finance/exchange rate policies, and environment, as well as sustainable development' – issues which may become of dominant importance for the future agenda of trade negotiations.

Chapters 3, 4 and 5 scrutinise in more detail the consequences of the UR for major country groupings.

In Chapter 3, **Fritz Franzmeyer** examines the expected impact of the agreement on Organization for Economic Cooperation and Development (OECD) countries. Starting with the observation that OECD countries are responsible for three-quarters of all world trade (despite the fact that newly industrialising countries (NICs) have increased their share) and that only one third of this OECD internal trade is subject to most favoured nation (MFN) duties under the GATT because of more far-reaching rules within the various trading blocs, Franzmeyer identifies three major areas where OECD countries will be affected by the UR agreements: (i) trade relations within the Triad; (ii) OECD trade with developing countries; (iii) the impact of horizontal measures, like the new rules on dispute settlement mechanisms, safeguards, anti-dumping procedures and so forth. With regard to trade within the Triad, Franzmeyer notes that although MFN tariffs on manufactures will be reduced by an average of one third, this is less impressive once it is realised that those tariffs have already been very low, and that the problem of informal trade barriers (the 'Japan problem') has not been solved on a multilateral base. But also in other sectors Franzmeyer is sceptical of the effective results. The progress in bringing down trade barriers in non-tropical agricultural products may be slowed down if the conversion of non-tariff barriers into tariffs results in a somewhat inflated 'dirty tariffication', not to mention remaining loopholes in the fields of agriculture and – in particular – in public procurement.

As far as OECD trade with developing countries is concerned, the author notes that much of this is still governed within the framework of preferential agreements, either of the regional variety, under the Generalised System of Preferences (GSP), or under the Lomé Agreements with the African, Caribbean and Pacific (ACP) countries. Due to this reason, the removal of quantitative restrictions such as the Multifibre Arrangement, not MFN tariff cuts, will stimulate OECD imports. But this may occur very late as the removal of barriers on especially sensible products can be postponed to the very final phase in the year 2005. Franzmeyer therefore expects that most changes will come from the third area, the horizontal measures. While in the short run OECD imports from developing countries are likely to increase because the horizontal measures partly strengthen their position, in the longer run a recourse on anti-dumping/anti-subsidy tariffs remains a threat to developing countries. The agreements on intellectual property rights will probably increase import prices for OECD countries as the licensing cost will be marked up on product prices, thus leading to less imports and more service exports (licence fees). In the longer run, it can be expected that a positive effect on the rate of innovation may occur. Franzmeyer concludes that while the expected growth effects of the UR will undoubtedly create jobs, the structural change involved will destroy jobs, especially in the low-skilled segment of the labour market. Overall, job losses may be relatively small.

Franzmeyer therefore suggests that the additional income generated by productivity increases through trade liberalisation should be used for shortening working time, improving the level of the 'human capital stock' to support a structural change towards more labour-intensive, high-quality services, and to accompany the trade liberalisation offensive by 'an equally decisive educational offensive'.

In Chapter 4, **Christopher Stevens** looks more closely at the other side of the story. His account of the consequences of the UR for developing countries starts with the general warning that this is a 'slippery subject', for three reasons. First, the UR has carried substantial intellectual (i.e. technical, theoretical and even ideological) baggage. Second, the agreement is a formidable document, difficult to digest and assess in all its details. Third, there is always the remaining and considerable uncertainty as to what extent what is written on paper will be implemented in that very spirit.

In his analysis, Stevens points to the active participation of developing countries in the UR – a novel and important feature. Three reasons are given for this: first, the non-tariff protectionism by industrial countries which, second, was sought to be brought back under multilateral disciplines, and finally, because the traditional protectionist stance of many developing countries has given way to greater openness, sometimes voluntarily, sometimes under pressure from the Bretton Woods organisations. In a way, it may be said that the developing countries accepted the higher cost of importing technologies and knowledge-intensive goods as an outcome of the TRIPs agreement for the virtues of a better and more secure market access for their export goods, especially in textiles, agricultural goods and some other labour-intensive manufactures. With respect to manufactures, Stevens notes the reduction of the average level of MFN tariffs and the phasing out of the Multifibre Arrangement (MFA) by the year 2005. The higher security in market access is acknowledged, but the author remains sceptical regarding the remaining protectionism of the non-tariff variety, such as misapplied anti-dumping regulations and safeguard clauses which – according to Stevens – have been altered in a way that they can be applied selectively, probably against successful developing country exporters of 'sensible' products.

As far as temperate agriculture is concerned, three issues stand out. First, increased market access through 'tariffication' of the current quota system which – according to the author – will not result in 'substantial liberalisation'. Second, the danger of a surge in food prices, negatively affecting net food importers, especially in Africa. Third, the impact on the development of the agricultural sector in the South. Stevens' overall conclusion is that next to the expectation that middle-income countries are likely to gain modestly, but not insignificantly, and that the African situation deserves special concern, the UR is only one factor which affects world trade. Rather, it is the place of African countries in the world trading system that constitutes the problem. Surely, the UR limited the concept of special and differential treatment of developing countries more than before, but according to Stevens this does not mean that the new agreement will force unwilling governments to dismantle import controls. Overall, developing countries are today more dependent on a more stable trading environment under multilateral disciplines that help to retain a new protectionist wave. It is in this respect that Stevens concludes that developing countries' interests are at stake and need to be defended.

In many respects the GATT is subsidiary to more far-reaching regulations, mainly because regional trading blocs set their own rules both inside and outside their territory. The EU policy towards what was earlier the Eastern trading bloc and towards a selection of countries in Africa, the Caribbean and the Pacific region, the so-called ACP countries, are the most relevant examples. While the 'countries in transition' still have to find their new place in the world trading system, the position of the ACP countries is more obvious as they indeed fear to undergo a 'preference erosion'. Because their trade with the EU is on preferential terms, a lowering of trade barriers on an MFN level also lowers their relatively more favourable treatment.

Chapter 5 on the survival of special preferences under the Lomé Convention, provided by **Adrian Hewitt** and **Antonique Koning**, scrutinises this issue. Preferences that violate the most favoured nation principle and discriminate against other developing countries have traditionally been seen as a mechanism at least to assist the industrialisation and diversification process of the favoured economies. The authors start by giving a number of indications of 'what prevented ACP countries from taking full advantage of the provisions'. They note that expectations should not be too ambitious as the share of ACP exports which enter the European market with a significant preferential margin *vis-à-vis* other suppliers is rather small. Furthermore, making use of preferences requires diversification into products where the preferential margins are high. While some countries succeeded in doing so, this cannot be attributed solely to the Lomé provisions as they are neither a necessary nor sufficient condition for developing a dynamic export sector. The whole array of structural, capacity and procedural reasons may have prevented most ACP countries from exploiting the preferences. Additionally, the Lomé provisions require adherence to the rules of origin. Therefore they can act as a disincentive to integrating efficiently into the division of labour accompanying the process of globalisation.

Given these problems, will the ACP win or lose from the Uruguay settlements? According to the authors, four areas are important to answer this question. First, the erosion of preferences, second, the changes in agricultural trade, third, the phasing-out of the MFA and, fourth, the global liberalisation of trade in services. In total, the authors expect a negative, though small impact on ACP export earnings, but acknowledge better market access to other than EU markets, as well as the more secure market access. For the survival of the Lomé preferences the authors see certain threats in the medium-term future. In the meantime and according to the authors' view, ACP countries should actively seek to exploit market access to the EU more intensely, and the EU could help by removing some of the remaining obstacles for ACP countries, such as too restrictive rules of origin, and improving the coherence of its trade and aid provisions. At the same time, however, the ACP countries need to diversify both the structure and the destination of their exports and to make trade a real priority.

The chapters presented in Part II examine more closely the perspectives for the world trading system after the Uruguay Round with special reference to the new issues arising.

In Chapter 6, **Jeffrey J. Schott** elaborates on the future role of the new World Trade Organization (WTO). In his view, the most significant aspect of the WTO agreement is its 'single undertaking', that is that GATT members must adhere not only to the GATT rules, but also to the broad range of trade pacts which have been negotiated under GATT auspices during the past two decades. This implies little change for many developed countries that are signatories of those pacts, but demands much from developing countries. This new institutional structure facilitates not only further trade negotiations, but also talks on new areas, like General Agreement on Trade in Services (GATS), TRIPs and other issues (such as the interface between trade and environment) under the umbrella of the WTO.

While Schott is sure that the UR 'made great strides in strengthening the multilateral trading system', he identifies four major challenges that need to be addressed in the future. First, the UR needs to be completed in the sense that unresolved problems have to be tackled, like the negotiations on financial services and that new negotiations have to be launched to build on the results of the UR. Second, the WTO has to react, in one way or another, to the pressures to deal with an increasingly broad array of issues which have traditionally not been on the agenda of trade negotiations, like labour and environmental standards, a 'GATT for investment', the harmonisation of competition policies. Third, the WTO should accommodate for negotiations between regional trading areas and close the loopholes in the trading rules to ensure that regional trading blocs do not undermine the multilateral trading system. The challenge the WTO is facing here is to act to ensure that regional trading blocs will in effect become building blocks for multilateralism. Fourth, the WTO institutional reform needs to be fine tuned in various aspects. Among these are improved procedures to accommodate the entrance of new members, especially powerful entrants like China and Russia, and an improved management structure of the WTO itself to work against the temptation for major trading countries to resort to ad hoc extra-legal processes. Although Schott is positive about the achievements in strengthening the multilateral system, he urges to pre-empt a protectionist backlash – by means of domestic policy reforms with a view to reviving productivity, and to deal with the new emerging issues as soon as possible within a multilateral framework.

Two of the new emerging issues, social and environmental standards, are discussed in more detail in Chapters 7 and 8. In Chapter 7, **Harald Grossmann** and **Georg Koopmann** scrutinise the recently raised concerns about social standards in international trade. As trade liberalisation requires sometimes painful adjustments, it can provoke tensions and defensive attitudes which may result either in a protectionist backlash by an increasing use of the available mechanism of 'contingent' protectionism, or in efforts to reduce the differences in the various social systems themselves in order to create 'a level playing field'. The authors note that four major reasons are given for including social standards in international trading rules. First, the motive of defending one's own social standards and achievements, which are perceived as being threatened by liberalising trade with countries with considerably lower standards. As far as this is interpreted as an attack on trade with low-wage countries, the argument reflects the old pauper labour argument of unfair trade which is orthogonal to the insights of international trade theory that such differences are at the roots of mutual beneficial trade. A second line of argument refers to basic human rights, like the freedom of unions, health and safety standards, non-discrimination of female workers, and the abolition of child, prison and forced labour. Yet another rationale is the altruistic and humanitarian concern about the welfare in countries with a low social standard. Finally, it is argued that an international adoption of a social (minimum) standard would act as a facilitator for further trade liberalisation.

Addressing the problem of low wages either by resorting to trade barriers or by 'imposing' higher wages, the authors insert that this could be counterproductive if not supported by productivity increases. Raising other labour standards can also be a mixed blessing for the people in the countries concerned. For example, the abolition of child labour can result in even greater poverty. Therefore, it is difficult to define the 'right' social standards in individual cases *ex ante* – and thus in general. With regard to the impact of social standards on international trade and imports, the authors note that low social standards could contribute to a migration of production sites to low-standard locations, but that actual empirical data are not confirming this 'threat', at least not on a large scale. There may, however, be pressure on less skilled workers in industrial countries. But again, evidence here is at least mixed. According to the authors, this would neither justify a new protectionism nor efforts to create a 'level playing field'. Judging from a purely economic point of view, for the authors the WTO is not the right forum in which to tackle these issues, including those of fundamental human rights, but rather a broader framework is needed, including the International Labour Organization, the United Nations and the Bretton Woods organisations. While the authors do not address the issues of international income distribution (and additional policy measures like active labour market policies, human capital formation, promoting socially compatible structural changes) it becomes clear that beyond the pure economic point of view the world trading system may reach its frontiers, an issue later addressed by Murray Gibbs in Chapter 10.

The interface between trade and environment is disussed in Chapter 8. **Nevin Shaw** and **Arthur J. Hanson** scrutinise the potential positive and negative linkages with a view on promoting sustainable development. The main linkages to which attention is drawn are: (i) the link between trade and economic growth and the supposed negative level effect of the latter on the environment; (ii) the limiting effect of free trade on national environmental standards and the flexibility of environmental policy; (iii) a distorting impact on competitiveness because of uneven environmental regulation which may lead to a migration of industries, jobs and income to 'pollution havens'; (iv) the fear of developing countries that imposed environmental standards (and probably different 'preferences' of the rich) would undermine their comparative advantages; (v) the possibility of a protectionist abuse of the issue.

The authors argue that, first of all, trade is only one factor among others which may promote economic growth, and the latter has varying effects on the environment. Some are positive (as higher incomes free resources for addressing environmental problems) and some are negative (in the usual way they are perceived). The issue is that, first, policy responses need to be context specific. Second, the competitiveness effects of high environmental standards seem not to have played the major role feared by many 'environmentalists'. Third, misallocation of resources induced by protectionist distortions of free trade can lead to tremendous environmental costs. After a detailed review of trade rules related to the environment at various levels, Shaw and Hanson contrast the perspectives of Northern 'environmentalists' and Southern 'developmentalists'. Rather than leaning to one side or the other, in their view it is essential to make globalisation and sustainable development more compatible, stressing both sustainability and development. Therefore, they argue that in the presence of neither simple nor clear linkages between environment and trade, careful assessments are needed and these fundamental assessments should be made at home as each country has a different set of competing priorities and goals. Second, it is imperative to develop a system which adapts and responds to a spectrum of competing values and interests, of both the rich and the poor. In the authors' view, 'we need proactive and rule-based bilateral, trilateral, regional, plurilateral and multilateral institution to promote sustainable development', because there is a subsequent need to 'conduct reform in a way which enables governments and international institutions to more easily adapt to a more co-ordinated view of an increasingly integrated economy and environment'. They therefore suggest that active use should be made of what an international working group, composed of nine members of the trade, environment and development communities proposed as the Winnipeg Principles. These principles for trade and sustainable development seek to enhance the ability of different countries to negotiate and adhere to trade and environment agreements. They suggest efforts to internalise environmental cost, in order to reflect the true environmental burden coming with economic activities and to improve economic/environmental efficiency, to preserve environmental integrity in a multilateral way in cases where cost internalisation cannot capture environmental values, to build in efforts to promote greater equity in the world economic system by sharing capital, knowledge and technology on a broader base, to apply subsidiarity (i.e. to respond to transborder, regional and global problems in an appropriate institutional way by approaching global problems globally and regional problems regionally, etc.), to develop further the multilateral system of international cooperation, to encourage a precautionary approach to the adoption of environmental policies in advance of conclusive scientific evidence, and – last but not least – to provide timely, easy and full access to information by and to all affected or interested parties, as openness is critical in support of sustainable development.

With the end of the cold war, the former Council for Mutual Economic Assistance (CMEA) countries need to be reintegrated into the world trading system. The issue has at least three dimensions: the design of national trade policies, the integration into the world trading system, and – eventually – the countries' position towards regional arrangement. In Chapter 9, **András Inotai** and **Judit Kiss** analyse these partially interrelated issues for the Central and Eastern European countries (CEEC). In particular they focus on: (i) the heritage of the transition period and the impact of an overhasty import liberalisation; (ii) the likely consequences of the GATT Agreement on CEECs; (iii) the shorter and medium-term consequences of the Association Agreements with the EU. With respect to the first issue Chapter 9 surveys the external and domestic conditions of import liberalisation and calls attention to the unique features of this policy step in the CEEC in the early 1990s. Import liberalisation preceded and, to an increasing extent, started to hinder genuine export orientation. The authors argue that the opening up was carried out in an extremely unfavourable environment due to the collapse of the CMEA and the dramatic decline of domestic output and demand. In addition, the elimination of tariff barriers was not accompanied or preceded by the establishment of a secondary protection based on technical norms, health and sanitary measures, widely known and used in OECD economies.

In the section on the impact of GATT the authors question whether, and if so to what extent, the transforming economies can expect improving market access. All non-tariff barriers in industrial trade with the EU and EFTA countries will be eliminated well before the GATT schedule. However, the future of agricultural exports is more complicated. In the longer run, cuts in farm support and export subsidies seem to benefit agricultural exports from transforming economies. In the shorter run, however, substantial tariff increases partially replacing previous quotas may aggravate the situation. On the side of agricultural imports the new GATT rules leave less room for market protection for the transforming countries. In sum, it is argued that market access will improve in general. The success, however, will largely depend on the development of production pattern and efficiency in the transforming countries, as well. The final issue of trade relations of CEECs with the EU has developed dramatically in recent years. This process has been revealed both in the rapid geographical shift of trade relations and in the substantial 'upgrading' of the CEECs' export pattern. Interestingly, except for clothing, the most dynamic export commodities included higher value-added and skill-intensive goods. This development was only partially due to the Association Agreement with the EU which has also shown some shortcomings in the last years. Growing trade deficits despite trade 'asynchronity', problems of agricultural exports due to the Common Agricultural Policy of the European Union and to serious domestic policy errors, as well as still unclear consequences of ongoing import liberalisation, as stipulated by the Association Agreement, belong to the issues of major concern. The chapter argues for a more comprehensive and coordinated effort in order to mitigate the potential negative impacts and to strengthen the overall competitiveness of the transforming economies.

The role of developing countries in the world trading system has changed considerably over recent years. Some emerged as successful exporters, others – among them many debt-ridden countries – opened up their economies extensively and in a unilateral way, but were often less successful in terms of export performance. Globalisation is increasingly changing the 'rules of the game'. All this contributed to a much more active participation of developing countries in the UR. Under the governance of the new WTO, developing countries need to define their positions not only in this new institution, but also within the international economic order and its various institutions. These issues are addressed in Chapter 10 by **Murray Gibbs** with a view to searching for a development-oriented trading system. He observes that while the debate on involving developing countries in the international trading system in coherence with their needs and aspirations had resulted in such institutions as UNCTAD, the Group of 77, and a clause for differential and more favourable treatment within the GATT system, the pendulum has swung back in the early 1980s. Rather than receiving more favourable treatment, developing countries were facing a proliferation of 'grey area' measures against their exports, including regulated sectors like textiles and agriculture, bilateral pressures by major importing countries to offer them trade concessions, an extension of developed countries trading blocs, and a conditional application of preferential treatments under the Generalised System of Preferences (GSP). These developments have shifted those countries' interests towards actively defending the integrity of an unconditional MFN clause. The UR brought the developing countries improved market access, and especially 'stricter multilateral disciplines that were to provide secure access to markets and eliminate bilateral pressures and unilateral actions

11

by the major trading countries'. On the other side, developing countries made important concessions to reduce trade barriers and in other trade-related issues such as investment measures and intellectual property rights. In a way, the various disciplines of the UR agreement may deprive latecomers (including countries in transition) of the opportunity to copy the economic development strategies of the successful newly industrialised economies.

According to Gibbs, developing countries are facing two challenges in the post-Uruguay trading system. First, they must protect the achieved gains made in the UR and insist that what is written on paper will be adhered to in practice. Second, they must try to regain the initiative in the establishment of the future agenda, both in the light of the new issues that have already been raised, such as the trade environment link, labour standards, regionalism, trade and investment, and also the linkages existing between trade on the one hand and such diverse issues as migration, competition policies, monetary and fiscal policies, development and poverty alleviation. With regard to policy harmonisation in the various fields, Gibbs warns not to overload the international trading system which could finally undermine its efficacy in the field of trade.

Another important point raised by the author is the coherence in the international system which has to be addressed. Unilateral openings during structural adjustment programmes, sponsored by the Bretton Woods organisations, and the virtual absence of multilateral disciplines over national monetary policies illustrate this need for a closer cooperation between the WTO and the Bretton Woods organisations. The necessity to establish a safety net to protect the weakest trading nation in the process of globalisation and liberalisation is another case in point. As a consequence, Gibbs states that 'the international community is thus faced with the question of the extent to which these issues can be dealt with in multilateral trade agreement under the WTO umbrella, that is, to define "the frontiers" of the multilateral trading system'. He suggests that more active use should be made of the experience of regional trading arrangements in integrating economies at different levels of development. On the one hand, the more advanced nations need to address the problem of structural change coming with globalisation and liberalisation which may especially penalise unskilled workers and may lead to a greater inequality of incomes. A policy response is needed to avoid resort to protectionist measures. On the other hand, 'the experience of freeing trade in Europe has shown that policies involving massive transfers of resources are required to enable peripheral and disadvantaged regions to derive benefits from the process of trade liberalisation and economic integration. It has also shown that the freer movement of labour is a particular important element in this process.' The South needs to make its presence felt both on these and other matters and with regard to the new emerging issues. It should therefore reform and streamline its coordination mechanisms and should also draw on the expertise of UNCTAD as the latter's major role is in policy analysis and consensus building. An important albeit general conclusion reached by Gibbs is as follows:

> It may be more than a cliché to state that the adjustment to globalisation will require a global response involving not only the WTO and the Bretton Woods institutions, but the whole international system. While certain aspects of the issues identified for a possible new trade agenda could appropriately be dealt with through new trade obligations or the interpretation of existing ones and brought within the WTO umbrella, it is obvious that the whole gamut of economic and social problems facing the world in the next century cannot be dealt with through a series of trade arrangements enforced through the threat of trade sanctions, nor through structural adjustment and low interest loans. It is also clear that the frontiers of the multilateral trading system should be established through a process of consensus building which takes account of the interdependence among the issues and not merely reflect short-term responses to political pressures nor relative bargaining strength in establishing a negotiating package. It is also crucial that simplistic ideological approaches be abandoned in favour of a new pragmatism based on actual experiences, and serious analysis of current trends.

Part I

THE WORLD TRADING SYSTEM AND THE URUGUAY ROUND: ISSUES, RESULTS AND CONSEQUENCES

1

MULTILATERALISM, REGIONALISM AND GLOBALISATION

The challenges to the world trading system[1]

Harald Sander

INTRODUCTION

The Uruguay Round of the General Agreement on Tariffs and Trade (GATT) was the most comprehensive round in the succession of multilateral trade talks, both in scope and duration. Ironically, its ambitious agenda was set up and had to be negotiated during a time when the GATT system of multilateral and non-discriminatory trade policy was facing two serious challenges: an increasing non-tariff protectionism by industrial countries and a new wave of regionalism, visible in the proliferation of new trading blocs around the globe as well as in the extension and deepening of existing ones.

The rise in protectionist practices was more than just a backlash against multilateral tariff reductions negotiated in earlier GATT rounds. As those measures predominantly surfaced as non-tariff barriers to trade, directed against particular trading partners, they violated the spirit of the GATT which stands for a 'fix-rule' trading regime, with these rules applying to all GATT members without discrimination (except under specific, multilaterally agreed criteria). Likewise, regionalism almost by definition discriminates against non-members of a trading bloc as the latter receive less favourable treatment than club members.

These threats to the multilateral trading system must be seen against the background of a changing economic geography, both in terms of an uneven relative growth performance by individual countries and regions in the world economy and, of special interest here, in terms of changing patterns of trade, investment and production, a process commonly referred to as globalisation. Globalisation is visible in the financial sphere, in trade, and in cross-border investments. It is predominantly driven by microeconomic forces, like new technologies and globally oriented corporate strategies, but at the same time it has been propelled and reinforced by the market-oriented policy frame-work prevailing since the early 1980s. The subsequently increased intensity

17

of international competition resulted more often than not in shifting comparative advantages.

Since productivity growth slowed down in the major industrial countries when the so-called 'Golden Age' – the post-World-War-II era of increasing global prosperity – came to an end approximately around 1973, a tremendous catching-up process of developing countries has also become visible. However, this was concentrated on some newly industrialising economies (NIEs), mainly in the Far East. Many NIEs are now 'first-rank fighters' for trade liberalisation – often after having gone through long periods of nurturing and protecting their domestic industries.

As globalisation is coinciding with a relatively weakened position of industrial countries, signalled by high unemployment rates, it has contributed to a higher sensibility of those countries towards foreign competition which is increasingly being perceived as unfair and threatening the standard of living in the rich part of the world. The problem is aggravated further by bilateral trade imbalances (such as the US trade deficit with Japan), which is partly a result of (earlier) exchange rate misalignments. Globalisation may thus have conditioned the build-up of protectionist pressures – including calls for competitive devaluation – as well as the proliferation of those regional initiatives directed towards isolating the respective region from the perceived threats of globalisation. At the same time, the internationalisation of production has made domestic and regional 'beyond-the-border' policies more powerful in competing for production locations and thus jobs.

These developments have been casting doubts on the appropriateness of the GATT system to govern the world trading system in the future. Although the successful conclusion of the Uruguay Round is commonly viewed as a victory for multilateralism, neither the protectionist nor the regionalist challenges to the world trading system have been eradicated. The words of the Uruguay Round agreements point in the right direction. The success of multilateralism, however, will depend on to what extent the major players in the world economy will act in the spirit of the agreement and develop the multilateral system further in a direction capable of coping with the challenges emanating from globalisation in a mutually beneficial way.

The objects of this chapter are the threats to the multilateral trading system, in particular in relation to the challenges of globalisation. The second section, pages 19–26, discusses the major threats to multilateralism: the new protectionism and the new regionalism. The third section, pages 26–33, reviews the structural changes in the international division of labour and the challenges of globalisation for the multilateral system thereof. The fourth section, pages 33–4, concludes by calling for a combination of a national/regional policy response with an institutional response at the multilateral level, the latter both within the sphere of multilateral trade negotiations and beyond the 'frontiers' of the international trading system.

MULTILATERALISM, PROTECTIONISM AND REGIONALISM

The multilateral approach of the GATT

The General Agreement on Tariffs and Trade was signed in 1947 by twenty-three countries in order to restore an open international trade environment and to rebuild international economic integration. While the initial efforts to create an international trade organisation as the third pillar of the post-war international economic order (next to the Bretton Woods institutions) did not succeed, the GATT system – which is essentially a contract between signatory states – established the instrument of periodic multilateral trade negotiations, the so-called GATT rounds, directed at reducing tariff and non-tariff barriers to trade.

The approach adopted in the GATT rounds is based on the principle of multilateralism with the major elements of non-discrimination and reciprocity. Reductions in import impediments are offered in return for reciprocal market access concessions by the other trading partners. Non-discriminatory treatment[2] is ensured by the most favoured nation principle (MFN) which demands that concessions granted to individual trading partners are extended to all signatories of the GATT. To avoid a free-rider problem and thus to ensure reciprocity, multilateral trade negotiations are required.

While multilateralism is the backbone of the GATT system, it is neither a necessary nor a sufficient condition for establishing a liberal world trading order. In theory, even unilateral trade liberalisation can enhance national welfare because it would result in lower import prices and thereby free resources for a higher demand of those domestic products where the home economy is more efficient. This would constitute an incentive for individual countries to liberalise unilaterally. If all countries would follow this textbook advice, a liberal world trading system would evolve even without any multilateral mechanism. There are, however, a number of (valid as well as non-valid) arguments against the textbook case, and these arguments more often than not govern the more reluctant approach of policy-makers towards free trade. This is why the GATT is important and necessary for reducing trade barriers in practice. But the same arguments simultaneously expose the GATT to the threat that important signatory states may attempt to circumvent its very principle of non-discrimination.

It would be a mistake, however, to view the GATT as well as its successor, the World Trade Organization (WTO), as a free trade organisation *per se*. From the point of view of individual countries, GATT is often primarily perceived as instrumental to gaining access to foreign markets rather than as an unconditioned commitment for opening up the home market. The GATT system can be understood as the outcome of a compromise between neo-mercantilist sentiments and free trade arguments. As Paul Krugman

(1992: 429) noted, the 'theoretical' underpinnings of GATT negotiations can be related to what he calls 'GATT-think': 'a simple set of principles that is entirely consistent, explains most of what goes on in the negotiations, but makes no sense in economics'. According to Krugman, it is based on three 'rules' about the objectives of the negotiating countries: (1) exports are good, (2) imports are bad, and (3) an equal increase in exports and imports is good. The principles (1) and (2) are – strictly speaking – economic nonsense. The implied trade surpluses are impossible to achieve by all trading partners simultaneously as the surplus of one group necessarily requires a combined deficit of all remaining countries, and trade surpluses would ultimately invoke upward adjustments in wages, prices or the exchange rate, resulting in a correction of the trade imbalance. But the rules are in line with the political economy of protectionism (if one adds 'for the exporting industry' and 'for the import competing domestic industry' to rules (1) and (2), respectively). Rule (3), however, is compatible with the economists' belief in mutual beneficial trade expansions.

Consequently, GATT members speak of concessions when 'granting' market access to foreign exporters and demand 'reciprocity' – a 'compensatory' access to the foreign country's market.[3] Armed with and assisted by the MFN principle, the success of the GATT in reducing MFN tariffs is easy to understand. Countries interested in market access in a foreign country would approach it and offer concessions in return. By means of the MFN principle, the concessions made are extended to all GATT members. Reciprocity then calls for compensating concessions from all 'benefiting' countries. The free-rider problem potentially involved in such a process, however, can only be overcome by multilateral trade talks that force all members to the negotiation table. MFN and reciprocity thus work as accelerators of multilateral trade liberalisation, while backsliding is prevented by binding the lowered (average) MFN tariffs.

The item-by-item negotiations in the first GATT rounds, however, proved to be too time-consuming, and balancing concessions for thousands of goods and with many countries simultaneously became a formidable task that slowed down the progress considerably. Therefore, a formula approach was implemented in the Kennedy Round (1963–7) and thereafter. The formula requires a certain average tariff cut for all but some excluded products. This tariff cut applies to all industries unless certain industries can convince their governments that they need more protection. The formula approach brought considerable tariff reductions (see also Baldwin 1987: 42–3) of about 35 per cent in the Kennedy Round, some 30 per cent in the Tokyo Round (1974–9), and 38 per cent in the Uruguay Round. Post-Uruguay Round MFN tariffs on manufactured goods in developed countries will come down to below 4 per cent.

The political economy of trade policy therefore makes the multilateral approach of the GATT a more promising and necessary way towards an open world trading system. But at the same time, it is this particular political economy that tends to undermine the GATT's very principle of non-discrimination in practice.

Protectionist motives

While free trade is mutually beneficial in theory and in principle (but not in general), policy-makers and their electorates rarely share the economists' beliefs. The reasons given for resistance against multilateral liberalisation are manifold. Some of them are simply economic nonsense, partly because they are the outgrowth of successful lobbying efforts by vested interest groups, partly because they are being based on purely nationalist arguments or 'feelings'. Others refer to concerns over adjustment costs caused by rapid structural changes that may follow an external liberalisation. And a final group of arguments draws on the insights of the 'new trade theory' (which partly incorporates elements of the infant industry protection argument advanced by Friedrich List in the first half of the nineteenth century) as a rationale for a strategic trade policy.

Adjustment cost can become important if declining industries are not replaced at the same speed by new industries and/or if resources are specialised in a way that they will not or cannot be used by the new industries. Structural unemployment can surface and lead to a period of output losses. However, the root of the problem is the structural adjustment capacity of the resources rather than the actual structural change. Several policy responses are possible. First, attempts can be made to slow down the speed of the structural change by means of protectionism and/or 'beyond-the-border' policies (e.g. subsidies). Second, efforts can be made to promote new or to expand existing activities, by means of improving overall market conditions, support to certain industries, or by attempts to open foreign markets that are considered too closed (e.g. 'Japan-bashing', or demands for reciprocity addressed to developing countries enjoying GSP preferences). Third, attempts can be made to increase the mobility of resources, especially labour, for example by means of active labour market policies. Finally, the immobility of resources can be taken for granted and socially acceptable (but sometimes very costly) ways of handling the retreat from active labour market participation (e.g. early retirement) can be organised. Under the current world economic conditions where industrial countries are confronted with previously unknown high levels of unemployment, almost all of them have resorted to some kind of a mixture of these policy elements. Although the recipes vary from country to country, more often than not they show some bias towards measures directed against foreign competitors.

On the strategic side, the 'new trade theory' has given a sophisticated rationale for protecting high-tech industries in order to enhance national welfare. Market failures are at the root of the diagnosis that trade and industrial

21

policies can increase national economic welfare by supporting industries with a high potential in terms of productivity spillovers (technological externalities) and average-cost-reducing learning and scale effects. While these policies can be justified in theory, they can be difficult to apply in practice as informational problems entail the risk of picking losers rather than winners and they may provoke foreign retaliation, especially when they aim at redistributing monopoly rents between countries. Finally, large countries can improve their terms of trade by raising tariffs – a strategy that works against the economist's case for unilateral import liberalisation and points to the protectionist temptation to which large trading blocs are exposed.

The new protectionism

Multilateral trade liberalisation negotiated in the various GATT rounds has often been followed by a protectionist backlash. While the road back to increasing tariffs is closed by GATT-bound tariffs, bureaucratic creativity was never short of finding new protectionist ways by innovating new instruments, in particular those of the non-tariff variety. Examples are voluntary export restraints (VERs), 'orderly market arrangements' (OMAs), voluntary import expansions, or a misuse of countervailing duties and anti-dumping duties against alleged unfair trade. The 1980s witnessed a proliferation of such measures, especially directed against East Asian producers which led some observers to state that GATT is suffering from its own success in bringing down MFN tariffs. Not only old and declining industries, like steel and textiles, have been the targets of the new protectionism, but increasingly also high-tech industries, like microelectronics, which are often being viewed as strategic sectors (see Table 1.1).

The crucial issue is that unlike their protectionist cousins of the tariff variety, non-tariff barriers (NTBs) can be applied selectively and thus directly violate the principle of multilateralism. And – even worse – goods may be added to the list of 'sensitive products' at exactly the very moment when a competitor is becoming a successful exporter of this particular good. While the GATT is well equipped to act against a backlash in tariff protectionism, its instruments are relatively blunt in the case of NTBs. For example, a voluntary export restraint arrangement is directly negotiated between two trading partners. Rather than resorting to import quotas (which would violate the GATT principles), the restrained partner is being 'convinced' to cut back his exports. If he agrees, neither the protectionist country nor the trading partner will complain at the GATT. From the point of view of the exporter, agreeing to a VER is much more favourable than facing tariff protection or foreign retaliation. The reason is that he will receive a rent from selling (less) goods at higher prices in the foreign market, a rent that in the case of tariff protection would otherwise constitute a tariff revenue for the protectionist

Table 1.1 Export restraint arrangements, 1987–90 (by number of arrangements)

	9/87	5/88	3/89	12/90
Total number of arrangements:	135	261	289	284
By sectoral composition				
– Steel	38	52	50	39
– Agricultural and food products	20	55	51	59
– Automobiles and transport equipment	14	17	20	23
– Textiles and clothing	28	72	66	51
– Electronic products	11	19	28	37
– Footwear	8	14	18	21
– Other	15	32	56	54
By protected markets				
– European Community	69	137	173	n.a.
– United States	48	62	69	n.a.
– Japan	6	13	13	n.a.
– Other industrial countries	12	47	32	n.a.
– Eastern Europe	–	1	1	n.a.
By restrained exporters				
– Japan	25	28	70	n.a.
– Eastern Europe	20	45	41	n.a.
– Korea	24	25	38	n.a.
– Other industrial countries	23	59	57	n.a.
– Other developing countries	42	98	83	n.a.

Note: n.a. = not available
Source: IMF 1993: 117

country.[4] Third countries will usually also not object to such agreements as they facilitate their own exports to the selectively protected market.

Next to NTBs (including arrangements which exempted various sectors, e.g. agriculture and textile), 'beyond-the-border' policies, like industrial and competition policies, can to some extent replace border protection. Moreover, increasingly all kinds of differing standards (health, safety, environmental, social), regulations and practices can restrict market access. Informal barriers to trade can also limit the effectiveness of multilateral trade agreements. Examples are alleged informal import barriers in Japan and government procurement regulations that favour domestic over foreign supplier. And especially social and environmental standards and regulations may and can be used for protectionist rather than for the mentioned altruistic reasons by making more extensive use of anti-dumping and countervailing duties (see Chapters 7 and 8). The threat remains therefore that despite the successful conclusion of the UR a disguised new protectionism may remain and probably increase.

The threat of regionalism

By the end of 1994 the GATT had been notified of 108 regional arrangements, 33 of them alone in the 1990s (*Financial Times*, 28 April 1995). Almost every country of the more than 120 WTO members is involved in some kind of a trade group, albeit with a varying intensity. This second wave of regionalism – after the first one in the 1960s and early 1970s which was mainly a regionalism of developing countries seeking a critical mass market to realise economies of scale in their industrialisation efforts – is being hotly debated among economists and policy-makers alike. However, it is important to distinguish between regionalisation, signifying a market-driven process of trading more intensively with close neighbours, and regionalism which attempts (not always successfully) to promote regional economic integration on a *de jure* base. Regionalism may therefore either lead or follow a de facto process of regionalisation.

By definition, *de jure* trading blocs – custom unions and free trade areas – are violating the principle of non-discrimination by giving preferential treatment to members of the club but not to outsiders. Moreover, trading blocs often tend to regulate their trade affairs *vis-à-vis* other trading partners on a special base, for example, the EU's preferential treatment of ACP and Eastern European countries (see Chapters 5 and 9). The GATT, Article XXIV, allows for the formation of a regional trading area under two vague conditions. First, most of the trade should be subjected to the lowering of intra-regional trade barriers. Second, the external tariffs are not to be raised. These conditions never failed the test of GATT compatibility (see Chapter 6: 111).

In 1992, around 45 per cent of world trade was conducted under the rules set by preferential regional agreements. The figure, however, is dominated by preferential trade within Western Europe (32.5 per cent of world trade) and – to a lesser extent – the North American Free Trade Area, NAFTA (7.6 per cent). Judged by such figures other regional groupings are of minor importance. Their intra-regional trade typically does not exceed 2 per cent of world trade (Borrmann and Koopmann 1994: 367). Even in the much discussed ASEAN Free Trade Area (AFTA) intra-regional trade accounts for less than 1 per cent of world trade.

Western Europe surely fits best into the picture of a fragmented world of trading blocs because intra-regional trade accounts for more than 70 per cent of the region's trade (GATT 1994). North America is trading around one third with itself (or somewhat over 40 per cent when Mexico is included). Intra-regional trade in the whole of Asia is around 45 per cent; if one looks at East Asia only the figure is around 35 per cent. North America and what now constitutes the NAFTA, as well as East Asia are thus regions still exposed to the world economy in a somewhat triangular structure. To be more precise, in all major regions intra-regional trade grew over the 1980s by more than the decade's world trade expansion rate of 5.5 per cent. But so did trade among the so-called Triad – North America, Japan and Western Europe. In a way, it may be argued that the visible growing importance of regional markets in the 1980s, so intensively discussed in recent years, is also in part the statistical effect of a relative and sometimes absolute disintegration of the Triad with Latin America, Eastern Europe, Africa, and in particular the Middle East (see Table 1.2).

The evaluation of regionalism as a threat to the multilateral trading system has to consider two effects. First, the static effect of what it does to world welfare compared to a situation without preferential arrangements, and, second, the dynamic effects, that is what kind of trade policy stance such blocs will take *vis-à-vis* the rest of the world and whether they will act as and become building blocks or stumbling blocks for the multilateral trading system (Bhagwati 1992b).

With regard to the static effects, every trading bloc has the potential to create trade among its members by lowering or abolishing internal trade barriers. While this would be appreciated by trade theorists, the overall assessment looks less convincing when imports from more efficient non-member countries are being replaced by imports from a member country. If such trade diversion effects are exceeding the trade creation effects, a regionally limited trade liberalisation can be worse than no liberalisation at all in terms of global welfare and will surely hurt external exporters. In general, the probability that a trading bloc will be a net trade creator is higher the more the region at hand constitutes something like a natural trading bloc (i.e. an economic space where market forces already brought about a high level of de facto regional integration in absence of such an integration scheme).

Evaluating regional initiatives by their trade creating and diverting effects alone could, however, be too narrow because this would neglect the fact that they can also 'send a signal to potential third country investors' – which was one of the arguments put forward by a Singaporean official when launching the AFTA (Oman 1994: 82). Investment diversion from third countries may thus constitute another threat to the multilateral system. But as the benefits of a regional integration scheme could be derived from an intra- and extra-regional rationalisation of production, the risk of excluding the least cost producer may be less than traditional analysis assumes, especially if extra-regional investors are transplanting similar sites in different countries (Summers 1991: 299). Furthermore, regional initiatives may offer 'political economy gains' from 'locking in good policies' (Summers 1991: 300), partly by curbing the influence of special interest groups (Oman 1994).

These observations already touched upon the issue of the dynamic time path and the behaviour of trading blocs. A case has been made in favour of regional blocs by highlighting that few but more homogeneous groups may succeed faster in organising multilateral trade talks than more than one hundred nations. North America and East Asia both need open world markets more urgently than Western Europe. Regionalism in the aforementioned regions could thus be less threatening to multilateralism than European regionalism.

25

Table 1.2 Trade growth by major regions 1980–90 (average annual percentage changes in value of exports and imports)

	North America	Western Europe	Asia	Latin America	Central and Eastern Europe	Africa	Middle East
North America	8.0	7.0	10.0	4.0	1.0	-6.0	-1.5
Western Europe		8.0	11.0	2.0	3.0	-0.5	-4.5
Asia			10.5	4.5	-4.5	0.0	-2.5
Latin America				-1.5	2.0	-9.0	-3.5
Central and Eastern Europe					n.a.	-1.5	-3.5
Africa						2.5	1.0
Middle East							-4.5

Note: n.a. not available
Source: GATT 1992: Table III.4

In the case of East Asia, most observers agree that the chances for a successful formation of an East Asian trading bloc are relatively low and – judging from trade creation/trade diversion exercises – relatively unpromising (Panagariya 1993; Sander 1995).[5] Nevertheless, even if such a bloc were to be formed it would be more likely to be supportive of multilateralism because of the region's dependence on a reliable access to the world markets.

On the other hand, trading blocs are easily tempted to raise the effective level of protection as this could lead to an improvement in the region's terms of trade. It has been estimated that in Western Europe the level of external protection 'tends to be higher on average at the beginning of the 1990s than it was 20 years ago' (Preusse 1994: 160). The mushrooming of the new protectionism may therefore not be independent from the new regionalism, and both have shown that the provisions of the GATT, Article XXIV, of not 'raising duties and other regulations of commerce' can be too weak to prevent trading blocs from taking the road to protectionist trade diversion (Bhagwati 1992a, b). Moreover, as the real obstacles to effective market access are increasingly buried beyond the border in differing standards, regulations and procedures, the behaviour of regional blocs in building up or bringing down those regulations is important for whether or not the international system will face more fragmentation and inter-regional conflicts. While regional organisations may therefore have some positive effects of curbing the influence of special interest groups, this is by no means guaranteed. Rather, it is quite possible that regulations, standards and procedures – which are also to a good part the outcome of lobbying effort – are adding up to considerable market entry barrier. Among others, such concerns have led to proposals for a Transatlantic Free Trade Area (TAFTA).

Whether trading blocs are likely to become protectionist stumbling blocks or not depends very much on whether the general economic conditions are supportive of protectionism, such as low growth and high unemployment. Restoring the economic conditions of the 'Golden Age' would be the best advice to turn stumbling blocks into building blocks. But this is easier said than done. However, rethinking the international economic order, as well as developing international, regional and national policy responses other than a negative-sum protectionism and aimed at restoring full employment are in high demand today. In this respect it has also been said that a new, open regionalism aimed at improving international competitiveness in the world markets would constitute no challenge to the multilateral trading system.

THE CHALLENGES OF GLOBALISATION

What is globalisation?

Globalisation has become a prominent catchword for describing the processes of international economic integration. Three areas stand out:[6]

- The dramatic internationalisation and global integration of financial markets over the past two decades – the size of the world financial markets was estimated at $43,000 billion in 1992, nearly a threefold increase over the decade and roughly twice the value of world gross domestic product (GDP) (UNCTAD 1994: 129).
- A world trade volume expanding faster than world production and thus leading to a higher degree of trade integration of nations in the world economy.
- A surge in foreign direct investments, particularly in the second half of the 1980s when cross-border investments increased with an annual rate of more than 20 per cent.

The crucial issue is, however, whether these trends towards globalisation signify a new quality in international economic integration or whether they merely reflect a continuous but essentially unaltered process of increasing global integration. It is therefore the causes and effects of the above-mentioned trends rather than the trends themselves which could make the difference.

A first important qualitative consequence of globalisation is the reduction in national economic policy autonomy, especially in the field of macroeconomic management, both *vis-à-vis* the market and other governments. Given the high mobility of international financial flows and the sheer size of the world financial markets, national governments are virtually unable to stabilise their exchange rates and to counter speculative capital flows. The recent real appreciation of the Japanese Yen and the German Mark, as well as the various crises of the European Exchange Rate Mechanism prove this point. Such developments demonstrate that the global financial markets have essentially paralysed uncoordinated monetary and fiscal policy for managing the macro-economy in a traditional Keynesian way. The Maastricht accord to establish a European Monetary Union may therefore – at least in part – be interpreted as an attempt to regain control over the instruments of monetary and fiscal policies on a regional level. Moreover, unpredictably over- and undershooting exchange rates expose firms to considerable exchange rate risks, to which they react partly by using – and thus spurring – innovation in the global financial market, like futures and options, which in turn tends to reinforce the globalisation process in the financial sphere. On the real side, establishing production sites in each of the major currency areas of the Triad is yet another response that contributes to the process of globalisation of production, and eventually to higher trade integration on both the regional and global level.

Second, while the process of increasing trade integration continued from post-World War II onward, with the 1980s even witnessing a slowing down of this process, it is important to note that in the latter period higher trade integration took place despite an increasing non-tariff protectionism, while in the former period it was spurred by the predictable outcome of multilateral tariff reductions. Most periods of capitalist development have witnessed trade growing faster than real production. From 1820 to 1989, the international trade of sixteen industrial countries has grown significantly faster than their output – with an average annual rate of 4 per cent compared to a GDP growth rate of 2.7 per cent (Maddison 1991: 74). An exception to this rule was only the neo-mercantilist phase of disintegration between 1913 and 1950 when trade grew at a rate of only 1 per cent while GDP was increasing by 2 per cent per annum on average. When the liberal trading system was restored after World War II, trade increased by an annual average of 8.6 per cent during the 'Golden Age' period from 1950 to 1973, exceeding the excellent growth performance of industrial countries by 3.7 per cent. Since then trade and output growth slowed down to 4.7 per cent and 2.6 per cent respectively for the period from 1973 to 1989. But as trade still exhibited stronger dynamics, the openness of the national economies increased. Maddison (1991: 326–7) reports ratios of merchandise exports to GNP for the sixteen-country sample of 15.1 per cent in 1950 and 24.1 per cent in 1987, measured in current market prices.

Two important notes should be added. First, the growth rates of international trade among the major regions are in line with the Golden Age trade growth average (see Table 1.2). Second, although there was a relative disintegration of some developing country regions, the developing countries' share in world manufacturing production increased between 1965 and 1985 from about 14 per cent to 18 per cent, and their world export share in manufactured goods increased even more sharply from 9 per cent to 18 per cent. Over the 1980s Third World manufactured exports grew with an annual rate of 12 per cent two to three times faster than the corresponding number for industrial countries (Singh 1994: 177).

As the intensity of global competition has increased, globalisation exhibits 'a tendency to disrupt entrenched oligopolies, effectively changing the "rules of the game" in the struggle for competitive advantage among firms within, as well as between and among, countries' (Oman 1994: 33). The resulting pressures for corporate restructuring and downsizing, and the subsequent acceleration of structural change, often involving at least temporary unemployment, have all contributed to a growing perception that the process of globalisation is closely intertwined with an increasing level of uncertainty and vulnerability.

Cross-border trade is a form of economic integration which has been dubbed a 'shallow integration' as opposed to a 'deep integration' at the production level. While the latter establishes longer lasting and deeper linkages between economic agents located in different countries, arm's length trade ends with the initial transaction (UNCTAD 1994). Globalisation's third dimension, the strategies and behaviour of transnationally active firms – increasingly also small- and medium-sized enterprises – seeking to be present in each of the major economic regions of the Triad, has led to an increase in the intensity of international inter-firm competition and a subsequent acceleration of structural change. Moreover, the internationalisation of production has been considerably increased by technological and organisational innovations.

On the technological side, new information and communication technologies are contributing to a changing international division of labour, increasingly in the realm of services. Organisational innovations, such as the various new forms of international corporate equity and non-equity cooperation, like 'strategic alliances', and the so-called 'flexible production system' with its various elements of 'just-in-time' production, close supplier and customer relations, steady and incremental product improvements, also speed up the process of structural change. The flexible production system especially has the potential of contributing to the globalisation and regionalisation of production simultaneously: with regard to globalisation, because internationally competitive firms seek to be present in all major regions of the world economy; with regard to regionalisation, because the emerging flexible production system is essentially one which relies heavily on highly integrated regional production networks (UNCTAD 1994). Again, perceptions of greater insecurity and vulnerability are – justified or not – among the consequences to which regional integration initiatives and the new protectionism are in part a response.

One can therefore characterise globalisation as a centrifugal process of economic outreach which is essentially driven by the microeconomic forces of technology, strategies and behaviour of entrepreneurs, innovators, investors and consumers (see also Oman 1994: 33–4). In consequence, and according to Oman, globalisation is having three major effects: a heightening perception of growing 'interdependence', a diminished national policy sovereignty, and a greater uncertainty and instability.

The challenges of globalisation of production

While all three elements of globalisation contributed to sentiments towards global free trade, the challenges from globalisation of production are perceived as especially intrusive. However it is not the quantitative surge in overseas investments which is startling, but the changing character of those investments. According to Dunning (1992: 128–33) the most significant features of international business activities since 1960 have been:

- A shift from market-seeking and resource-seeking investments to rationalised and strategic asset-acquiring investment, with the former activities increasingly being viewed from a global perspective as a part of a geocentric or transnational organisational strategy of multinational enterprises.
- Changing and more pluralistic organisational forms of international business, including all forms of non-equity cooperative ventures like cross-border strategic alliances and networks of suppliers and customers.

- Frequent revisions of organisational forms and decision-taking structures to meet new environmental and technological challenges, with multinational enterprises increasingly performing as a controller of a system of interlocking value-added activities.

With the globalisation of production trade may become increasingly intra-firm especially in the manufacturing sector. Intra-firm trade is not directly governed by market prices and thus exhibits elements of a regulated trade where the allocation of resources is subordinated to strategic considerations of the involved corporations and not simply directed by elaboration on short-term allocative efficiency governed by market prices.[7] Moreover, the evolution of regional production networks and the resulting pattern of intra-firm (and, since non-equity partnerships are increasing, also inter-firm, cross-border trade) is often directly influenced by divergences in national and international regulations and their changes over time. The standard examples are divergences in taxation and regulation levels to which companies may respond by moving production locations or resorting to transfer pricing practices in order to reduce tax payments. Similarly, preferential treatment (or the loss of it) under the Generalised System of Preferences (GSP) can result in industrial relocations and give tremendous rise to foreign direct investments, nowadays also increasingly involving transnational corporations from the NIEs as can be seen from the example of Singapore. Since the loss of its GSP status Singaporian companies are increasingly engaged in the surrounding region like Johor State in Malaysia and Bantam Island which belongs to Indonesia. A new regional growth pole is thus developing fast with the active involvement of Third World Multinationals, responding in part to international trade policy developments.

A first important conclusion is that globalisation and regionalisation are not mutually exclusive events, but two sides of one coin. Both are increasingly driven by microeconomic forces of strategies and behaviour of firms coming along with the international diffusion of the new 'flexible' or 'lean' production systems and are supported and facilitated by government deregulation, the advances in information technologies and the globalisation of financial markets (Oman 1994: 13). In such a competitive environment firms tend to set up highly integrated regional production networks in each of the major economic regions of the Triad. Regionalisation and globalisation occur simultaneously on a de facto base. Although foreign direct investment is better than trade in spanning different regions, FDI also exhibit a pattern of regional concentration (see Table 1.3) (i.e. 'Geography still matters').

Second, under those conditions locational advantages of nation – or more precisely of economic regions – may become more rather than less important in shaping the international division of labour. Those advantages include not only natural and human resources, but a complex set of factors such as public and private infrastructure, specialised capabilities and experiences,

31

Table 1.3 Intensity ratios[a] for two-way trade and FDI of 10 major investor countries, 1990

Trading region/investor region	Partner/host region		
	North America	Europe	East Asia
North America			
Trade intensity	4.53	0.37	1.20
FDI intensity	2.03	0.84	0.80
Europe			
Trade intensity	0.46	1.49	0.37
FDI intensity	0.97	1.30	0.55
East Asia			
Trade intensity	1.54	0.38	2.27
FDI intensity	1.28	0.50	1.95

Notes:
[a] Trade intensity: share of partner region in total trade (exports and imports) of a given country, divided by share of partner region in worldwide trade, excluding trade with the given country.
   FDI intensity: share of host region in outward investment stock of a given country divided by share of host region in worldwide FDI stock, excluding FDI stock in the investor country.
Source: UN 1993: Tables VII.4 and VII.6

proximity to customers and suppliers, and so forth. It is important to note that there is a certain paradox in national policy-making. In a world where the mobility of goods, services and factors of production – with the exemption of labour – has increased tremendously, locational advantages like quality and quantity of the labour force, complementary research and development facilities, infrastructure in general, size and dynamics of markets, and regulations of various sorts can play an important and increasing role in shaping locational competitive advantages (UNCTAD 1994: 151–2). The point, however, is that those policies are, on the one hand, becoming increasingly difficult and complex to implement in an efficient way, and, on the other hand, entail a considerable risk of destructive competition for production locations in the absence of a multilateral agreement, like a 'GATT for Investment' that seeks to curb unfair and discriminatory practices in attracting foreign investments; a competition which poorer and disadvantaged nations chronically short of funds cannot win.

Third, the emergence of highly integrated regional production networks may require more policy harmonisation and coordination. *De jure* regionalisation may thus follow a de facto and sharply increasing deep integration at the production level which may have the potential of raising productivity tremendously. If and when such regionalist patterns tend to reinforce themselves, intra-regional trade may become more intensified. This region-alisation is thus as much a consequence of the globalisation process as it is – at times – the unintended outcome of policies. For example, Japan's much discussed industrial policy, which essentially appeared to have been forward-looking in that companies have been encouraged to relocate 'old' industries into neighbouring countries – a pattern now copied by some Asian NIEs – may have contributed to the building of the regional economy as much as the deliberate open-door policy of the host countries.

Fourth, as competition increases and unfolds both the centrifugal processes of globalisation and the centripetal processes of regionalisation, a policy response is needed on the global, regional and national/local level in order to reconcile the imperatives of economic efficiency with the needs and aspirations of the people.[8] It seems sensible neither to return to beggar-thy-neighbour policies nor to search for responses to globalisation alone on the global (multilateral) level. As any process of economic structural change involves some winners and losers, the distributional issues have to be addressed on the various levels at which they occur – probably necessitating compensation schemes (as they are common ground in regional integration programmes; see also Chapter 10).

Finally, the globalisation-cum-regionalisation process could involve consid-erable problems for a number of developing countries located apart from the major economic centres. As cheap, low-skilled labour becomes a less important element for locational decisions, many poor countries ironically may not benefit from the process of localised globalisation at just the time when most of them gave up (voluntarily or under advice from the Bretton Woods organisations or bilateral donors) their resentments against foreign direct investments (Oman 1994: 17–20). In this way, globalisation may exhibit tremendous implications for an unequal international distribution of gains from the changing pattern of trade and investment.

CONCLUSIONS

The full impact of globalisation is far from clear at the moment, but it seems likely that the pattern of trade and investment may change more rapidly than in earlier times, that insecurity and vulnerability are increasing, and that distributional consequences both within and between countries will be very complex.

All this calls for a global institutional response to coordinate the economic, social, environmental and political problems involved. Coordination is required with regard to an overlapping of issues like trade and environment, the interface between social and trade issues, and the interdependencies between monetary and trade policies. Likewise it is essential to coordinate national and regional responses to the challenges of globalisation. The task here is to avoid destructive policy competitions, be they in the field of trade (protectionism and exchange rate policies) or in the field of competing for production location (read: jobs). Among such measures the most important are in the fields of international investment, technology, competition policies, and labour, social and environmental standards, issues which will surely dominate the future agenda in international trade negotiations and the international economic and social system beyond the likely 'outreach' of the WTO.[9]

Nevertheless – somewhat paradoxically – globalisation also makes national and regional policies more important. A policy response on these sub-global levels is needed to address the issues of high unemployment, low productivity growth and the distributional consequences within national borders and within and among economic regions. As globalisation tends to foster rather than weaken regionalisation, it also calls for a subsequent policy harmonisation on a regional level which should be in line with the non-discrimination rules of the multilateral trading system.

As these issues expose countries to new risks and adjustment pressures it is important to contribute to the development of the international economic system which, alongside coordination, also encourages national and regional policy responses that aim at reconciling the imperatives of economic efficiency with the needs and aspirations of people. Without such efforts the threats to multilateralism will prevail or even increase, be it protectionism or be it 'fortress-type' regionalism. Both could ultimately work against the weakest – within countries and between countries. Their position is threatened and needs to be addressed and improved.

NOTES

1 Comments on an earlier draft by András Inotai, Nevin Shaw, Ann Clarke, Andreas Gettkant and Stefanie Kleimeier are gratefully acknowledged. The author is, however, responsible for all remaining errors.

2 Non-discriminatory treatment is further ensured by the national treatment principle which demands that like imported and domestic products are treated alike.

3 In practice 'reciprocity' cannot be separated from other elements of economic relations, like economic strength, structure and growth, secondary protection, and so forth. In effect, rather than 'reciprocity' it may happen that 'asynchronity' occurs which favours the stronger 'partner'. See, for example, Inotai and Kiss (Chapter 9) on the experience of Central and Eastern Europe with the Association Agreements with the European Union.

4 The foreign producer may use this extra rent for upgrading and diversifying his production. Non-tariff protection can therefore be a double-edged sword as it can contribute to creating new competition in other areas, often including higher value-added activities.

5 An exemption would be an 'open regionalism' which was suggested by World Bank circles as a concept for a non-discriminatory regionalism for the Asia–Pacific Region. It advocates negotiating tariff reductions regionally and extending them to non-members of the regional arrangement (Panagariya 1993). In effect, 'open regionalism' is thus a regionally based version of GATT-style most favoured nation liberalisation. Because reciprocity from all beneficiaries is not required, 'open regionalism' entails a free-rider problem.

6 Another important area of globalisation is cross-border ('global') environmental effects, as pollutants and greenhouse gases do not stop at national borders. Although this problem is not new, it was only recently that it became an issue on the international agenda, partly because of improvements in scientific monitoring of environmental impacts, partly because of changing preferences in affluent societies. The linkages between trade and environment are more closely examined in Chapter 8.

7 In the United States 34 per cent of all exports and 41 per cent of all imports were intra-firm trade in 1989. The corresponding figures for Japan are 33 per cent and 29 per cent, respectively (UNCTAD 1994: 143).

8 For a discussion of the policy implication on the multilateral level see also Chapter 10.

9 See especially Chapters 7, 8 and 10, which address the issue of to what extent these concerns should be tackled under the umbrella of the world trading system, or rather, what are the 'frontiers' of the world trading system.

BIBLIOGRAPHY

Baldwin, R.E. (1987) 'Multilateral Liberalisation', in J.M. Finger, and A. Olechowski, (eds) *The Uruguay Round. A Handbook for the Multilateral Trade Negotiations*, Washington DC: The World Bank.

Bhagwati, J. (1992a) 'The Threats to the World Trading System', *The World Economy*, Vol. 15: 443–56.

—— (1992b) 'Regionalism and Multilateralism: An Overview', New York: Columbia University Department of Economics Discussion Paper Series No. 603.

Borrmann, A. and Koopmann, G. (1994) 'Regionalisierung und Regionalismus im Welthandel', *Wirtschaftsdienst*, No. VII: 365–72.

Dunning, J.H. (1992) *Multinational Enterprises and the Global Economy*, Wokingham: Addison-Wesley.

Franzmeyer, F. (1996) 'The Consequences of the Uruguay Round for the OECD Countries', in this volume: Chapter 3.

GATT (1992) *International Trade 1991–92*, Geneva: GATT.

—— (1994) *International Trade 1993–94*, Geneva: GATT.

Gibbs, M. (1996) 'The Future Representation of the South in the International System', in this volume: Chapter 10.'

Grossmann, H. and Koopmann, G. (1996) 'Social Standards in International Trade: A New Protectionist Wave?', in this volume: Chapter 7.

Hewitt, A. and Koning, A. (1996) 'The Survival of Special Preferences under the Lomé Convention: The ACP Countries and Europe after the Uruguay Round', in this volume: Chapter 5.

IMF (1993) *Issues and Developments in International Trade Policies*, Washington DC: International Monetary Fund.

Inotai, A. and Kiss, J. (1996) 'Central and Eastern Europe's Integration into the World Trading Systems', in this volume: Chapter 9.

Krugman, P. (1991) 'The Move towards Free Trade Zones', in Federal Reserve Bank of Kansas City (ed.) *Policy Implications of Trade and Currency Zones*, Kansas City: Federal Reserve Bank of Kansas City.

—— (1992) 'Does the New Trade Theory Require a New Trade Policy?', *The World Economy*, Vol. 15: 423–41.

Maddison, A. (1991) 'Dynamic Forces in Capitalist Development. A Long-run Comparative View', Oxford: Oxford University Press.

Oman, C. (1994) *Globalisation and Regionalisation: The Challenge for Developing Countries*, Paris: OECD.

Panagariya, A. (1993) 'Should East Asia Go Regional? No, No, and Maybe', Washington DC: World Bank, Policy Department Working Paper No. 1209.

Preusse, H.G. (1994) 'Regional Integration in the Nineties. Stimulation or Threat to the Multilateral Trading System?, *Journal of World Trade*, Vol. 28, Iss. 4: 147–64.

Sander, H. (1995) 'Deep Integration, Shallow Regionalism, and Strategic Openness: Three Notes on Economic Integration in East Asia', in F.P. Lang and R. Ohr (eds) *International Economic Integration*, Berlin: Physica Verlag.

Schott, J.J. (1991) 'Trading Blocs and the World Trading System', *The World Economy*, Vol. 14: 1–17.

—— (1996) 'The Future Role of the WTO', in this volume: Chapter 6.

Shaw, N. and Hanson, A.J. (1996) 'Linking Trade and Environment to Promote Sustainable Development', in this volume: Chapter 8.

Singh, A. (1994) 'Global Economic Changes, Skills, and International Competitiveness', International Labour Review, Vol. 133, No. 2: 167–83.

Stevens, C. (1996) 'The Consequences of the Uruguay Round for Developing Countries', in this volume: Chapter 4.

Summers, L.H. (1991) 'Regionalism and the World Trading System', in Federal Reserve Bank of Kansas City (ed.) *Policy Implications of Trade and Currency Zones*, Kansas City: Federal Reserve Bank of Kansas City.

UN (1993) *World Investment Report 1993*, New York: United Nations.

UNCTAD (1994) *World Investment Report 1994. Transnational Corporations, Employment and the Workplace*, New York and Geneva: United Nations.

2

THE URUGUAY ROUND OF MULTILATERAL TRADE NEGOTIATIONS

A preliminary assessment of results[1]

United Nations Department of Economic and Social Information and Policy Analysis

A period of stagnation in world trade, pervasive drift to protectionism and erosion of confidence in the multilateral trading system followed suprisingly close on the heels of the Tokyo Round of multilateral trade negotiations, completed in 1979, which was designed to strengthen the system and liberalise trade. Already in the early 1980s these developments were beginning to be seen as a danger signal to the trading system. The GATT Ministerial meeting of November 1982, considering the multilateral trading system to be in serious danger, took a number of decisions on strengthening the system and initiated an elaborate work programme to this end. The sharply deteriorating international economic situation, the large amount of unfinished business from the Tokyo Round and lack of progress in the GATT work programme soon made it clear, however, that a new round of multilateral negotiations had become necessary. Those negotiations, the Uruguay Round, started with the Punta del Este Ministerial Declaration of September 1986 and were completed in December 1993. Some three years behind schedule, the agreement under the Uruguay Round comes into effect on 1 January 1995, subject to ratification, with implementation of some of its major elements spread over the next 10 years.

The major aims of the Uruguay Round, as set out in the Punta del Este Declaration were (a) to bring about further liberalisation and expansion of world trade in goods to the benefit of all countries, especially less developed countries, through improvement of access to markets by reduction and elimination of tariff and non-tariff barriers and (b) to strengthen the role of GATT, improve the multilateral trading system and bring about a wider area of world trade in goods under effective multilateral disciplines. The Declaration also agreed to an immediate stop to further trade-restrictive measures inconsistent with GATT rules and to minimise the use of restrictive measures which were legal under GATT rules and to roll back all measures that were inconsistent with GATT rules before the completion of the Uruguay Round. In parallel with negotiations to liberalise trade in goods, a major decision was taken to launch negotiations on trade in services – which now accounts for over 20 per cent of world trade – having the objective of establishing a 'multilateral framework of principles and rules for trade in services' with a view to expansion of such trade.

In its coverage of issues, the Uruguay Round has been the most ambitious of the multilateral trade negotiations.[2] Important areas, such as textiles and agriculture, which had so far remained largely outside the purview of GATT, were to be brought under GATT discipline. Negotiations were extended to services, intellectual property and trade-related investment, areas which had never before been regarded as concerns of the multilateral trading system. The widespread use of trade-distorting measures which evaded or ignored GATT rules and the perceived weakness of GATT in such areas as dispute settlement clearly called for action. Some of the GATT rules needed review and clarification. The number of issues negotiated was thus very large.

The number of countries participating in the Uruguay Round had also been far larger than in any other round. In all, as of December 1993, 117 countries took part in the Uruguay Round; of these 113 were contracting parties (full members) of GATT.[3] In the Tokyo Round, about 100 countries participated in the negotiations; of these, 70 were contracting parties. Unlike other multilateral trade talks, the involvement of the developing countries in the Uruguay Round was extensive. They fully participated in practically all major aspects of the negotiations and played a large role in bringing the Uruguay Round to a successful conclusion. A total of 88 developing countries participated in the Uruguay Round compared with 70 in the Tokyo Round. This reflected an increased realisation among those countries that the rapid globalisation of the international economy was a process from which no country could afford to be left out, as well as the continuing need of many of those countries for differential treatment, which could be met only through participation in negotiations.

A SUMMARY OF THE RESULTS OF THE NEGOTIATIONS

The negotiators sought to achieve the objectives of further trade liberalisation and strengthening of the multilateral trading system through simultaneous negotiations in a large number of areas. Some of the negotiations related directly to the opening up of markets, some others sought to extend the rules of multilateral trade to specific areas, and still others concerned the clarification and strengthening of these rules and institutional questions. The following paragraphs contain a brief survey of the main results.[4]

Market access

Increased access to markets was one of the critical, as well as one of the most complex, areas of negotiations. The negotiations aimed at reduction of tariff and non-tariff barriers, and binding of tariffs (in other words, undertaking not to raise the agreed rate) in agricultural and non-agricultural goods, and involved scores of country offers covering tens of thousands of tariff lines. By 15 December, when the Round was formerly completed, a number of market access offers were still to be completed and the least developed countries had been allowed an extra year to lodge their tariff schedules.

The assessment of the results of market access negotiations can only be partial at this stage. Based on offers as of mid-November 1993, the GATT secretariat estimated that the trade-weighted average tariffs on developed country industrial imports from all sources should decline from the pre-Round level of 6.4 to about 4 per cent, representing a reduction of 38 per cent.[5] Tariffs on their imports from developing countries should decrease from 6.8 to 4.5 per cent, or by 34 per cent. Though the average tariffs were small to start with, large differences in tariffs existed across product categories. For example, the developed country average tariff offered on imports of textiles from developing countries was estimated at 11.5 per cent (compared with 14.6 per cent at present) which was two and a half times the average tariff on industrial imports.

There has been a large increase in the proportion of duty-free developed country imports. This proportion is expected to increase from 20 to 43 per cent for imports of industrial products. In agriculture, significant reductions in tariffs are expected as a result of the Uruguay Round. As of mid-November 1993, the tariff reduction (including tariff equivalents resulting from tariffication of quantitative restrictions) offered by developed countries was 36 per cent.[6]

The importance of tariffs as a trade barrier has, in general, declined over the years as successive multilateral negotiations cut them down, while quantitative trade restrictions have gained in importance. A major objective of the Uruguay Round was to reduce non-tariff barriers. In so far as this will have been successful, the extent of reduction of trade barriers expected to be achieved through the Uruguay Round negotiations will exceed that indicated by the reduction of tariffs alone, probably very considerably. Major examples of non-tariff barriers are the Multifibre Arrangement (MFA), most trade in agriculture, import restrictions imposed under the safeguard clauses of GATT and the various 'grey area' measures like the voluntary export restraint (VER). Among the successes of the Uruguay Round are the phasing out or reduction of those barriers.

Textiles and clothing

The objective of negotiations has been to bring trade in textiles and clothing, which has been dominated for so long by MFA, fully under GATT rules and disciplines. The agreement envisages integration of this trade into GATT in three phases beginning 1 January 1995 and to be completed by 2005. It also provides for a formula for a progressive increase in the growth of trade for products remaining under restraints during the implementation period. Non-MFA restrictions will also be brought into conformity with GATT within the same time-frame. A Textiles Monitoring Body will be set up to oversee the implementation of the agreement.

Agriculture

Agriculture was an issue of protracted negotiations in the Tokyo Round. Except for limited agreements on dairy products and bovine meat, however, the negotiations foundered, mainly on basic disagreements between the EU and the United States. It would be another 15 years before an agreement on agriculture could finally be reached.

The agreements on agriculture provide a framework for long-term reform of agricultural trade and domestic policies. At the core of the agreements lie commitments on market access, domestic support and export subsidies. In addition, under a Ministerial decision concerning least developed and food-importing developing countries, the possible adverse effect of liberalisation on those countries will be closely monitored and their food requirements considered. A related agreement on sanitary and phytosanitary measures seeks to discourage arbitrary application of rules concerning food safety and animal and plant health regulations that impede trade.

On market access, non-tariff measures are to be replaced by their tariff equivalent, and total tariffs (that is, tariffs combining this tariffication process and existing tariffs) are to be reduced by an average of 36 per cent in the case of developed countries and by 24 per cent in the case of developing countries. The developed countries are to undertake this reduction over six years while the developing countries have ten years to achieve their target. Least developed countries are not required to reduce their tariffs.

Domestic support to agriculture, which has been a major source of distortion in trade in agriculture, is to be significantly reduced. An agreed measure of such support, called the Total Aggregate Measurement of Support (Total AMS), is to be reduced by 20 per cent during the implementation period in the case of developed countries. For the developing countries, the reduction required is 13.3 per cent, while the least developed countries are not required to undertake any reduction. For all countries, support measures that have a minimal impact on trade ('green box' policies), including payments under structural adjustment assistance and environment programmes, are exempted from these requirements.

Direct export subsidies to agriculture are to be reduced, in the case of developed countries, to a level 36 per cent below their 1986–90 base period level over six years, and the quantity of subsidised exports is to be cut by

21 per cent over the same period. There is some flexibility regarding the base period but not on the period of implementation. In the case of developing countries, the reductions, which are two-thirds of those for the developed countries, are to be made over a ten-year period. The least developed countries are exempted from these requirements.

Services

Considering the growing importance of trade in services for growth and development of the world economy, the negotiators sought to bring services under multilateral rules and disciplines and create a framework for continuing trade liberalisation. The agreement recognises, however, the right of member countries to regulate supply of services within their own territories in order to meet national policy objectives and the particular need of developing countries to exercise that right.

The basic agreement on services, which applies to all member countries, defines services as being covered by multilateral rules, and as including services supplied by one country to another, services supplied by the territory of one country to the consumers of another (for example, tourism), services provided through the presence of service-providing entities of one country in the territory of another (for example, banking) and services provided by nationals of one country in the territory of another (for example, construction projects and consultancies).

The basic agreement also sets out the general obligations and disciplines. The MFN obligation is extended to trade in services. It recognises, however, that MFN treatment may not be possible for every type of service and therefore envisages that parties may indicate specific MFN exemptions. Those exemptions are to be reviewed after five years and generally limited to a ten-year duration. The agreement includes the important general obligation to provide national treatment to foreign suppliers. It also recognises that domestic regulations, as distinct from border measures, significantly influence trade in services and requires that such measures should be administered in a reasonable, objective and impartial manner. The basic agreement further emphasises transparency and requires all parties to enhance it through publication of all laws and regulations concerning trade in services.

The agreement of course goes far beyond basic principles. One of its major components contains rules and disciplines relating to particular services (telecommunications, financial services and air transport services) and movement of labour. The agreement on labour movement permits countries to negotiate specific commitments applying to movement of people providing services. The agreement does not apply to measures affecting persons seeking access to the employment market of a member or to measures regarding citizenship, residence or employment on a permanent basis.

A third major component of the agreement provides the basis of progressive liberalisation of trade in services through successive rounds of negotiations and the development of national schedules of market access commitments. A large number of national offers of commitments on market access are already on the table in this area. Countries are free to decide which services they would include in the offer and may also impose limitations on market access and national treatment with the agreement of other participants.[7] The agreement also allows parties to withdraw or modify, through negotiations, their schedules after three years.

Trade-related aspects of intellectual property rights (TRIP)

Infringement of intellectual property rights and trade in counterfeit products have often been a source of international tension. The agreement addresses the applicability of GATT principles and those of relevant international intellectual property agreements, provision of adequate enforcement measures for intellectual property rights, and multilateral dispute settlement.

Under its basic principles, the agreement extends, for the first time, the requirement of MFN treatment to intellectual property. It then takes up each type of intellectual property and, where necessary building on existing international agreements, lays down the guidelines and requirements of each type. Among the major features of the agreement are the following: it requires parties to comply with the substantive provisions of the Berne Convention for the protection of literary and artistic work; it ensures that computer programs will be protected as literary work; it seeks to protect the rights of authors of computer programs and producers of sound records to authorise or prohibit the commercial rental of their work and to protect live performances from bootlegging. In trade marks, the agreement defines what type of signs should be eligible for protection. Industrial designs are similarly protected under the agreement.

The agreement sets out the obligation of member governments to provide adequate protection under their domestic laws to the intellectual property rights of foreigners as well as to those of their own nationals. Settlement of disputes over infringements of intellectual property rights between member countries are to be brought under the GATT dispute settlement procedures.

For developed countries, the agreement envisages a one-year transition period to bring their national legislation and practices into conformity with the guidelines of the agreement. Developing countries and economies in transition to the market system have a five-year transition period and the least developed countries have an eleven-year one.

Trade-related investment measures (TRIM)

The agreement provides that no member shall apply any trade-related investment measure (TRIM) that is inconsistent with GATT rules of national treatment and prohibition of quantitative restrictions. It provides an illustrative list of TRIMs that violate those rules. The agreement requires notification of all non-conforming TRIMs and their removal within a specified period: two years for developed countries, five years for developing countries and within seven years for the least developed countries.

Safeguards

GATT article XIX, which allows a member country to take temporary action to protect ('safeguard') a domestic industry from 'serious injury' due to a sudden and large increase in imports, has often been used as a pretext for protection and its provisions have often been skirted around through 'grey area measures', such as 'voluntary' export restraints. Strengthening of article XIX was a major objective of the Tokyo Round but little was achieved. Among the achievements of the Uruguay Round was its prohibition of the grey area measures and its setting of definite time-limits (the 'sunset clause') to the duration of action that could be taken under the article.

The agreement provides, *inter alia*, that all existing safeguard measures taken under article XIX shall be terminated not later than eight years after the date on which they were first applied, or five years after the date of entry into force of the agreement establishing the World Trade Organization (WTO), whichever comes later. It lays down criteria for determining 'serious injury' to domestic industry and provides that safeguard measures can be applied only to the extent necessary to prevent or remedy the injury. The safeguard measures should not normally discriminate as to the sources of import. Time-limits of all safeguard measures have been laid down. The duration should not generally exceed four years, though this could be extended to a maximum of eight years. Safeguard measures should not be applied to a product from a developing country if the imports of the product from the country do not exceed a minimum share defined in the agreement (around 3 per cent, given other conditions).

Anti-dumping measures

GATT rules provide for a member country's right to take measures against imports of products that are priced by their exporters below their 'normal value'. In recent years there has been an increasing use of such anti-dumping measures which have become a major mode of protection.

Rules governing the application of such measures have been more clearly spelled out under the new agreement, in particular the method of determining whether a product is being dumped, the criteria for determining that the dumped imports have caused injury to the domestic industry, the procedure to be followed in anti-dumping investigation and the duration of anti-dumping measures. The agreement also calls for prompt and detailed notification of all anti-dumping action to the GATT Committee on Anti-Dumping Practices.

Subsidies and countervailing measures

Subsidisation of domestic industries has been a major source of trade distortion. By seeking to reduce or eliminate subsidies, the negotiations under the Uruguay Round aimed at reducing these distortions as an important way to liberalise trade. Reduction of subsidies in agriculture is a major example of this effort but subsidies are by no means limited to that sector.

Subsidies that the agreement sought to address are those that are specific to industries rather than general subsidies. The agreement establishes three categories of subsidies. In the first category are subsidies that enhance competitiveness of exports or import-competing industries. These are to be prohibited under the agreement and are subject to the new dispute settlement procedures. In the second category are subsidies that adversely affect the interest of other member countries, for example, through injury to domestic industry ('actionable' subsidies). Members affected by actionable subsidies may take up the matter with the Dispute Settlement Body. The third category of subsidies are either non-specific or involve assistance to industrial research or to disadvantaged regions, and are non-actionable.

The agreement also covers the use of countervailing measures against subsidising imports. It lays down rules for initiating countervailing cases and for investigation by national authorities. Countervailing duties have normally to be terminated within five years.

While subsidies distort, they also play an important role in economic development policies of developing countries. The agreement exempts the least developed countries and developing countries with per capita income under $1,000 from the disciplines of 'prohibited' export subsidies. For other developing countries, prohibition of export subsidies would take effect eight years after the establishment of WTO. For countries in transition to the market system, the prohibited subsidies are to be phased out within a period of seven years from the date of entry into force of the agreement.

Dispute settlement

The working of the multilateral trading system depends critically on the speed and effectiveness of its dispute settlement procedures. Indeed, a major source of dissatisfaction with the present system has been its perceived weakness in this area. Bilateral or unilateral action is often seen as far more competitive by comparison. One of the major results of the Uruguay Round has been the Understanding on Rules and Procedures Governing the Settlement of Disputes (DSU) which significantly strengthens rules and procedures. In particular, the new Understanding provides for greater automaticity in decisions on the establishment, terms of reference and composition of dispute settlement panels in that they no longer depend on the consent of the parties to the dispute.

The DSU requires a member state to enter into consultation within 30 days of a request for consultation from the complaining member; and if there is no settlement within 60 days, the latter may request the setting up of a dispute settlement panel. The DSU sets out the panel procedures. The panel, normally consisting of three persons of appropriate background, from countries not party to the dispute, and approved by the Director-General if there is no agreement among the parties on its composition, will complete its work within six months or, in urgent cases, within three months. A Dispute Settlement Body (DSB), exercising the authority of the General Council of WTO, will adopt the report within 60 days of its issuance, unless the DSB decides, by consensus, not to adopt it or if one of the parties wishes to appeal.

Appellate review is an important new feature of the dispute settlement mechanism. The DSU provides for an Appellate Body which will examine only the issues of law covered by the panel. The proceedings of the Body should not exceed 60 days and the resulting report shall be adopted by the DSB and accepted unconditionally by the parties to the dispute, unless the DSB decides, by consensus, against its adoption. The DSB will keep the implementaion under review till the issue is resolved. The agreement provides for rules of compensation for the party concerned, or suspension by the party of its concessions or other obligations to the other party, where the recommendation is not implemented. The DSU explicitly provides that the parties will not themselves make the determination of the violation or suspend concessions, but rather will use the DSU mechanism.

Customs unions and free trade areas (article XXIV)

The agreement recognises that the number of regional trade blocs, in the form of customs unions and free trade areas, has greatly increased in recent years and notes the contribution they might make to the expansion of world trade. It reaffirms the general principle contained in article XXIV of the GATT that these regional trading agreements should be such that they cover all trade among the constituent territories because the contribution of the expansion of world trade is diminished if any major sector of trade is excluded. It stresses that the purpose of such arrangements should be to facilitate trade between the constituent territories and not to raise barriers to trade of other member countries with such territories. The agreement clarifies and reinforces the criteria and procedure for the review of new or enlarged regional trading arrangements and for evaluation of their effects on third parties.

Trade Policy Review Mechanism

An early result of the Uruguay Round, achieved in December 1988, was an agreement on the Trade Policy Review Mechanism under which trade policies of member countries are already being examined in detail by GATT. The objective of the Mechanism is to approve the adherence by all members to rules, disciplines and commitments made under multilateral agreements by achieving greater transparency of national trade policies. The final agreement of December 1993 confirms the Mechanism and encourages greater transparency in national policy-making in trade.

Achieving greater coherence in global economic policy-making

The Uruguay Round negotiators recognised the importance of the interrelationship between international monetary and financial conditions and international trade. A separate decision sets out proposals for achieving greater coherence in global economic policy-making and called on WTO to develop cooperation with the World Bank and IMF with this objective in view.

The World Trade Organization (WTO)

The agreement creates the World Trade Organization (WTO) which will encompass the GATT, as modified by the Uruguay Round, and all agreements and arrangements concluded under the Round. The highest body of the organisation will be the Ministerial Conference, which will meet at least every two years, and under which the General Council will oversee the operations of WTO agreements and ministerial decisions on a regular basis. The General Council will also act in the capacity of the DSB and the Trade Policy Review Body. Like GATT, WTO will conduct decision-making on the basis of consensus. Where voting is necessary, decisions will be taken by a majority vote, except in cases where an interpretation of the WTO agreement is involved, where a two-thirds majority will be required.

The main functions of WTO will be to facilitate the implementation of multilateral agreements on trade and provide the forum for multilateral trade negotiations; to administer the dispute settlement mechanism; to administer the trade policy review mechanism; and to develop cooperation with international organisations dealing with other major issues such as money and finance.

IMPACT ON WORLD TRADE AND INCOME

The liberalisation of trade resulting from the Uruguay Round should lead to a significant increase in world trade and income. Quantification of such aggregate results is difficult, however, and results obtained by the various studies so far should be seen as reflecting only broad orders of magnitudes. A GATT study suggests that world trade (in 1992 prices) in 2005 should be some $745 billion or 12 per cent higher – owing to the effects of trade liberalisation through improved market access as a result of the completion of the Uruguay Round – than it would otherwise be.[8] Some of the largest projected increases in trade are in sectors of great interest to developing countries, such as clothing (60 per cent), textiles (34 per cent), and agriculture, forestry and fishery products (20 per cent). The assumption used in estimating what the trade volume in 2005 would be without the Uruguay Round results was that trade would grow at around 4 per cent, the rate at which it had been growing over the period 1980–91. One implication of the aggregate numbers is that the average annual growth rate of world trade would rise by a full one percentage point over the period 1995–2005.

Trade liberalisation resulting from the success of the Uruguay Round will bring about a corresponding increase in world income. The GATT study estimates that world income will be some $230 billion (in 1992 dollars) higher by 2005 than it would be without the Round. This is broadly in line with the results of other studies on the impact of the Uruguay Round.[9] These numbers represent approximately 1 per cent of world income in 1992. According to one study, income in developing economies would increase by some $80 billion as a result of trade liberalisation from the Uruguay Round.

While these aggregate numbers represent only broad orders of magnitude and appear merely modest, they almost certainly underestimate the gains from the Uruguay Round. First, as the GATT study points out, they do not take into account the gains in trade in services due to liberalisation measures taken in the Uruguay Round. Furthermore, the estimates assume that international trade and world income would have continued to grow at the same rate as in the past even if the Round had failed. The possibility of a deterioration in the international economy directly linked with a failure of the negotiations was real, however. Thus, in so far as a 'without the Round' situation underestimates the potential cost of failure, the aggregate number also underestimates the net gain due to the success of the Round. There are also other important gains that are not easily quantifiable. The conclusion of the Round, for example, is expected to increase confidence in the trading system through the strengthening of the multilateral rules of trade, and this should by itself encourage investment in trade-related activities leading to higher volumes of traded output. It is also likely that the success of the multilateral trade negotiations will help to weaken regionalism.

While the completion of the Uruguay Round is expected to result in significant gains for the world economy, its impact will vary greatly among industries and economic groups within a given country and among countries and regions of the world. Within individual countries, there will be gainers and losers among both producers and consumers, with consumers in general tending to gain from any import liberalisation. The gains or losses, in absolute and relative terms, will also differ greatly among countries, though the gains from trade liberalisation should in general outweigh any losses in the long run. Particular concern has been expressed regarding the net impact of the Round on some developing countries.

The relative gain or loss of a country as a result of any trade liberalisation measure will depend on the role of international trade in the national economy, the pattern of its imports and exports, the extent of liberalisation in specific areas of trade, and the time-horizon considered relevant for the assessment of the results. For trade negotiations as vast and complex as the Uruguay Round, it is too early to assess gains and losses of individual countries with any degree of accuracy, although a number of observations on the broad directions of the relative gains and losses can nevertheless be made.

The developing countries as a whole should gain significantly as some of the impediments to exports that are of interest to them fall down. As pointed out above, the expansion of exports of textiles and clothing due to the phasing out of MFA is expected to be substantial. More important, since the fastest growth of trade is expected to take place in manufactures in general rather than in primary commodities, and given the past experience of high rates of growth of manufactured exports from the developing countries, a considerable share of the benefit of liberalisation in manufactures should accrue to those countries.

The gains from trade expansion will, however, differ greatly among developing countries. Though the structure of an economy does indeed change over time, the ten-year time-horizon in which most of the negotiated measures are expected to take effect is not long enough for radical changes in many developing countries to take place. In a large number of primary-producing developing countries, diversification into manufacturing to take advantage of the potential expansion of trade in manufactures will be a slow process. Those countries will probably gain only little from liberalisation. In terms of regions, many countries in Africa would fall within this category. Most of the gain is likely to accrue to the more diversified economies of Asia and Latin America. Even in the relatively simple labour-intensive industries like clothing, where new producers are likely to emerge as MFA is phased out, a large gain for Africa is not assured in the next ten years.

Many African and other primary-producing countries could also find themselves among the least benefited, partly because of the low price elasticity as well as the low income elasticity of demand for many primary commodities and partly because trade barriers to some of those commodities are already low. Barriers to most tropical foods are already low in the industrialised countries and the further reduction in tariffs resulting from the Uruguay Round would probably not lead to a significant expansion of their exports. On the other hand, developing country exporters of food grain should see a substantial increase in their exports. Once again, most African countries will not benefit from an increase in this trade.

Some of the net food-importing developing countries, many of them African and West Asian, may face an increase in the cost of imported food as world food prices rise as a short-term result of the Uruguay Round. However, in so far as food is obtained as grant, the price increase should leave the cost to the importers unchanged. On the other hand, continuing dependence on food aid cannot be a long-term choice for any country. In any event, the question of whether to buy food from abroad or produce it at home is one that policy-makers have to decide early in any programme of sustained economic development.

As MFN tariffs are cut and non-tariff barriers in general come down, the preferences given to developing countries under special arrangements such as the Generalised System of Preferences and the Lomé Convention will tend to erode. The extent of the erosion will depend, however, on how those arrangements, which have limited durations, are renewed and adjusted to take into account the general reduction of trade barriers and how the new margins of preferences are worked out.[10]

BEYOND THE URUGUAY ROUND

The Uruguay Round has been a major step towards liberalisation of world trade and strengthening of the multilateral trading system. The cuts in tariffs and reduction of non-tariff barriers through such measures as reduction in subsidies in agriculture and phasing out of MFA, and other agreements that further discourage the use of arbitrary border measures, should lead to a significant increase in world trade. The agreement brings under the multilateral framework the important new area of trade in services which should expand faster as a result. The creation of a permanent and more effective body – the WTO – to oversee world trade and provide a forum for continuing trade liberalisation is a major achievement. In a fundamental sense, the agreement is also a commitment not to practise 'managed' trade. A number of steps have been taken to increase transparency of national trade policies, and to strengthen multilateral disciplines and rules. In the final analysis, however, these results will depend on how member countries live up to the agreements. Above all, it will depend on whether the Uruguay Round's multilateralism will be upheld in letter and spirit.

A nation may often be tempted to bend its own rules, however liberal they might be for international trade, to accommodate special interests or to pursue short-term gains, and thus diminish its own long-term economic well-being as well as that of the world. Binding international rules are meant to guard against such temptations. The Uruguay Round does strengthen multilateral rules of trade. Yet threats of unilateral action, which usually come from the powerful countries, can undermine even the most elaborately designed multilateral system. As the Secretary-General of the GATT points out, there is evidence since the signing of the accord in December that 'major economic powers are still ready to take the unilateral approach to trade problems. We have clearly not heard the last of managed trade, an idea which is the antithesis of an open multilateral system. Arguments for protectionism based on the alleged threat of low-cost competition to production and jobs will not just fade away because the Round is a success.'[11] A willingness of all countries to adhere fully to the agreed multilateral rules of trade thus lies at the heart of the ultimate success of the Uruguay Round in liberalising world trade.

The obvious first step is a speedy ratification of the agreement by national governments. While ultimate ratification by most signatories is not in doubt, concern has been expressed over the prospect of only a slow process of ratification in some cases. With the Final Act of the Round formally signed on 15 April 1994 in Marrakesh, it is imperative that all signatories proceed to ratify the agreement without delay.

While implementation of the various agreements on market access and removal of trade distortions, such as subsidies, and unfinished business in liberalisation of trade in services, will be some of the major tasks in the years ahead, two sets of issues are likely to be important concerns of international trade policy: developing country import competition and labour standards, and the relationship between trade and the environment.

Increasingly, concern is being expressed in the industrialised countries over the impact of increased imports of labour-intensive commodities on employment and wages in those countries. Since the *sine qua non* of the trade liberalisation measures of the Uruguay Round is increased trade and trade arises out of differences between countries, concern over increased competition from developing countries, which have a comparative advantage in some products but not in others, appears to question the very rationale behind the Round. However, the question has been greatly complicated by the issue of labour standards. The argument is being increasingly made that labour is cheap in developing countries because their labour standards are lax, while high labour standards make labour expensive in developed countries. Violation of human rights, including use of child labour, has also been seen as a way of keeping wages low in developing countries and giving them an unfair competitive advantage. Such issues have great social, cultural and moral ramifications. However, they can also be used as a pretext for protection against imports from developing countries. A balance must be struck between the recognition of the fact that trade arises because countries are different and the incontrovertible need to protect human rights; but it would be essential to separate the two issues.

The relationship between the environment and trade is receiving increasing attention at national and international levels. Environmental considerations were never completely ignored in GATT and a number of GATT articles take those considerations into account. Multilateral discussions of these issues are bound to increase in importance in the coming years, despite the reservations of many countries regarding the competence of trade organisations in this area. A GATT/WTO programme of work is being drawn up including items on trade, labour standards, competition policy, investment rules, finance/exchange rate policies, and environment, as well as sustainable development. WTO, unlike GATT, already embodies the question of sustainable development in its preamble.

NOTES

1 Source: United Nations Department of Economic and Social Information and Policy Analysis, 'World Economic and Social Survey 1994. Current Trends and Policies in the World Economy', 79–88; Copyright: United Nations 1994. Permission for reproduction granted 16 December 1994.
2 Though world trade still faces numerous barriers, the post-war world has seen an unprecedented degree of trade liberalisation. Much of this has taken place through a series of rounds of multilateral trade negotiations under GATT auspices. These were: Geneva Round: 1947; Annecy (France) Round: 1949; Torquay (England) Round: 1951; Geneva Round: 1956; Dillon Round: 1960–1; Kennedy Round: 1964–7; Tokyo Round: 1973–9.
3 For further details, see *Focus, GATT Newsletter*, No. 104 (December 1993).
4 These paragraphs draw heavily on the press summary of the results issued by GATT on 14 December 1993 and its addendum of 15 December 1993 and partly on GATT, Final Act Embodying the Results of the Uruguay Round of Multilateral Negotiations (MTN/FA, 15 December 1993), and GATT, 'An analysis of the proposed Uruguay Round agreements, with particular emphasis on aspects of interest to developing countries' (MTN.TNC/W/122, MTN.GNG/W/30 and corrigendum). In several cases, the language of the press summary and the Final Act has been retained.
5 GATT, 'An analysis of the proposed Uruguay Round agreements, with particular emphasis on aspects of interest to developing countries' (MTN.TNC/W/122, MTN.GNG/W/30 and corrigendum), p. 24, table 11.
6 Ibid.
7 Ibid.
8 See GATT, 'An analysis of the proposed Uruguay Round agreements, with particular emphasis on aspects of interest to developing countries' (MTN.TNC/W/122, MTN.GNG/W/30 and corrigendum), November 1993, based on offers as of mid-November 1993.
9 Organization for Economic Cooperation and Development (OECD), *Assessing the effects of the Uruguay Round*, Trade Policy Issues, No. 2 (Paris, 1993). The study suggests that net world welfare will be around $270 billion higher in the year 2002. Of this, some $86 billion will accrue to non-OECD countries.
10 A study by the GATT secretariat – based on the assumption that preferential rates are adjusted to retain their current relationship with MFN rates and that rates that are currently at zero remain at zero – suggests, however, that the overall results will be a net expansion of trade receiving preferential treatment. See GATT, 'An analysis of the proposed Uruguay Round agreements, with particular emphasis on aspects of interest to developing countries' (MTN.TNC/W/122, MTN.GNG/W/30 and corrigendum), p. 42.
11 GATT, 'Global trade – the next challenge', address by Peter D. Sutherland to the World Economic Forum, Davos, 28 January 1994 (NVR 082, 28 January 1994).

3

THE CONSEQUENCES OF THE URUGUAY ROUND FOR THE OECD COUNTRIES

Fritz Franzmeyer

PROBABLE DEVELOPMENTS IN TRADE CREATION AND TRADE DIVERSION: AN OUTLINE

The Organization for Economic Cooperation and Development (OECD) countries are responsible for just under three-quarters of all world trade. Similarly, three-quarters of the total trade of these countries consists in the mutual exchange of goods, of which one-fifth relate to manufactured products (GATT 1994: 80–1, 92–5). Only in trade with developing countries do the import and export structures of the OECD differ in any marked way in terms of product groups. The greater part of OECD trade in services also takes place between its own members (Petersen *et al.* 1993: 98–100). Given these relations, it would seem obvious that, as far as the OECD countries are concerned, the results of the Uruguay Round are of relevance chiefly in terms of their reciprocal trade. However, there are two reasons why this is not the case.

For one thing, 60 per cent of internal OECD trade is within the European Economic Area, consisting of the European Union (EU) and the remaining European Free Trade Association (EFTA) countries. But Western Europe has regulated both its internal trade (except for trade in agricultural goods between the EU and EFTA) and the rules governing freedom of establishment, according to its own set of laws, which are more far-reaching compared with those of GATT. Tariff-free trade between the North American Free Trade Area (NAFTA) countries (USA, Canada, Mexico) and between Australia and New Zealand has, similarly, to be excluded. Overall, a residue of only a little less than one-third of total internal OECD trade remains which is subject to the most favoured nation (MFN) duties agreed in the GATT – in other words to which the Uruguay Round is relevant.

Second, the internal trading relations of the OECD countries, or country groupings, do not contain as much potential for conflict as do their external ones. Much of what has now been agreed in Geneva for all GATT countries, or (viz. the so-called plurilateral agreements) for particular signatory states, had already been regulated by the OECD some time ago, within its own framework. This applies in particular to mutual guarantees to investors, the protection of intellectual property rights, the freedom to provide services, and public procurement. To this extent, the Uruguay Round may have brought the OECD some marginal improvements in legal security and freedom to trade, but it has not brought anything fundamentally new as far as trade with the remaining members of GATT is concerned. Again, the OECD countries in the main engage in the exchange of goods on which the most favoured nation tariffs are already extremely low.

This does not mean that, in particular cases, trade between the major OECD actors will not be massively affected by various outcomes of Uruguay. This is true, for example, of certain Japanese manufactured goods exported to the USA and the EU which up to now have been subject to voluntary export restraints (VERs) – that is to say, informal quantitative restrictions that have come about as a result of pressure from the importing country, or group of importing countries, and which GATT has up to now had no means of influencing. The same is true of agricultural trade. This issue – which, in the final phase of the talks, was almost exclusively negotiated on by the USA and the EU – threatened for a time to lead to the breakdown of the whole Uruguay Round. In contrast, there were other areas which, because the USA and EU or other major OECD partners were unable to agree in Geneva, remained unresolved within the framework of the Uruguay Round, but were not crucial for the progress of the negotiations as a whole. This was the case, in particular, for audiovisual services. The reason for the varying pressure for regulation is that in the case of agricultural products, the USA and EU are mainly competing in outside markets, whereas in service domains there is reciprocal market access, which can also be – or, as in air transport, is – regulated bilaterally. It would in any case be a mistake to suppose that within the future international economic order, bilateralism in trade relations will play only a subordinate role.

Yet even within OECD trade with third countries there are trade flows on which the results of the Geneva negotiations will have no great influence because they are already regulated along liberal lines, and in a way that is satisfactory for the countries concerned in terms of outward direct investments. This applies in particular to EU trade with the African, Caribbean and Pacific (ACP) countries, and, recently, with the countries in transition in eastern Central Europe. Within the framework, respectively, of the Lomé Convention and the Europe Agreements, these two sets of countries enjoy, or will soon enjoy, unrestricted, tariff-free access to the EU market for their industrial products; in addition, freedom of establishment, investment protection, and protection of intellectual property are more comprehensively regulated here than in the Uruguay Round. Moreover, preferential market access for industrial products and for specific agricultural goods is given by the industrialised countries to the remaining developing countries, and by the EU to the countries in transition, within the framework of their Generalised Systems of Preferences (GSPs).

Taking into account, on the one hand, the special contracted regulations within different geographic groupings, and, on the other, the geographic variation in the potential for conflict, it is possible to identify an initial group of trade relations, and product-specific or comprehensive regulations, in which OECD trade will be appreciably affected by the Uruguay Round:

- As far as internal OECD relations are concerned, there will be an expansion of mutual trade in industrial goods, particularly within the Triad (North America/Japan/EU). This trade is subject to most favoured nation tariffs and is, therefore, one of the areas of trade for which tariff barriers still have some significance.
- As far as external OECD relations are concerned, the effective factors here will be not only the numerous agreements on the facilitation of trade – notably in regard to agricultural products, textiles and clothing – but also the General Agreement on Trade in Services (GATS), the Agreement on Trade-Related Aspects of Intellectual Property Rights (TRIPs), and the Agreement on Trade-Related Investment Measures (TRIMs). Tariff reductions will primarily affect trade with the newly industrialising countries (NICs). The elimination of agricultural protectionism will be of benefit chiefly to Latin America, and the expiry of the Multifibre Arrangement (MFA) chiefly to South East Asia. (Exports of textiles and clothing to the EU by the countries in transition in eastern Central Europe will shortly be regulated along liberal lines within the framework of the Europe Agreements.) The greatest curtailment to be suffered as a result of the TRIP agreement will be in the flow of imports into the USA – but also into Western Europe – from countries with a particular penchant for pirating intermediate technology products and fashion goods. The TRIM agreement favours OECD exports to NICs (see pages 58–60).
- The whole of OECD trade could be greatly affected by the horizontal agreements, particularly those regarding dispute settlement procedures, safeguards, and the more transparent and objective formulation of anti-dumping/anti-subsidy procedures – including the standardisation of non-preferential rules of origin that is crucial in this context (pages 61–3).

Some of the attempts that have been made in the Uruguay literature to assess the quantitative effects of the Geneva negotiations on the OECD and its subregions in terms of welfare and growth are discussed on pages 63–8 of this chapter. The concluding section of this chapter is devoted, albeit in a general way, to the effects of Uruguay on the job market and on employment – a subject rarely dealt with in the literature.

TRADE WITHIN THE TRIAD

As highly industrialised countries, OECD members trade with each other chiefly in machinery, electrical equipment, motor vehicles, and technology intensive chemical products. In many cases, tariffs are now to be completely eradicated in these areas – including tariffs on pharmaceuticals, medical technology, construction machinery and steel. Initially, this will apply to mutual trade within the group of four countries (Quad group) – the USA, Canada, EU and Japan – who concluded the decisive package of reciprocal tariff reductions in Tokyo in 1993 (UNCTAD 1994: 139). However, because of the most favoured nation principle, the imports which the group receives from all the other MFN countries will also benefit from this total removal of tariffs. Relative cuts in duty charges – some quite impressive – were also agreed for other products. On average, MFN tariffs for industrial goods are to be reduced by a third – although this tends to disguise the fact that in each case only a few percentage points are involved. The high reduction rates in relative terms are explained by the fact that the MFN tariffs in many product groups had already sunk to the low average level of 4–9 per cent even before the Uruguay Round. In the case of major trade flows, MFN tariffs are now, following the Uruguay Round, still significant only in the case of cars – and in Europe also in the case of office and telecommunications equipment.

The particularly generous looking concessions made by Japan in, most notably, the area of technological goods, is the price that country is having to pay for what, despite sizeable reductions, remains its extremely high level of residual tariffs on non-tropical agricultural products. They also show that Japan, in its long-established demesne, is not dependent on tariff-based protection, because its high level of productivity ensures a competitive advantage in prices that exceeds the remaining tariff differential. In addition, informal import protection in this area functions well in conjunction with the country's vertical corporate structure.

The European Union had the most difficulties in coming to terms with the liberalisation regarding cars. The EU reduced the average tariff by only 1.5 points from 9.5 to 8.4 per cent, leaving itself with the highest residual tariff level of all product groups and all major participating countries. In addition, there is the protection afforded by a voluntary restraint agreement with Japan. This outcome was undoubtedly also influenced by the state of the European car industry in the concluding phase of the negotiations, when sales stagnation due to the business cycle situation was combined with a crisis in cost and structure. One is quite justified in asking whether a branch of industry which, globally, is competing in oligopolistic markets, and which relies on competition as a motor for innovation, is not hamstringing itself by insisting on a relatively high level of import protection.

On average, however, the Quad country that remains the most protectionist in regard to the whole range of investment goods is Canada. Given its high starting level, however, it also had the greatest adjustment to make. As an indication of new flexibility, this is all the more significant in that, at the same time, Canada has had to remove tariffs relating to its most important trading partner – the USA – within the framework of NAFTA. The tendency towards alignment runs through all the agreements on tariff reduction: countries with a high starting level have to make higher reductions, in absolute terms, than those with a low one. As a result, the principle of approximate equality in tariff protection is gaining general acceptance to an extent that was not the case in previous GATT Rounds.

Mutual tariff reduction will intensify intra-industrial exchange between North America, Western Europe and Japan in the areas of machinery, plant and pharmaceuticals. However, the OECD countries do not trade with each other only in technologically sophisticated industrial goods, but also to a considerable extent in non-tropical agricultural products, products involving low levels of raw material processing, textiles and clothing. In the case of agricultural products, all non-tariff barriers will be converted into tariffs (tariffication) and all tariffs, including the new ones, will be reduced by an average of 36 per cent, with a 15 per cent minimum for any single item. However, 'dirty tariffication' – that is to say, calculating inflated tariff equivalents of non-tariff trade barriers – may diminish real results. In the case of Japanese rice imports, which are very strongly protected, quantitative restriction of tariff concessions will actually remain permissible for the time being. The maintenance of a relatively high average level of tariff protection for agricultural products in the temperate area has also been made possible by reducing tariffs on tropical products at a high rate (albeit a very small amount in absolute terms; the starting level for these products in North America was only about 2 per cent). The starting tariffs for products involving low levels of raw material processing are, in most cases, equally low. In the case of textiles and clothing, which is characterised by higher tariff protection, the reductions, measured in percentage points, are appreciable only in Canada and (with reservations) Japan. If one considers the size of each of the trade flows between the Triad regions, together with the relevant tariff reductions, the following changes may be seen to be of potential significance: increased imports of cereals and meat by the EU from the USA, and of cereals, meat, fruit, and vegetables by Japan from the USA; some increase in North American imports of upmarket clothing from Europe.

Another integral aspect of the GATT results, however, is the Blair House compromise of late 1992 between the EU and USA, which provides, amongst other things, for limits on subsidised agricultural exports. Thus, over the six-year transitional period, export subsidies on the individual products are to be reduced by 36 per cent, and the volume of subsidised exports by 21 per cent. Within the EU, a reduction in the cereal price of 15 per cent – and thus also in the implicit subsidy – had already been agreed as part of the EU's 1992 internal agricultural reform, but the impetus for this had emanated largely from the GATT negotiations (Schomerus 1994: 97). Independently of the Blair House compromise, it was agreed to reduce the total of all production-related subsidies to agriculture (Aggregate Measure of Support, AMS) by 20 per cent. However, apart from the fact that a whole range of subsidies are not included under the AMS, and so in principle remain permissible, certain individual products can continue specifically to be protected through subsidies as long as the new, reduced AMS as a whole is adhered to. (The only product-specific undertakings that had to be made as part of the Blair House compromise – under pressure from the USA – were those of the EU in respect of oilseed.) In addition, where there is a marked increase in market penetration (trigger level), or a great fall in prices (trigger price), recourse may be had to a protective clause – in other words, the subsidy can be reintroduced.

If, nonetheless, it proves possible to bring the subsidy competition between the EU and the USA in regard to agricultural products to an end, and to achieve a marked reduction in the level of protection, prices on the world market will rise, with the result that a large proportion of EU supplies will remain competitive even without subsidies, and there will, to this extent, be no fall in exports (Toepfer International 1994: 42). Overall, however, because its level of productivity in agriculture is higher compared with that of the EU, the USA will be better able to withstand the combined pressure of subsidy reductions, cuts in import prices, and expanded access to markets (from 3 to 5 per cent of respective domestic consumption according to the GATT negotiations), and will even gain extra shares of the market both in the EU and at home, and in outside markets. The associated structural changes that will take place in the USA are, it must be admitted, unusual for a highly developed country. In as much as the increase in exports and in imports create a surplus in the trade balance, the dollar will tend to be revaluated, resulting in a downward pull on price competitiveness, particularly that of industrial products.

Another way in which trade between the industrialised countries will be intensified is via the liberalisation of public procurement. The main relevant instrument here is 'National Treatment'. A 'code' concerning this – and binding on all signatory states – had already been negotiated during the Tokyo Round. It did not prove possible to 'multilateralise' the issue during the Uruguay Round, and so, as in several other cases, only a 'plurilateral' ruling was agreed, which basically covered only the OECD (plus Israel and Korea). The area of applicability was, however, greatly extended, and it is estimated that in the EU alone orders worth 350 billion ECUs (about US$ 420 billion) per year are now accessible to foreign suppliers as well – whereas under the terms of the Tokyo Round the total market volume of all the signatory states was only 45 billion Special Drawing Rights (UNCTAD 1994:

138), about US\$ 63 billion. However, practice within the European Single Market shows that it is one thing to put public procurement out to international tender, but another to refrain from exploiting the discretion which it is always possible to exercise in awarding contracts to the advantage of domestic suppliers, especially in cases where government research funds have been poured in.

OECD TRADE WITH DEVELOPING COUNTRIES

The industrialised world obtains less than a third of its total imports (including intra-bloc trade) from developing countries. A large proportion of these imports – currently just under one-fifth under MFN terms, plus a considerable proportion within the framework of regional trade agreements and General Preference Systems – are tariff-free. Of those imports that are subject to tariffs, more than half carry tariffs of under 10 per cent. Given these conditions, the overall effect of the tariff reductions on the OECD cannot be substantial, although sizeable reductions in tariffs were agreed in some areas. However, there could be marked shifts in regional import structure following the reduction in MFN tariffs, as many supplier countries who previously enjoyed a privileged status will now lose their preferential advantage (Möbius 1994: 32–4; see also Chapter 5).

The low level of the average tariff cuts means that individual OECD countries will feel the pressure of increased price competition in certain branches. This is especially true in Japan of textiles, clothing, leather and shoes – branches of industry which, in any case, play an even less important role there than in other industrialised countries. Unlike the other industrialised countries, whose tariffs in these areas remain high despite significant cuts, Japan is clearly engaging in a systematic withdrawal from these kinds of wage-intensive branches of industry. In the case of non-tropical agricultural products, it is the USA in particular that will be open to increased price pressure from developing countries.

What will stimulate OECD imports from Third World countries to a much greater extent than tariff cuts, however, is the removal of the quantitative restrictions common in certain branches of industry. Thus, after a period of four (in exceptional cases five) years, no voluntary restraint agreements, orderly marketing arrangements, or other forms of quantitative restrictions may be practised. The most important liberalisation measure in this connection – although it will be slower to come to fruition than others – is the expiry of the Multifibre Arrangement, whose origins go back to the early 1960s. After repeated extensions and expansions, this is now to be definitively brought to an end by the year 2005. A dual strategy will be used to accomplish this. First, an increasing number of products are to be integrated into the GATT regime in a four-stage process. Second, bilaterally agreed maximum import quotas are to be raised annually. However, no kind of linear liberalisation process has been agreed. Importing countries may decide from within four broad product groups – each of which must be involved at each stage – which products they will decontrol first, and which last. The basis for this decision will, in each case, be the 1990 total of relevant imports – in other words, including those that have already been liberalised, so that, at the initial stage, it is merely a case of enshrining the liberal status quo for particular products. Also, importing countries may postpone the decontrol of 49 per cent of all imports until the last minute. Finally, where 'serious damage' could result in the case of particular products that have not yet been 'integrated', there is a 'transitional safeguard mechanism' available. Therefore it may be assumed that the most sensitive products will be decontrolled only in the very final phase of the removal of quantitative restrictions.

Whereas the industrialised countries – albeit only in the longer term – are required to liberalise mainly in the area of textiles and agricultural trade, many developing countries are required to do so in the field of trade-related investment measures (TRIMs). This will affect OECD exports. Because of the globalisation of markets and the growing pressure to safeguard export markets by having one's own assembly, intermediary and after-sales services located close to the market, transnationally active production enterprises had focused investment in the South East Asian area and in Latin America. Partly in order to prevent foreign domination of their own industries, which were still in their infancy and striving to achieve autonomy, and partly in order to link these industries into the experience and dynamics of foreign-based firms, the governments of the host countries imposed special conditions on the countries of origin, forcing them to use the resources of the host country (local content), to forgo any transfer of profits, or to improve the country's foreign currency situation (trade balancing); or else they creamed off part of the profits via special taxes (no 'National Treatment'). Although this protectionist practice was originally brought up for discussion as part of a GATT dispute between two industrialised countries – the USA and Canada – it rapidly became a broad issue within the context of the relationship between the industrialised countries and the advanced developing countries, who perhaps suspected that the matter was being used as a vehicle for pushing through a generalised freedom of establishment. This aim was successfully opposed by a group of developing countries, with the result that the agreement was ultimately confined to investment measures relating to trade in goods (UNCTAD 1994: 136). However, there is no guarantee, as yet, that the agreement will be effective, since the prohibited measures were enumerated item by item. The complexity of the subject, however, makes it susceptible to circumvention, and the question of which deviations from current practice will still be considered permissible will depend entirely on the expertise and independence of the competent WTO Trade Council.

The restriction of the TRIMs agreement to trade in goods does not mean that service-related investments are excluded. It is just that they are regulated elsewhere: in the new General Agreement on Trade in Services (GATS). This is potentially where one of the greatest achievements of the Uruguay Round is to be found. The GATS covers all four possible kinds of supply and use of services: transborder export in the traditional sense (e.g. transport, data communication); the movement of consumers to the location of supply (e.g. tourism); commercial presence (e.g. branches of foreign banks); and, last, the free movement of natural persons as producers of services. The fundamental principles are National Treatment and unrestricted most favoured nation status. However, the achievement is only potential because liberalisation of trade in services is not defined as a general rule, to which exceptions are then allowed, but initially takes place only within the framework of national, widely differing schedules (Senti 1994: 28–9). Each country can cite anticipatory exceptions to the most favoured nation status, and for air transport, financial services, telecommunications and services produced by natural persons, there are special restrictive or temporary regulations – though with an undertaking to continue negotiations. Only for the areas of tourism, entrepreneurial services, telecommunications related value-added services, and financial services do the national schedules tally very closely (UNCTAD 1994: 153).

UNCTAD (1994: 152) finds itself unable to quantify the concessions contained in the GATS, let alone assess their effect on trade in services. However, there are grounds for supposing that it will be service and capital transactions between industrialised countries and developing countries (and among developing countries themselves – but this is not relevant to the topic of this chapter) that will be most affected. This is because the agreement essentially represents an enshrining of the status quo for the OECD countries. In the important area in which the major parties involved – namely the USA and EU – had already failed to arrive at an agreement in connection with the legislation on the internal European market (namely, audiovisual services), the Uruguay Round also brought no advance. As regards the relationship between the OECD and the developing countries, any analysis of effects requires a thoroughgoing study of the schedules of concessions. Within the segment that has largely already been liberalised, the OECD countries have export interests and comparative advantages chiefly in business services, value-added services and financial and insurance services. In these areas there is a large and growing market potential, but it is one that advanced developing countries will also strive to secure control of. Success – or failure – in trade in goods and trade in services is mutually dependent here. With further liberalisation – which, admittedly, still has to be negotiated – the OECD countries, and in particular the USA, will conquer shares in the market in basic telecommunications services, air transport, and audiovisual services. Because of lower manpower costs and safety standards, developing countries enjoy advantages in ocean freight – although the practice of 'flagging out', the now common 'second register', and increasing international safety requirements are eroding these advantages.

THE HORIZONTAL MEASURES

Future world trade flows will be greatly affected by a good number of Uruguay Round agreements that do not relate to specific product groups or sectors but apply horizontally, across all trade flows – though it must be said that some of these cross-sectional agreements themselves have variants relating to specific sectors and are included in the relevant special agreements. Under discussion here are safeguards, anti-subsidy measures, anti-dumping procedures, and trade-related aspects of intellectual property rights (TRIPs). In general, the negotiations have resulted in an extension of the area of applicability, not only geographically (to all WTO countries), but also, in the case of TRIPs, materially (all products are declared patentable in principle). Moreover, they have brought greater legal security through transparency and the introduction of more objective procedures, and greater liberality, through stricter requirements in regard to discipline in trade policy. Thus the industrialised countries, particularly the EU, were obliged to bid farewell to the demand which they had been advancing since the Tokyo Round for 'selective safeguards' allowing for discrimination between countries; the most favoured nation principle is upheld. Countries that subject themselves to the stricter disciplinary regime when having recourse to safeguards are rewarded by no longer having to compensate adversely affected third countries for a period of three years, as they have had to do up to now. Anti-subsidy measures presuppose 'specificity', and a definition is provided of which are 'actionable' and which 'non-actionable'. In addition, the importing country must provide more stringent proof that the subsidy has truly caused the injury complained of.

However, UNCTAD (1994: 132) highlights the fact that the 'cumulation of injury' that is now permissible – that is to say, the adding together of minor injuries caused by individual supplier countries into one major overall injury – also encourages the use of safeguards. At the same time, it points out (1994: 128) that deviation from the most favoured nation principle, as allowed – though on strictly substantiated grounds – by the safeguard regime (see Agreement on Safeguards, Sect. II.9b), opens the way to abuses. Another fear is that because of reduced recourse to quantitative measures, the number of anti-dumping procedures will greatly increase. Finally, it is a cause for concern to UNCTAD (1994: 135) that the USA and EU have successfully prevented a more stringent standard of review in regard to the settlement of anti-dumping disputes – as compared with other agreements. These standards leave much scope for interpretation and thus bring with them the danger of 'grey' (i.e. informal) quotas in a new guise. Here again, it becomes clear that the effectiveness and general acceptance of the regime that has now been established will depend to a great extent not only on the arbitration practice of the new Committee on Safeguards, but also on the overall institutional structure of the WTO.

The horizontal measures will have multifarious effects on OECD trade. As far as the short-term effect of increased procedural objectivity is concerned, it is scarcely possible to make any quantitative assessment. The dominant tendency could be one of increased imports, especially from developing countries, since their position up to now has been relatively weak and there will either be a greater tendency on the part of the industrialised countries to refrain from seeking safeguards or from anti-dumping/anti-subsidy procedures, or a greater tendency on the part of the developing countries to lodge complaints, which would then be settled to their advantage. The previously described measures facilitating recourse to safeguards or to anti-dumping/anti-subsidy tariffs do, it is true, work against this. In the long term, however, one can say with some certainty that the hindrances to OECD trade that result from these instruments will decrease – when less distorted production structures have established themselves in the wake of the implementation of the Uruguay package, and when the remaining companies' need for safeguards has further declined as a result of the effects which a more intensive international division of labour will have on growth.

The greatest reduction which the increased protection of intellectual property rights will bring will occur in exports to industrialised countries from the advanced developing countries. It is mainly these countries which engage in brand-name piracy and the illegal imitation of technological products, exploiting their huge labour cost advantage in the process. One such example is the dispute that flared up at the end of 1994 between the USA and the People's Republic of China, and which temporarily at the beginning of 1995 threatened to develop into a full-blown trade war, hindering, among other factors, the dialogue on the inclusion of China as one of the founding members of the WTO. The USA asserted that China's illegal copying of CDs, computer programs and other products was damaging American companies to the tune of $2 billion annually. Stopping such practices will cause the flow of exports from developing countries to industrialised countries – which consume large quantities of these products – to be replaced by a flow from countries in which the relevant companies enjoy legal protection of property. North–South trade will reassume a more marked inter-industrial character, and North–North trade a more strongly intra-industrial one. (To the extent that the owner countries are also consumer countries, external trade will be replaced by internal trade.)

In some cases, however, there will not be a shift in flows of goods, but an increase in the export of services (licences) by owner countries to countries that were previously imitators, and also a rise in the price of the relevant imports in the consumer countries. The size of the flow (and of consumption in the owner countries) will decline, but not to the same extent as prices will rise, because the price elasticity of the products involved is generally low. This will initially diminish the welfare effects of the international division of labour, since the imitator countries were – technically speaking – fully capable of producing this type of product. If, in the absence of property rights, the input costs of developing these products (which are likely to be high) could no longer be earned via product prices, all efforts at innovation would cease. The products, and thus also the trade in them, would not exist. Efficient international division of labour according to the principle of comparative advantage would be eroded and the overall welfare of all those involved would unavoidably be diminished, since potentially innovative countries would be unable to develop the same levels of demand for imports as previously due to a lack of foreign currency earnings. Property rights are thus an indispensable element in any international system of competition that seeks to achieve free trade.

ATTEMPTS AT QUANTIFICATION

Generally speaking, what can the national economies within the OECD expect from the Uruguay Round? A distinction must be drawn here between an immediate effect of liberalisation, and a series of lagged effects. The immediate effect, in relation to tariff reduction, is a spontaneous increase in the real incomes of consumers (price reduction) and/or foreign suppliers (increased profit margins). Where quantitative restrictions are removed, prices also fall – though as a result of an increase in the number of imports available; at a stroke, scarcity rents disappear for foreign suppliers. The dynamic effects depend on several factors: the level and geographical configuration of the effect, the type of product (whether elastic or not), the dependency of production costs on unit number (returns to scale or not), the structure of the market (perfect or oligopolistic competition), and propensities to save and invest. To the extent that liberalisation of trade consists in the reduction of subsidies, no further taxes have to be raised to finance these – thus producing positive effects on savings and consumer spending – and those branches of industry that are viable even without subsidies have a better chance of success in the competition for scarce resources. This fiscal effect is likely to be greater than would result from a change in tariff revenue, since the reduction in the rate of duty may be offset, at least in the long term, by an increase in tariff revenue from imports. The primary effects on real income, and their distribution, depend essentially on the way the elimination of barriers to trade is structured and on the new patterns of specialisation that result; the additional effects on income (multiplier effects) for their part depend on behaviour in relation to savings. Depending on how much new economic growth is triggered, and a higher degree of utilisation of productive capacities then ensues, a new need for investment may arise, which in turn fuels economic growth. All this will bring new patterns of trade, with new effects in terms of welfare and growth; the level, product structure and regional structure of these effects will depend on the particular constellation of parameters – which will itself, however, be subject to constant change depending on the level of income attained.

63

It is not possible, within the confines of this chapter, to attempt an assessment or forecast of the effects of the Uruguay Round on the size of the various trade flows or – since these are only a means to a greater end – on real incomes and employment in the OECD countries. Given the complexity of the subject, the calculations required would be far too great, and the results such calculations would produce could themselves only be indications of scale. Econometric models such as these, for measuring liberalising effects, were applied to the Uruguay Round (see Table 3.1), by, among others, the World Bank/OECD (Goldin *et al.* 1993) and Nguyen *et al.* (1993), and also within the environment of the GATT secretariat (Francois *et al.* 1994). The two former studies were conducted before the end of the negotiations and are based on interim results. All three are so-called 'equilibrium models'. One thing they have in common is their distinction of a number of regions and product groups – albeit differingly constituted. As regards products, a very prominent role is played on the one hand by agricultural goods, and on the other by textiles and clothing, the reason being that these enjoy a high degree of import protection in most of the industrialised countries, but are to undergo a marked degree of liberalisation when the Uruguay Round is implemented. World Bank/OECD and Nguyen *et al.* assume perfect competition and constant returns to scale. In the GATT-associated study, figures are calculated for a variant involving imperfect competition (existence of market leaders), increasing returns to scale (disproportionate growth in company results following increased inputs of labour, capital and know-how prompted by international division of labour) within specific industries, and dynamic effects (triggering of effects on savings, investments and growth). This undoubtedly makes the study the most comprehensive and most differentiated of the sets of calculations presented here. However, from the description of the individual agreements it should be obvious that, due to the many regulatory gaps, opportunities for circumvention, and imponderables, the overall package of undertakings cannot be clearly defined – which again produces a host of uncertainties as far as the results of the calculations are concerned.

According to World Bank/OECD, the world increase in real income resulting from an average reduction in tariffs of 30 per cent will be US$213 billion in 2002 (at 1992 prices). No less than $190 billion of this will be accounted for by agricultural products, and $120 billion of that figure by the OECD, with its exceptionally high starting position. In the case of manufacturing industry, the figure is $15 billion out of a total of only $23 billion. These relations between the product groups are, of course, distorted because no account is taken either of non-tariff barriers (in the case of manufactured products) or of services as a whole – the latter being particularly hard to quantify. The same is true of the dynamic effects of intensified competition and of the transfer of technology. The authors actually estimate the non-computed effects as being greater than the computed ones. Given that

Table 3.1 Effects on real income, in OECD countries and regions, of major elements of the Uruguay Round, as calculated according to three different models

	Goldin et al.[1] — In the year 2002, % of GDP				Nguyen et al.[2]						Francois et al.[3] — % of GDP[7]					
	With 'labour market rigidities'[4]	Without 'labour market rigidities'			% of GDP[6]	$billion, by segment within treaty complex					Underlying model		Modern model			
		Total	Agric.	Industry		Total	Agric.	Textiles	Services	Other	Traditional[8] 1990: $106 billion 2005: $173 billion[10]	Modern[9] 1990: $223 billion 2005: $364 billion[10]	Agric.	Industry	Tariff	NTBs[11]
		$138 billion[5]	$120 billion[5]	$18 billion[5]												
USA	0.7	0.2	0.2	0.0	0.8	36.4	9.3	21.6	2.0	3.5	0.5	1.3	0.1	0.2	1.1	1.1
Canada	-0.3	0.2	0.4	-0.2	0.9	3.7	1.2	1.6	0.4	0.5	0.4	1.3	0.2	0.1	1.0	1.0
Japan	2.3	0.9	0.7	0.3	2.0	27.0	21.6	-0.5	1.0	4.9	0.4	0.6	0.1	0.4	0.0	0.0
Australia/New Zealand	1.2	0.1	0.5	-0.2	1.1	2.4	1.0	1.1	0.2	0.1	0.4	1.0	0.4	0.6	0.1	0.1
EC (12)	3.6	1.4	1.3	0.2	1.8	61.3	29.5	17.2	7.0	7.6	0.8	1.7	0.2	0.4	1.2	1.2
EFTA	3.0	1.4	1.4	0.0	2.1	8.1	3.4	2.4	0.7	1.6	1.2	2.4	0.4	0.7	1.3	1.3

Notes: [1] Not including GATS or agreements not expressible in quantitative terms. Includes only tariff reductions and cuts in subsidies (30% in each case). [2] Effects of 'Draft Final Act'. Reduction of all border barriers in agriculture by 40% and of agricultural production subsidies by 30%. In the case of textiles, tariffs remain at the post-Tokyo level; all quotas are increased by a factor of 4, all other non-tariff barriers are abolished. In the case of high-tech goods and major intermediate products, tariffs are reduced by 30%, and equivalents of non-tariff barriers by 50%; in the case of other goods, tariffs are reduced by 30%, equivalents of NTBs, including those relating to services, by 40%. [3] Not including GATS or agreements not expressible in quantitative terms. [4] Wage-levels not compatible with full employment. [5] At 1992 prices. [6] No date specified. Price-base that of starting position. [7] At 1990 position. [8] Constant returns to scale; perfect competition. [9] Increasing returns to scale, imperfect competition. [10] At 1990 prices. [11] Non-tariff barriers.

Sources: Goldin et al. (1993); Nguyen et al. (1993); Francois et al. (1994)

in a second study (OECD 1993: 22), in which non-tariff barriers outside agriculture are also taken into account, the OECD indicates welfare effects of $274 billion, we are left with a difference of $61 billion which can be ascribed to the elimination of these non-tariff restrictions.

The computed effects are unevenly distributed across the world. The EU will rank among those deriving most benefit, particularly if only OECD countries are considered. The industrialised countries of the Pacific, and especially the USA, lie far behind (Goldin *et al.* 1993: 100). Particularly in those countries where agriculture is highly protected, the gap in income between industry and the service sector on the one hand and agriculture on the other will shift even further to the detriment of the latter. Farmers in the EU will be the ones to lose most. World prices for wheat, sugar and dairy and meat products will indeed rise (and so will, albeit to a lesser extent, those for cotton, wool and vegetable oil). However, previously protected domestic prices will unavoidably fall at the same time. But these losses bear no relation to the increases in real income for consumers; and, what is more, by the year 2002 the stimulatory secondary effects of these increases will have offset the decline in farming incomes.

According to the model advanced by Nguyen *et al.* two-thirds of the welfare effects similarly go to the OECD, and the USA again profits less from liberalisation than do the EU and Japan. The scale of the effects for the world as a whole, which the authors set at $212 billion, is, again, almost identical to that posited in the World Bank/OECD study. However, this indicates a relatively low estimate of the effects of tariff reduction, since the study by Nguyen *et al.* also takes into account the removal of quotas. This also affects the sectoral configuration of the effects. Thus the results for the agricultural domain are only a third of those cited in the parallel study, and those for manufactured products, estimated at $62 billion (of which $43 billion are accounted for by textiles and clothing), are more than four times higher. In addition, there is a calculated effect from the service sector (though at $11 billion this is probably set at much too low a level), a category which is considered neither by the World Bank/OECD nor by François *et al.*

The developers of the GATT-associated model estimate that the welfare effects of a thoroughgoing implementation of the results of the Uruguay Round will amount (roughly) to $510 billion by 2005 (at 1990 prices) (Francois *et al.* 1994). This tallies with the assumption by the World Bank/OECD that their own calculations encompass less than half the total effect. However, the highly differentiated simulations produced with the GATT-associated model relate to 1990 and reflect a liberal 'counter-world' to the protectionist actual conditions prevailing at that time, using a model specification which guaranteed that the actual market results were generated as an 'initial equilibrium'. A comparison of the variants in findings highlights the decisive influence of the market structure: only when account is taken of the fact that in many markets there is oligopolistic competition, with only a handful of large-scale enterprises leading the market, does the full extent of the trade-creating effect – based on intra-industrial specialisation and product differentiation – of the mutual opening up of markets become clear. The biggest potential for opening up markets lies in the developing countries, the countries in transition, and China.

In the OECD this process will bring an enormous change in trade patterns. Thus, in the EU in particular, clothing exports will decrease markedly in real terms – by more than a tenth – while exports of chemical products, transport equipment and 'other manufactured products' will rise between a fifth and a half. When this additional specialisation is, in turn, translated into effects on real income, the overwhelming influence of dynamic impulses becomes clear. If these are taken into consideration, the overall effect is 50–70 per cent higher. The factor that plays the greatest part here, as far as the EU and USA are concerned, is the reduction in quotas for industrial goods. In the EU, however, tariff reduction and the diminution of agricultural protectionism are also reflected, although both these effects taken together are not equal to the influence exerted by quantitative liberalisation in the field of industrial goods. In Japan – as in China and the other growth countries of South East Asia – the elimination of quantitative restrictions actually has a negative effect, under conventional model assumptions, on real income. This has to do with the disappearance of the 'scarcity rents' which suppliers in these countries currently reap: by charging the consumer in the importing country the same as the alternative course of imposing tariffs would provide, they rake in the tariff equivalent of a quota as extra profit. The effect of the liberalisation of the agricultural market is astonishingly small in the USA, as compared with Western Europe and Japan. This results from the different ways of subsidising agriculture. Although aid in all three regions is concentrated on the cereals sector, in the USA the focus is on aids to production, in Western Europe on aids to exports, and in Japan on tariffs and quotas. It goes without saying that the elimination of direct export subsidies is what most directly affects trade patterns. In addition, the starting level in terms of protection is particularly high in Western Europe.

Faced, at various stages, with failure of the Uruguay Round (May 1994: 106–7), the world economy, as a whole, has undoubtedly emerged as a winner from the successful conclusion of negotiations. But there are relative winners and losers. Allowing for the variations in findings resulting from differences in methodology, the empirical evidence presented here indicates, without exception, that Western Europe and the USA will be the ones to derive the greatest benefit in relative terms. The benefits to them will, however, result chiefly from the opening up of their own markets (Langhammer 1994: 15). One can therefore also say that the OECD has only itself to blame for becoming the main victim of the status quo in world trade relations, since it bears especial responsibility for having distorted world trade through subsidies and high levels of import protection. In line with the logic underlying the mechanism of achieving increases in real incomes through increased international specialisation, the biggest losers within the OECD are the producers of agricultural goods, textiles and clothing. These areas are required to undergo massive structural change, though this is to be absorbed by the dynamic effects of liberalisation. Nevertheless, the concentration of losses in only a small number of branches will cause the mobilisation of a powerful protective lobby, with the result that the achievements of the Uruguay Round will be permanently, and perhaps increasingly, under threat. Much will depend on whether the new WTO and its arbitration bodies prove themselves competent, independent, and capable of enforcing their decisions (see Chapter 6).

THE URUGUAY ROUND AND EMPLOYMENT

The main argument that is continually brought up against liberalisation is the need to safeguard jobs. Except for Nguyen *et al.*, the studies mentioned here do not make any explicit reference to employment. However, even the analysis by Nguyen *et al.* does not show the probable employment effects of the Uruguay Round in terms of total job numbers but only of sectoral structure. The dominant concern of the studies is rather welfare and real income. The vehicles for these are price reduction, growth, structural change and increases in productivity. Where liberalisation of trade leads to price reductions on the domestic market, the effect on real income, in cases where unemployment results from rigidities on the labour market, is, according to World Bank/OECD (Goldin *et al.* 1993: 84), greater, because wage cost pressure also declines and unemployment is reduced. Given that the study diagnoses a markedly more pronounced labour market rigidity in Europe than in North America, this kind of relaxation will result in appreciably stronger stimuli for employment and real incomes in Europe (Goldin *et al.* 1993: 95, 100). However, only the effects on income are quantified. Thus, after the Uruguay Round has been implemented, real income in the EU is said to be set to rise by 3.6 per cent by the year 2002, but in the USA by only 0.7 per cent more than it would have done without the Round.

Growth undoubtedly creates jobs. Structural change, on the other hand, destroys many of them – but at the same time creates more. Such change, however, requires greater individual acceptance of professional and regional mobility of a kind that workers – particularly older ones – do not always have. Moreover, it presupposes that the necessary opportunities for retraining are available. Initially, increases in productivity actually imply labour saving, in other words destruction of jobs, and only promise new and additional jobs at subsequent stages, via increased competitivity and greater demand. This means that advances in productivity reduce the effectiveness of growth in terms of job creation. Yet structural change and increased productivity are two things which the OECD will not be able to forgo, because in a dynamic world economy it would be ousted from its leading position if it were without them. Indeed, increased productivity offers the only means of maintaining the high standard of living that has been achieved. But the effectiveness of productivity gains in terms of employment can be increased if part of it is used for shortening working time. At the same time, there is an inherent tendency, within structural change at high income levels, to go back to more labour intensive, high-quality services (Franzmeyer 1994), a major precondition for which is a high level of 'human-capital stock' (Schumacher et al. 1995). It is therefore essential that politicians should ensure that their trade liberalisation offensive is accompanied by an equally decisive educational offensive.

As far as mutual trade between OECD countries – with their comparable stages of development and comparable economic structures – is concerned, the positive and negative effects on employment should largely offset one another. A considerable proportion of competitive pressure, however, comes from developing countries. Since imports from these countries are more labour intensive than exports to them, the overall effect will initially be that jobs in the OECD area will be at stake. However, as is shown by empirical studies, the gap will probably be small – and the market potential that can be opened up as compensation, great. Moreover, the OECD countries should appreciate the fact that the developing countries in particular – who could adduce good reasons for protecting their still vulnerable industries (the 'infant industry' argument) – have responded with a high level of commitment by raising the proportion of their bound tariffs more than any other group of countries and at the same time reducing the average tariff level not much less than did, for example, the USA in percentage terms. The OECD countries should also refrain from trying to use the 'new issues' in the WTO – environmental standards, social clauses, international competition – as a way of restoring the protective barriers they have lost (see Chapters 7 and 8). Possible levers here are the agreement on technical barriers to trade, the agreement on sanitary and phytosanitary measures (Reiterer 1994: 491), and – outside the GATT context – the resort to conventions of the International Labour Organization (ILO) (Sautter 1995: 24). By engaging in such an attempt, the industrialised countries would in fact merely gamble away the liberalisation that had already been achieved, without contributing to the improvement of ecological or social conditions in the developing countries.

BIBLIOGRAPHY

François, J.F., McDonald, B. and Nordström, H. (1994) 'The Uruguay Round: A Global General Equilibrium Assessment', rev. version, 30 September, Geneva: WTO Secretariat.
Franzmeyer, F. (1994) 'Auf dem Weg in die Dienstleistungsgesellschaft? Zum wirtschaftlichen Strukturwandel in sechs Industrieländern', Wochenbericht des DIW, 13: 184–91.

GATT (1994) *International Trade 1993 Statistics*, Geneva: GATT.
—— (1994a) *The Results of the Uruguay Round of Multilateral Trade Negotiations*, Geneva: GATT.
Goldin, I., Knudsen, O. and van der Mensbrugghe, D. (1993) *Trade Liberalisation: Global Economic Implications*, Washington DC/Paris: World Bank/OECD.
Langhammer, R.J. (1994) *Nach dem Ende der Uruguay-Runde: Das GATT am Ende?*, Kiel: Kieler Diskussionsbeiträge, 228.
May, B. (1994) *Die Uruguay-Runde: Verhandlungsmarathon verhindert trilateralen Handelskrieg*, Bonn: Forschungsinstitut der Deutschen Gesellschaft für Auswärtige Politik e.V., Arbeitspapiere zur Internationalen Politik, 86.
Möbius, Uta (1994) *Auswirkungen der Ergebnisse der abgeschlossenen Uruguay-Runde im GATT auf die Industriegüterimporte der Entwicklungsländer in die Europäische Union*, Berlin: Gutachten des DIW im Auftrag des Bundesministeriums für Wirtschaft anläßlich der Import-Messe Berlin 1994, mimeo.
Nguyen, T., Perroni, C. and Wigle, R. (1993) 'An Evaluation of the Draft Final Act of the Uruguay Round', *The Economic Journal*, 103, Nov.: 1540–9.
OECD (1993) *Handelspolitische Fragen 2: Bewertung der Uruguay-Runde*, Paris: OECD.
Petersen, H.J., Franzmeyer, F., Lahmann, H., Schultz, S. and Weise, C. (1993) *Die Bedeutung des internationalen Dienstleistungshandels für die Bundesrepublik Deutschland*, Berlin: DIW-Beiträge zur Strukturforschung, 145.
Reiterer, M. (1994) 'GATT/WTO: Internationaler Handel und Umwelt, Bilanz der GATT-Arbeitsgruppe über "Environmental Measures and International Trade" (EMIT) sowie der Uruguay-Runde', *Aussenwirtschaft*, 49/IV: 477–94.
Sautter, H. (1995) 'Schritte zu einer Weltsozialordnung', *epd-Entwicklungspolitik*, 1/95: 22–5.
Schomerus, L. (1994) 'Die multilaterale Handelsordnung nach der Uruguay-Runde', *Wirtschaftsdienst*, II: 96–100.
Schumacher, D., Belitz, H., Haid, A., Hornschild, K., Petersen, H.J., Straßberger, F. and Trabold, H. (1995) *Technologische Wettbewerbsfähigkeit der Bundesrepublik Deutschland: Theoretische und empirische Aspekte einer international vergleichenden Analyse*, Berlin: DIW-Beiträge zur Strukturforschung, 155.
Senti, R. (1994) *Die neue Welthandelsordnung für Dienstleistungen*, Zürich: Institut für Wirtschaftsforschung der ETH, Zürich, Materialien, 94/2.
Toepfer International (1994) *Die Marktordnungen der EU für Getreide und Ölsaaten 1994/5*, Hamburg: Toepfer International.
UNCTAD (1994) *Trade and Development Report 1994*, New York and Geneva: UNCTAD.

4

THE CONSEQUENCES OF THE URUGUAY ROUND FOR DEVELOPING COUNTRIES

Christopher Stevens

INTRODUCTION

The nature of the debate

The consequences of the GATT Uruguay Round for developing countries is a slippery subject to assess, and discussion on it tends often to result in unproductive mutual misunderstanding between the protagonists. There are several reasons for the wide-ranging nature of the debate.

- First, the Round has carried with it a substantial intellectual baggage. The text, although highly technical and detailed, is underlaid by a broad theoretical view of the role of trade in growth and development, and the appropriate role of the state in relation to trade. Discussion easily slips from the narrowly technical to the broadly theoretical and even ideological level.
- Second, the agreement is an exceedingly complex document (or, rather, set of documents) which will take a very long time to digest. The process of understanding precisely what was being agreed during the negotiations was complicated because of the high degree of secrecy in which they were conducted and the tendency of most protagonists to use public statements as a negotiating tool. Hence, many hopes and fears were engendered during the negotiations about what might transpire, and the task of checking whether or not the final agreements bear these out is still far from complete. In the meantime, unproductive debates rage between those who fear the worst, and assume that their concerns have not been adequately addressed until it has been demonstrated conclusively that they have, and those who expect the best, believing that potential problems have been dealt with until it can be shown that they have not.
- Third, there is considerable uncertainty as to how the contracting parties will implement what has been agreed on paper. The agreements provide many areas in which contracting parties have discretion over the speed or the extent of change. In addition, there is every reason to expect on past

71

form that countries will flout the spirit, if not the letter, of what has been agreed.

The nature of the agreement

Developing countries played a more substantial role in the Uruguay Round than in any of its predecessors. Almost three-quarters of the 117 states involved in the Uruguay Round of multilateral trade negotiations were developing countries. Why did developing countries – which have traditionally viewed the GATT as a 'rich countries' club' – embrace the new agreement in such numbers? The answer relates partly to what is in the agreement and partly to what it represents. The Round was launched to assert some multilateral influence over the increasing diversity of trade-related policies by including new areas (such as temperate agriculture and services), by reinforcing the institutional framework for trade monitoring and adjudication, and by continuing the process of lowering tariff and non-tariff barriers to trade.

In understanding the potential implications of the agreement for developing countries, it is important to bear in mind all three elements and to realise that there are two main sets of products from the negotiations. The first is a collection of documents covering general principles and agreed rules for trade. These were signed in Marrakesh in April 1994. The second comprises the changes to trade policy that each contracting party agreed to make during the Round. A large part of these consist of lengthy tariff schedules listing the alterations to tariffs that will be introduced over the next six years. These run into thousands, probably hundreds of thousands, of pages. And, since the devil is in the detail, the precise changes that will occur to world trade are as likely to be found in the second set of documents as in the first.

Like its seven predecessors since 1947, the Uruguay Round was a compromise between theory (favouring the free flow of trade between countries) and practical politics which recognise the need to be able to set concessions (i.e. tariff reductions on imports) against gains (i.e. better access to export markets). This mix has been very successful in reducing tariff barriers to trade through successive Rounds. In the late 1940s tariffs on manufactures averaged 40 per cent in rich countries; the figure is now 5 per cent. But as tariffs fell, so non-tariff barriers to trade increased in number and complexity. Most were outside normal GATT disciplines. The rules for temperate agriculture came to be seen as inadequate. Also excluded were policies that had indirect effects on trade, such as those concerned with investment and most services trade. The Uruguay Round was launched to assert some multilateral influence over this diversity: by including new areas, and by reinforcing the institutional framework for trade monitoring and adjudication.

The spread of new forms of developed country protectionism and a greater openness to trade in their domestic policies (introduced either of their own volition or under pressure from the International Monetary Fund (IMF) and

World Bank) altered the balance of interest for many developing countries in strengthening GATT disciplines. This partly explains their willingness to invest political and human resources in the GATT negotiation. For their part the developed countries were concerned to engage developing countries, some of which are now major international traders, in the Round and were willing to include on the agenda issues (such as trade in clothing and textiles) of particular interest to them.

The result is a balance of gains and concessions, illustrated by their agreement to the accord on trade-related aspects of intellectual property rights (TRIPs). This may increase the cost of knowledge-intensive goods to developing countries as net importers. But the developing country negotiators set against this loss developed country concessions on goods of export interest to them (such as textiles) and the advantages of a multilateral agreement over possibly tougher unilateral accords being sought.

KEY FEATURES OF THE MARRAKESH AGREEMENT

A key feature of the Uruguay Round was its breadth of coverage, but not all elements are of equal importance for developing countries as a group. The full implications of the new regime will become clear only after country-by-country analyses have been completed, each of which focuses on the elements that are most important for the country in question. Until that stage has been reached, the identification of broad implications requires the classification of the Uruguay Round elements into those that are potentially of most importance for the largest number of developing countries, and those that are of lesser significance. This chapter focuses on four principal areas: institutions, industrial products, the 'new areas' and temperate agriculture.

The World Trade Organization

One of the main innovations of the Uruguay Round is the extension of the institutional framework for trade. The crucial questions on the World Trade Organization (WTO) for developing countries are:

- what sorts of trade regime will it seek to promote?
- how far will the new disciplines safeguard developing country export interests?
- can it impose trade policies on unwilling developing countries?

The Uruguay Round establishes a WTO as a single institutional framework to encompass the GATT, all agreements and arrangements concluded under its auspices, and the complete results of the Uruguay Round. The replacement of the GATT Secretariat with a WTO reflects both the broadening of the scope of the new agreement and the desire to strengthen the monitoring of trade policy.

The WTO is evolutionary rather than revolutionary. Like the GATT, it will not be a free trade organisation (the developed countries, let alone developing countries, are not willing to accept this), but it will promote adherence to predictable rules and the objective of reducing barriers to trade wherever possible. It has a much more limited remit, for example, than the ill-fated International Trade Organization (the intended third pillar of the post-war economic institutional framework, alongside the IMF and the World Bank).

The WTO is headed by a Ministerial Conference meeting at least once every two years. Day-to-day operations will be overseen by a General Council, which will also act as a Dispute Settlement Body and a Trade Policy Review mechanism. Its permanent staff replaces the GATT Secretariat. The General Council will spawn a host of specialist subsidiary bodies such as the Council for Trade in Goods (which will, *inter alia*, oversee the phase out of the Multifibre Arrangement, MFA), a Safeguards Committee (to oversee operation of a revised Article XIX), a Council on Services, and a Council for TRIPs.

Although the detailed *modus operandi* of the WTO is yet to be agreed, the key principles are:

- membership of the Councils will be open to all signatories of the agreement;
- when there is no consensus, some decisions can be taken by qualified majority (mostly three-quarters or two-thirds) but others require unanimity;
- voting will not be weighted;
- the WTO will not itself take sanctions against transgressors, but will authorise aggrieved parties to withdraw most favoured nation (MFN) treatment from them.

It has been suggested (with pleasure or concern, depending upon the commentator's viewpoint) that the WTO will impose a liberal trade straitjacket on all developing countries, regardless of their circumstances. The assumed universality of the liberal trade concept is, indeed, evident from the altered status for developing countries in the Marrakesh agreement. Part IV of the GATT provides for 'special and differential treatment' for developing countries and laid the basis *inter alia* for the most widespread forms of trade preferences offered by developed countries to developing countries. Although the concept of special and differential treatment has been continued, it is more limited and timebound than previously. After the end of a transitional period, developing countries (except the least developed) are expected to adopt most of the same disciplines as developed countries.

Despite this change in the status of 'special and differential treatment', the scope for the WTO to impose unwanted policies will be limited by the structure of decision-making and enforcement. The use of qualified, unweighted majority voting means that the developed countries cannot force upon developing countries as a whole unwanted decisions. The OECD states form only one-fifth of the signatories.

Despite the arithmetic, however, developing countries cannot take for granted that their interests will prevail in the WTO, for two reasons.

- First, they can only defend their perceived interests if they are aware of what is being discussed. Poorer developing countries will have to concentrate their resources, giving priority to the WTO, join with others and seek technical assistance to ensure that they are adequately represented in key councils.
- Second, the enforcement of rules will continue to be asymmetrical because it will be undertaken by aggrieved parties imposing penalties on trans-gressors. In a dispute, for example, between USA and Bangladesh the imposition of penalties by Bangladesh on US exports will have far less impact than those imposed in the opposite direction.

Industrial products: protectionism remains

The principal interest for developing countries in the Uruguay Round was:

- the reduction of high tariff peaks on items in which developing countries compete strongly with developed country producers, and the elimination of escalation (whereby tariffs increase with the level of processing);
- its treatment of non-tariff barriers, especially those on clothing and textiles contained in the MFA, and the growing misuse of anti-dumping actions as covert protectionism.

Following the Round, the proportion of developed country imports of indus-trial goods from developing countries entering duty free will increase, but some manufactures of particular interest to developing countries still face relative discrimination. An initial analysis of the changes has been made by the GATT Secretariat (GATT 1994). This claims that:

- developed countries have agreed to reduce their tariffs on industrial goods from an average of 6.3 per cent to 3.8 per cent, a 40 per cent reduction.
- the proportion of industrial products which enter the developed country markets under MFN zero duties will more than double, from 20 to 44 per cent. At the higher end of the tariff structure, the proportion of imports into developed countries from all sources that encounter tariffs above 15 per cent will decline from 7 to 5 per cent, and from 9 to 5 per cent for imports from developing economies.

The agreement provides for the removal of both MFA and non-MFA restrictions on clothing and textiles trade over the period to 2005. But transi-tional safeguards can be applied for up to three years to any product not yet integrated into the GATT. A Textiles Monitoring Body will be established to oversee the implementation of these commitments.

The MFA is to be phased out over the period to 2005 in stages. In each, importing states will transfer from the MFA to normal GATT rules a tranche of products of a size related to the share of the items in their total 1990 import volume. The phasing agreed will allow states to delay into the next century the bulk of the transfers.

The first phase, for immediate implementation, is to cover items which accounted for at least 16 per cent of 1990 imports. Phase two, which must be completed by the end of 1997, adds a minimum further 17 per cent. An additional 18 per cent (minimum) is to be integrated by the end of 2001. The remaining products (up to one half of 1990 imports) need not be integrated until the end of 2004.

In addition to liberalisation, the GATT Secretariat argues that developing countries will benefit from increased security of market access. In the case of industrial products, the percentage of bound tariff lines has risen from 78 to 99 per cent for developed countries, from 21 to 73 per cent for developing economies, and from 73 to 98 per cent for transition economies – results that provide a substantially higher degree of market security for traders and investors (GATT 1994: 7).

Such improved security relates only, however, to tariffs; there is a strong view that non-tariff barriers, such as misapplied anti-dumping regulations, nowadays provide a more serious form of insecurity to developing country exports to developed countries. Rules on anti-dumping have been made clearer and more extensive in the Marrakesh agreement, making it harder (but not impossible) for developed countries to blame the woes of particular firms on supposedly dumped imports from developing countries. The requirement for the importing country to establish a clear causal relationship between dumped imports and injury to the domestic industry is strengthened. Moreover, 'domestic industry' normally refers to all domestic producers, not just one company, and other factors influencing the commercial well being of the industry have to be taken into account.

Of particular potential importance to less developed and smaller developing countries is that there are now minimum injury/dumping thresholds, below which anti-dumping actions will not be taken. These preclude investigations in cases where the dumping margin is less than 2 per cent of the export price, or the volume of imports from a particular country accounts for less than 3 per cent of the total.

In keeping with the complex balancing of interests that the Marrakesh agreement represents, any improvement in security resulting from curbs on anti-dumping must be set against changes to Article XIX, the safeguards clause. This has been altered in ways that may increase its use against developing countries. In the past developed countries have been reluctant to use it as a justification for import controls because these have to be applied against all suppliers. The new agreement permits selectivity if it can be established that imports from certain countries have increased disproportionately. It is arguable whether this will be to the detriment of developing countries (by facilitating 'legal' import controls against them) or be to their advantage (by bringing within WTO disciplines actions that developed countries would otherwise have taken unilaterally). Safeguards can be imposed for a maximum of eight years or, if selective, four years.

TRIPs and services: the new areas

Although the agreements on TRIPs and services have generated much heat, relatively little may be stated with confidence about their potential implications for developing countries. This is largely because the Marrakesh agreement does little more than bring these areas into the remit of formal multilateral regulation for the first time: how they will be regulated has been deferred for future decision-taking. Moreover, to the extent that rules have been set, their precise implications are still unclear (and may well require legal adjudication before they become clear).

There are two elements to the agreement on TRIPs: all members have agreed to recognise minimum rights for owners of intellectual property, and to establish national enforcement mechanisms. Discussion of the former was contentious because, although most developing countries already provide legal protection for intellectual property rights, a group of states (including India, Brazil and Turkey) do not. On enforcement, members must provide within their existing domestic legal system procedures to enable rights to be enforced effectively by both foreign and national holders. Hence, in the first instance, any dispute over the implementation of what has been agreed will be a matter for the civil courts of particular states.

Services are covered by the General Agreement on Trade in Services (GATS). Initially one of the most contentious issues dividing developed and developing countries, the division between these groups was blurred by the decision to extend the negotiations from issues of particular developed country interest (such as a company's right to establish a commercial presence in a foreign state) to those with which developing countries are concerned (such as migrant labour).

The final agreement contains two elements: to bring services for the first time within the multilateral framework of rules; and to provide some degree of improved market access, although the extent of this will not be clear until the schedules have been analysed thoroughly. There is likely to be pressure for further liberalisation on migration (primarily from developing countries) and to include financial services in GATT (primarily from developed countries).

Agriculture

The Uruguay Round covered both tropical and temperate agriculture, but attention has been concentrated on the latter, which was the most contentious part of the Uruguay Round. Tariffs have been cut on tropical products, but were low before the Uruguay Round. What has been agreed on temperate agriculture is a compromise that will introduce normal market mechanisms into production and trade – but slowly. How slowly will not be clear until the voluminous tariff schedules – the second part of the agreement – are studied with care, but even by 2002 world trade in temperate agricultural goods will be significantly less liberal than is trade in manufactures now. The concerns of developing countries are focused on:

- the scope for increased agricultural exports, especially to protected developed country markets, like that in Europe;
- the danger of higher food import prices, since many are net food importers;
- the effect on their agricultural development.

The outcome under all three headings will be determined by what has been agreed to change market access, producer and export subsidies in the industrialised and developing countries, each of which is now dealt with in turn. Since the changes are complex, and of considerable importance to developing countries given the prominent position of agriculture in many of them, the broad terms of the agreement are now mapped out.

Improved market access for developing country exports

Agricultural protectionism (especially in developed countries) will be reduced . through two instruments:

- the conversion of all import restrictions to tariffs (a process known as 'tariffication');
- and guarantees of minimum market access.

As a result of tariffication border measures will be changed into customs tariffs. The contracting parties have some latitude in setting the level of these tariffs. As will be seen below, the EU proposes to set them at a very high level.

These tariffs will then be reduced by an average of 36 per cent over six years by developed countries and 24 per cent over ten years by developing countries. Least developed countries will not have to reduce their tariffs at all. This does not mean that all import tariffs will fall by over one-third, only that the average cut will be of this magnitude.

The broad distribution of tariff reductions that will be made is indicated in Table 4.1. The differences between products evident in the Table are possible because these average reductions will not be trade weighted. This has left scope for the developed countries to maintain higher-than-average levels of protection on some items. Hence, for example, if the tariff on an unimportant product imported negligibly is reduced by 45 per cent, the tariff on a major product need be cut by only 21 per cent to achieve an average reduction for the two products of one-third.

It is clear that these changes do not amount to 'substantial liberalisation'. This conclusion is reinforced by the consideration that further protection is

Table 4.1 Tariff reductions by developed economies on agricultural
product categories

	Value of imports (US$m)		Percentage reduction in tariffs
Product categories	All sources	Developing economies	
All agricultural products	**84,240**	**38,030**	**37**
Coffee, tea, cocoa, maté	9,136	8,116	35
Fruits and vegetables	14,575	8,887	36
Oilseeds, fats and oils	12,584	6,833	40
Other agricultural products	15,585	4,233	48
Animals and products	9,596	2,690	32
Beverages and spirits	6,608	2,012	38
Flowers, plants, vegetable materials	1,945	1,187	48
Tobacco	3,086	1,135	36
Spices and cereal preparations	2,767	1,134	35
Sugar	1,730	1,030	30
Grains	5,310	725	39
Dairy products	1,317	48	26
Tropical products	**24,022**	**18,744**	**43**
Tropical beverages	8,655	8,041	46
Tropical nuts and fruits	4,340	3,672	37
Certain oilseeds, oils	3,443	2,546	40
Roots, rice, tobacco	4,591	2,497	40
Spices, flowers and plants	2,992	1,987	52

Source: GATT 1994

provided by a variable element called a 'special safeguard clause', which is added automatically to the tariff when the actual import price falls more than 10 per cent below the average 1986–8 import price. Protection against exchange rate changes is given by the fact that import prices will be calculated in national currencies.

The capacity of developed countries to use these provisions to continue to restrict imports on their most vulnerable commodities will be limited only by two requirements. The first is that there be a minimum reduction of 15 per cent in every tariff line. The second is a set of rules that establishes the minimum level of imports for any product. The figure agreed for developed countries is an initial 3 per cent of 1986–8 domestic consumption. This will be expanded to 5 per cent over ten years. For developing countries, access must rise from 1 per cent to 4 per cent over the same period. The GATT Secretariat has calculated that such minimum access will create market opportunities for, among other products, 1.8 million tons of coarse grains, 1.1 million tons of rice, 807,000 tons of wheat and 729,000 tons of dairy products (GATT 1994: 6). But even this opening has been tempered by 'anti-surge' devices.

Domestic support reduction

The interest of developing countries in improved market access is primarily as potential exporters to developed country markets from which they were previously excluded, but their interests in other elements of the agricultural package are more wide-ranging. They may affect the ability of developing countries both to export and to defend their domestic markets from imports. They may also affect the prices developing countries have to pay for their food imports. Developed country subsidies to agriculture have depressed world food prices; the removal of subsidies may cause prices to rise.

Aggregate producer subsidies are to be cut by 20 per cent (13.3 per cent for developing countries and zero for the least developed) over six years. These cuts will be with respect to the levels applying in 1986–8. They are expressed in terms of an Aggregate Measure of Support which applies globally to all supported commodities, with credit allowed for actions already taken since 1986.

Supports in the so-called 'green box' would be exempt from this reduction. Such supports are defined as those 'having no, or at most minimal, trade distortion effects' and include publicly financed R&D, early retirement schemes for farmers and payments for long-term land retirement. There is a strong view that some of the green box supports are actually linked to production which will not fall, therefore, by as much as expected (Pryke and Woodward 1994). If production does not fall it is unlikely that world prices will rise.

Importantly, deficiency payments (as used in the US and EU arable sectors) and headage payments (as used in the EU livestock sector) are excluded from the reduction commitment for domestic support. This is despite the fact that these payments are only weakly 'decoupled' from production decisions. In the case of cereals, for example, Agra Europe (1994) estimates that this effect could increase EU production by some 20 per cent from what it would be without compensation payments in 2000.

Export subsidies limitation

The Uruguay Round agreed reductions in export subsidies which may assist developing country exporters in third markets but may increase the cost of supplies to food-importing developing countries. Developed countries have agreed to reduce by 36 per cent the value of direct export subsidies from their 1986–90 base level (often higher than current levels) and to cut the quantity of subsidised exports by 21 per cent over six years. For developing countries, the reductions will be two-thirds of those applying to developed countries and the implementation period is extended to ten years (with no reductions applying to the least developed). Food aid and unsubsidised exports are not covered by these commitments.

While significant, these cuts will still leave very substantial export subsidies in place. GATT has estimated the total level of export subsidies by developed countries in the base period as US$19 billion (Table 4.2). Cereals, dairy products and meat receive the largest subsidies.

IMPLICATIONS FOR DEVELOPING COUNTRIES

How is this welter of crosscutting effects to be organised in order to show the net effects on different groups of developing countries (and of communities within them)? There have been many quantitative estimates of the Uruguay Round's impact. But these should be treated with caution because of uncertainties about the translation of the agreement into actual changes in tariff schedules, over the time frame for implementation and on the dynamic effects of extended rules. However, the figures are useful in identifying the broad scale of impact and the sectors/geographical regions that will tend to see the greatest changes. More detailed analysis of particular products and countries can then be understood within this broader framework.

Table 4.2 Subsidised export reduction commitments by product

Product	Base period[a] export subsidies US$m	Reduction commitments
Wheat	3,483	−36
Beef	2,802	−36
Coarse grains	2,258	−36
Butter and butteroil	1,996	−36
Other milk products	1,877	−36
Sugar	1,731	−32
Cheese	819	−36
Fruits and vegetables	800	−35
Skim milk powder	746	−36
Live animals	623	−36
Pigmeat	505	−36
Poultry meat	323	−36
Rice	230	−28
Vegetable oils	199	−35
Oilseeds	130	−36
Eggs	125	−36
Wine	107	−36
Tobacco	96	−32
Cotton	85	−24
Sheepmeat	32	−34
Oilcakes	7	−34

Note: [a] 1986–90
Source: GATT 1994

Broad effects

The forecast static developing country gains from the GATT agreement are small but not insignificant. By the year 2005, the GATT Secretariat's model suggests that the export volume of developing and transitional economies will be between 14 per cent and 37 per cent higher (depending on the assumptions made) than they otherwise would be. When expressed in terms of income (how much richer countries will be in 2005 compared with the situation without liberalisation), the range of outcomes for developing and transitional economies extends from a high of US$70 billion (in terms of 1990 dollars) to a low of –US$2 billion. In other words, on some sets of assumptions developing countries could be worse off as a result of the Round than they otherwise would have been. And this remains true even when the GATT Secretariat's calculations take account of dynamic gains (i.e. resulting from the impact of income increases on the level of savings and investment) (GATT 1994: 32–5).

The potential for loss as well as gain is underscored when account is taken of the regional distribution of effects. The gains are unlikely to be shared equally. Most analyses suggest that Asia will gain most, that Latin America's gains are smaller, and that Africa (North and sub-Saharan) will tend to gain least or even lose compared with the status quo. The reasons for this differential impact are that:

- most of the gains will be in manufactures trade and therefore will tend to accrue to the countries most likely to increase their exports of these products as opposed to primary producers;
- African exporters already receive more liberal access to their main market, the EU, than will be the norm after the new agreement is implemented and have demonstrated limited capacity to increase exports to other markets where the Uruguay Round will result in improved access.

The sectoral areas of the Uruguay Round can be divided into three groups in terms of their potential implications for developing countries.

- The traditional concerns, notably barriers to industrial trade. The Round could have a substantial effect on developing countries, but the type of effect is well understood and can best be identified by country- and product-specific analysis.
- New concerns, such as TRIPs and services, which have been brought under a multilateral framework for the first time, but on which concrete change to past practice is for future negotiation. Relatively little may be said at this juncture on the potential implications.
- Temperate agriculture, which is *sui generis*. There are two reasons for giving it special attention. One is that the agreed changes are sufficiently arcane that it is important to explain the potential effects, yet well enough understood to permit the desired broad picture to be painted. Second, agriculture

is profoundly important for a very large number of developing countries, not only as a source of exports and of food imports but as a source of employment and a major contributor to the welfare of a substantial proportion of the population. For these two reasons, it is helpful to give it special attention.

Implications for agriculture

Overall, the absolute impact of the changes on world agricultural markets is likely to be small over the next six years. Hence, there are unlikely to be major opportunities for developing country agricultural exporters. By the same token, developing countries are not likely to be forced by the GATT agreement to abandon their domestic agricultural sector to foreign competition. Nonetheless, the effects may be asymmetrically onerous for food-importing developing countries.

Impact on developing country importers

A large part of world trade in cereals is currently undertaken outside normal markets through actual and quasi food aid. If markets firm up as a result of reduced supply from subsidised agriculture, developed countries' willingness to supply food on concessional terms may fall disproportionately while poor importers' needs rise, at least in the short term (in the longer term higher prices may induce greater domestic supply).

This is precisely what appears to have occurred in the case of European dairy products, for which the Common Agricultural Policy (CAP) was reformed in the early 1980s. The volume of food aid fell significantly over the period 1984–90.

The same pattern may not be repeated for cereals, but it is a potential problem that developing countries need to observe with care. In the case of dairy products the EU Commission switched resources during this period to the purchase of cereals for food aid. This was justified, almost certainly correctly, on the basis that cereals are more useful than dairy products in the food aid basket. It does not follow, therefore, that a decline in cereals carry-over stocks would be accompanied by a similar squeeze in availabilities for grant food aid (and there is even the possibility of an increase in loan food aid). Nonetheless, there is some danger that, at a time of fiscal stringency, cuts may be made in food aid budgets that are disproportionate to the effect of agricultural reform on overall world supply.

Impact on developing country agricultural development

The agreement provides several possible avenues for developing countries to protect their domestic agriculture from imports. Least-developed countries are exempt from any reductions in either tariffs or subsidies. Developing countries, like developed countries, may place some agricultural subsidies in the so-called 'green box' of measures deemed to have minimal trade distorting effects that are exempt from the subsidy reduction commitments. These include payments under environmental programmes, public stockholding for food security purposes and general agricultural development services (such as research, pest and disease control, extension and advisory services).

Additionally, some more general agricultural subsidies are acceptable for developing countries provided that they do not exceed 10 per cent of production value. They may exclude from their reduction commitments 'government measures of assistance, whether direct or indirect, to encourage agricultural and rural development ... which are generally available to agriculture in developing country members' (*Agreement on Agriculture*, Article 6.2).

Finally, extension to temperate agriculture of a wider range of GATT disciplines should permit developing countries to take anti-dumping actions against subsidised developed country exports which will continue to be a feature of trade. There is an increased willingness by developing countries to turn the weapon of anti-dumping against the developed countries that have used it with such abandon.

The EU's changes

It is important not to invest the figures reported in this chapter with more authority than they have. Given the uncertainties concerning the precise changes to trade policy that will result from the Round, let alone the impact of such changes on the economies of the contracting parties, their function is to serve as a broad framework within which country- and product-specific analysis should be viewed.

As explained above, in the area of merchandise trade the impact of the GATT Uruguay Round on developing countries will be heavily influenced by the detailed changes to tariff policy that contracting parties have agreed to make in order to give effect to their new obligations. These changes are voluminous, running to many thousands of lines for each contracting party. There is no short cut to a laborious product-by-product, country-by-country approach for those who wish to understand the true effects that the Uruguay Round will have on developing countries.

This section presents the findings of an analysis of the EU tariff changes from three perspectives (Stevens and Kennan 1994). Two were established in terms of product type, and one was geographically defined. In all three cases a similar methodology was used for identifying the products to analyse and for estimating the scale of the changes.

- The two product types were defined in terms of the initial level of EU protection. A review was made of the proposed changes, first on industrial and then on temperate agricultural products, that are of particular interest to developing countries and which have faced the highest tariff protection in the EU market heretofore. The analysis assesses the extent to which this protection will be reduced as a result of the Round.

- The geographical focus is sub-Saharan Africa, one of the regions of the world least likely to gain substantially as a result of the Uruguay Round. The analysis throws light on the extent to which sub-Saharan Africa will witness an erosion of its competitive position in the European market following the changes in MFN tariffs.

Industrial products

It seems likely, from this initial analysis, that the effect on developing countries of the EU's tariff liberalisation on industrial products will be mixed. On the positive side, when the implementation period is completed a large proportion by value of the items currently imported by the EU from developing countries will enter either duty free or with a tariff of less than 6 per cent. But, for items that are 'sensitive' the changes will be modest. The great majority of significant imports that currently face tariffs of between 11 per cent and 20 per cent will benefit from reductions of two percentage points or fewer.

Because of the enormous number and variety of industrial products the analysis focused only on a select group. However, this group was chosen on the basis of criteria related to their importance to developing countries. The static effect of the tariff reductions that the EU will introduce over a six-year period is equivalent to less than 5 per cent of the value of EU imports from developing countries of the items analysed. To the extent that there are gains, they will accrue largely to the East and South East Asian states.

It would appear that on the non-tariff barrier front, there will be very little change in the EU's effective quotas for clothing and textile items under the MFA in the short term. The EU's initial proposal for the first of the four steps that must be taken between 1994 and 2004 would have had virtually no impact on developing countries. Subsequently, there have been suggestions that some substantial changes might be made, but these have not yet been detailed. No further changes are required until the end of 1997.

Agricultural products

It seems even less likely that there will be substantial changes to the import regime for 'heartland' CAP products this century. The tariffs with which the EU is proposing to replace the existing variable import levies are sufficiently high that, even after subsequent liberalisation, they will still represent a formidable obstacle to imports (Table 4.3). The EU has expressed these tariffs

Table 4.3 Tariffication by the EU on cereals

	Initial tariff (ECU/T)	Ad valorem[a] (%)	Reduction by 2000 (%)
Durum wheat	231	134	36
Spelt, common wheat and meslin	149	89	36
Barley	145	141	36
Oats	139	108	36
Semi-/wholly-milled rice	650	128	36
Wheat and meslin flour	268	88	36

Note: [a] Calculated by applying the initial specific tariff to 1993 unit import values.

as specific duties (see column 2 of Table 4.3). In order to indicate their severity, they have been converted into *ad valorem* equivalents (column 3). The last column shows the reduction in these levels that the EU has agreed to make by 2000.

In the less sensitive temperate agricultural areas, however, there may be some liberalisation of importance to developing countries. Although the tariff cuts on floriculture, horticulture and fruits are small relative to the value of trade (in the region of 6 per cent of EU 1992 imports from developing countries), the products in question are of potential importance to a large number of countries. Many are Mediterranean or African, Caribbean and Pacific (ACP) states (which receive significant preferences over MFN levels and so may not, in practice, benefit), but there is a good sprinkling of countries with limited, if any, preferences, such as Chile, Brazil and South Africa. Various categories of winter flowers, winter potatoes and summer carnations will feel the greatest change.

Africa

Fears have been expressed that the EU's preferred suppliers will lose as a result of the Round, since the margin of preference will be eroded. As any such deterioration would be particularly serious for sub-Saharan Africa, the analysis focused on this region. A review of all the most important sub-Saharan African exports to the EU suggests that the erosion of preference *as a result of the GATT Round* will be modest: of the order of 4 per cent of total exports, of which over one-half is accounted for by a single product, coffee. The reason for the emphasis in the previous sentence is that the situation could change substantially if the GATT Round is followed by a reduction in the EU's tariffs under the Generalised System of Preferences (GSP). Until the rates applying under the proposed new EU GSP are known, the extent of the erosion cannot be calculated.

CONCLUSION

It is difficult to strike an appropriate balance between investing the Uruguay Round with more importance for developing countries than is justifiable and dismissing it as irrelevant. The Round will be important for developed and developing countries alike, but it is only one among many factors that affect world trade. Moreover, many of the most critical issues for developing countries, such as labour and environmental standards in trade, remain for future negotiation.

The symbolic importance of the agreement must not be overlooked. The success in Marrakesh will make it harder for developed countries to justify protectionism against developing countries, although it would be naïve to suppose that such practices will cease. The importance of this symbolic blow for liberal trade is enhanced if account is taken of what might have happened in the event of a collapse of the negotiations. The threats by USA, EU and other major actors to indulge in trade wars in the event of a GATT failure were probably negotiating tactics, but there was nonetheless a real danger that in the acrimony surrounding collapse trade hostilities might have increased.

At the same time, there has been a symbolic boost to the cause of liberalisation in developing countries. The new agreement retains the concept of special and differential treatment for developing countries, but it is more limited than before. By comparison with pressure emanating from the IMF/World Bank or from the domestic supporters of liberalisation, however, the tangible stimulus that the GATT agreement will provide to dismantle protection is slight. Fears that the new agreement will force unwilling governments to dismantle import controls have been much exaggerated.

The impact of the detailed changes agreed in the Round is not yet understood precisely because of the complexity of reforms. From what is known, however, it seems likely that middle-income developing countries will gain to a modest, but not insignificant, extent. Most concern is focused on Africa, which seems likely to gain least and might even lose. The reasons for this are to be found in Africa's place in the world trading system rather than the Marrakesh text and, in particular, in its reliance on exports of primary commodities facing low MFN tariffs and stagnant markets.

Possibly the most important feature of the Uruguay Round for developing countries is that it is likely to be the last such mammoth negotiating forum. Henceforth, negotiations on changes to the world trade regime are likely to take place on a continuous basis within the WTO framework. Developing country interests are likely to be at stake in many of these negotiations. They need to be defended.

BIBLIOGRAPHY

Agra Europe (1994) 18 February, cited in J. Pryke and D. Woodward 'The GATT Agreement on Agriculture: Will it Help Developing Countries?', *CIIR Seminar Background Paper*, London: Catholic Institute for International Relations, March.

GATT (1994) 'The Results of the Uruguay Round of Multilateral Trade Negotiations. Market Access for Goods and Services: Overview of the Results', Geneva: GATT Secretariat, November.

Pryke, J. and Woodward, D. (1994) 'The GATT Agreement on Agriculture: Will it Help Developing Countries?', *CIIR Seminar Background Paper*, London: Catholic Institute for International Relations, March.

Stevens, C. and Kennan, J. (1994) 'How Will the EU's Response to the GATT Round Affect Developing Countries?', *IDS Working Paper* No. 11, Brighton: Institute of Development Studies.

5

THE SURVIVAL OF SPECIAL PREFERENCES UNDER THE LOMÉ CONVENTION

The ACP countries and the European Union after the Uruguay Round[1]

Adrian Hewitt and Antonique Koning

Former colonies of the member states of the European Union (EU) have enjoyed preferential access into the EU market since the creation of the European Economic Community in 1957. Moreover, since 1975 successive Lomé Conventions have committed this specially privileged group of countries which now consists of seventy African, Caribbean and Pacific (ACP) states, and the European Union to achieving a 'better balance of trade'. Although that is a somewhat hazy concept, if one were to attempt to target the overall merchandise trade balance of seventy developing and now fifteen EU states combined, the thinking behind the concept as originally set out in the mid-1970s is at least clear. It aims at promoting and diversifying ACP exports to the EU market and at decreasing ACP dependency on primary exports. Since the Lomé Convention arrangements are hybrid, it was hoped to achieve this by means of aid provisions and non-reciprocal trade preferences. Nowadays, one may wonder what the meaning of such a commitment is in an international trade environment which is increasingly oriented towards trade liberalisation – as has been clearly marked by the completion of the Uruguay Round – rather than to preferential and discriminatory trade agreements such as the Lomé Convention.

In this chapter an analysis is made of the effects of the Uruguay Round on ACP exports to the European Union and other markets, with a special emphasis on the effects on their preferential access to these former markets. In order to understand these effects better, however, we start with an assessment of the Lomé trade preferences and their effects on ACP trade performance. In the final part of this chapter some conclusions will be drawn on the prospects and challenges which ACP exporters face under the regime of the new World Trade Organization (WTO).

Table 5.1 Preferential treatment of ACP exports to the EU (1992 exports)

	Tropical products	*Annex XL products*	*Protocol products*	*Total agr. products (CN 01–24)*	*Non-agr. products (CN 25-99)*
ACP exports 1992, m ECU	1,898	1,514	1,279	5,273	12,688
Share of ACP exports to EU, %	11	8	7	29	71
Preferential market access under the Lomé Convention	Duty free	Concessions on CAP	Quota arrangements	n.a.	Duty free

Notes:
Tropical products include coffee, tea, spices, cocoa.

Annex XL of the Lomé Convention offers concessions to certain agricultural exports, including some dairy products and meat, tobacco, fish, some fruit and vegetables, some of which are restricted in quantity, throughout the year and depending on the season others get only a reduction in their levies or face seasonal quotas.

Protocol products include sugar, rum and bananas, some beef and veal.

LOMÉ TRADE PROVISIONS AND THEIR IMPACT ON ACP TRADE PERFORMANCE

The trade provisions of the Lomé Convention include non-reciprocal prefer-ences for industrial ACP exports to the European market, preferential treatment for their agricultural exports and special protocols for exports of bananas, rum, sugar, and beef and veal. Altogether approximately 97 per cent of (1992) ACP exports get preferential access to the EU market, most of them without being restricted by any duty or non-tariff barrier (see Table 5.1). Such totals are, of course, only of limited significance. Agricultural products which face too high a barrier in the European market might simply not become ACP exports at all. The trade preferences are intended to give the ACP states a price advantage over industrialised and other developing country exporters to the EU – in other words, the Lomé preferences not only violate the most favoured nation (MFN) principle agreed in multilateral trade negotiations, they also discriminate against other developing countries. Traditionally, they have been seen as a mechanism to give an initial boost to industrialisation or are at least claimed to be an incentive for further processing of primary products, so as to reduce ACP reliance on resource-based products (a secondary meaning of the mid-1970s phrase 'better balance of trade').

90

Nevertheless, despite these preferences and other trade-related provisions of the Convention,[2] trade performance of the ACP has been rather disappointing. Table 5.2 which shows ACP export performance between 1976 and 1992 indicates that the share of ACP exports in the EU market has declined from 6.7 per cent to 3.7 per cent, while their dependence on the EU market for their export revenue is still significant (41 per cent on average between 1990–2). Twenty-seven (mainly African) countries depended on their EU exports for more than 75 per cent of their total export revenue from OECD countries. This shows that most ACP states have been unable to diversify, in any significant way, their exports to markets outside the EU. As a result, their poor overall performance within the EU market is all the more dramatic.

Table 5.2 Value of EU imports from ACP states in bn ECU and share of total EU imports (1976–92)

	1976 bn ECU	%	1980 bn ECU	%	1985 bn ECU	%	1990 bn ECU	%	1992 bn ECU	%
Africa	9.4	6.0	17.2	6.3	24.3	6.0	20.1	4.4	16.0	3.3
Caribbean	0.8	0.5	1.6	0.6	1.6	0.4	1.4	0.3	1.5	0.3
Pacific	0.2	0.1	0.4	0.1	0.7	0.2	0.4	0.1	0.4	0.1
Total ACP of which:	10.5	6.7	19.4	7.2	26.8	6.7	21.9	4.7	18.0	3.7
ACP non-oil exports	6.6	6.1	9.7	5.3	13.9	4.8	13.5	3.5	12.3	2.9

Note: All EU imports mentioned in this study are extra-EU imports, excluding intra-EU trade
Source: Eurostat data

Diversification away from primary commodities into non-traditional and processed products has also been less than was expected, or at least hoped. In the last five years up to 1992, 10 traditional commodities still accounted for almost 61 per cent of ACP exports to Europe on average. Apart from petroleum (the largest export product which has always heavily influenced the trend of ACP exports), these included coffee, cocoa, sugar, bananas, copper, aluminium and gold.

However, large differences in the volume and structure of exports exist among the 70 African, Caribbean and Pacific countries; they are by no means homogeneous although some of them might face similar obstacles in expanding their export base. Most ACP exports still originate from only a small number of countries. For instance Nigeria – by far the largest ACP country – accounted for 22 per cent of ACP exports to the Union in 1992: its exports were almost exclusively crude petroleum.

Perhaps paradoxically, and in contrast with ACP performance, developing countries which have enjoyed less favourable treatment in the EU market, in particular Asian countries, have been more successful in penetrating it.

91

Growth rates of developing countries' exports to the Union between 1976 and 1992 were only 2.3 per cent for the ACP countries, but 5.9 per cent for Mediterranean developing countries, 6.0 per cent for Latin America and almost 12 per cent for developing Asian countries (Cosgrove 1994).

WHAT PREVENTED THE ACP COUNTRIES FROM TAKING FULL ADVANTAGE OF THE PROVISIONS?

The above facts seem to indicate that the Lomé Convention, at least on an aggregate level, did not provide the essential provisions to achieve growth in ACP exports to the EU. What went wrong? To begin with the expectations for the expansion of ACP exports as a result of the preferences were too ambitious. According to calculations of the European Commission, 63.4 per cent of ACP exports do not enjoy a preferential margin since they enter the Union free of duties as a result of most favoured nation (MFN) treatment or – if from a developing country – under the Generalised System of Preferences (GSP) (CEC 1993). For the other exports that could potentially have benefited from Lomé, only 7 per cent received a significant preferential margin (i.e. a tariff differential greater than 5 per cent) *vis-à-vis* other exporters.[3] As most ACP countries have remained heavily dependent on primary exports, their ability to benefit from the preferences has been low. In addition to the existence of a preferential margin for a country's exports, the value of preferences depends on the response to price changes in demand for and supply of ACP products, expressed by their elasticities of demand and supply. As these are generally relatively low for (mainly primary) commodities exported by ACP countries, large benefits could not have been expected. (For more detailed description of the value of preferences see Davenport *et al.* 1995.)

If one looks at the disaggregated product or country level, evidence can indeed be found that those countries which knew how to diversify their exports towards products with a relatively high preferential margin might have benefited from the Lomé arrangements. At the product level a comprehensive study by McQueen and Stevens (1989) concluded that certain ACP exports that enjoyed a significant preferential margin had grown relatively fast during the existence of the Convention. These were canned tuna, bovine hides and skins, processed wood, some fabrics and clothing and furnishing and some others. However, it was admitted that little correlation between the size of the growth rate and the preference margin was found. Countries which have been able to expand their exports to the EU significantly over time are often described as success stories, and did so while exploiting Lomé preferences after they had moved into more processed and manufactured goods exports. The leading examples here are Mauritius, Jamaica and Zimbabwe. However, it is unlikely that these good performances can be attributed solely to Lomé preferences. Although in these countries the trade provisions of the Lomé Convention may have had a catalytic role in developing dynamic export sectors, experience in other countries suggests that they may be neither a necessary nor a sufficient condition for developing a dynamic export sector and that other critical factors restrict the accelerator role of preferences and limit the benefits that can be derived from them.

In other words, the Lomé Convention may not have provided sufficient incentives to overcome the structural problems of some ACP countries that limit trade development, such as the lack of adequate infrastructure to provide a reliable export supply, insufficient capacity to attract private investment, inadequately developed financial sector and the weak human resource bases in some countries (see also Agarwal *et al.* 1985). It could be argued that the non-trade elements of the Lomé Convention might have addressed precisely these deficiencies, and so complemented the trade provisions, but that would be asking a lot from a relatively modest instrument, after all.

Other factors hampering ACP trade are more germane to the implementation of the trade provisions. For instance, it has been found that in most ACP countries there is still limited awareness about the provisions, and the tariff concessions and quota arrangements, even after twenty years. Another problem is the complicated procedures that apply to the Lomé access provisions. The Lomé rules of origin have restricted potential ACP exports in some cases. These rules are designed to prevent non-ACP exports being sent through ACP countries (and claiming ACP preferences) but fail to take account of the increasing growth of outward processing. They are particularly restrictive in processed fish and clothing sectors, leading the ACP to suspect that the EU is protecting those sectors against them after all. The rules do not normally allow ACP exporters to cumulate inputs from non-ACP or non-EU sources, although it would often be more efficient to obtain inputs automatically from cheaper or nearer sources. They therefore affect the competitiveness of ACP exports and often appear to act as a disincentive to investment and diversification (Davenport *et al.* 1995).[4]

Most ACP states have had great difficulty in exploiting the Lomé preferences for structural, capacity and procedural reasons rather than a limitation of market access, except probably in the case of some agricultural exports where this has been restricted by quota. It needs to be mentioned, however, that the value of Lomé preferences has been decreased by the extension in recent years of some near-equivalent preferences to other developing countries.[5] More importantly still, the special status of the Lomé countries has been crucially affected by the subject of this book, multilateral liberalisation, most recently in the Uruguay Round.

DID ACP COUNTRIES WIN OR LOSE FROM THE URUGUAY ROUND SETTLEMENT?

The Uruguay Round will have its most obvious effects on ACP countries through the erosion of their preferences and the changes in the world prices for ACP exports and imports of temperate agricultural products, over the period when the Round is fully implemented in ten years' time. The phasing out of the Multifibre Arrangement (MFA) is likely to have an impact on relatively few ACP countries by increasing competition in the textile and clothing sector (because although ACP countries were not subjected to MFA quotas, few developed an efficient textile or garment industry for export, unlike the Asian and southern Mediterranean countries). Similarly, the liberalisation of services is likely to have little impact on ACP countries in the near future. The post-Uruguay Round effects of preference erosion and changes in world price levels, especially for food, together with new opportunities due to rising incomes and increased access to non-EU markets are estimated and described below.[6]

Preference erosion

The lowering of tariffs following the Uruguay Round will decrease the preferential margin for ACP states and subsequently cause a loss of competitiveness which in theory will lead to a trade diversion away from the ACP exporters to more competitive non-ACP suppliers. This is expected to further decrease ACP export earnings not only from the EU but also from other OECD markets in which ACP countries have enjoyed preferences. Countries which are most affected are the ones which depend on those few primary export commodities or processed tropical products for which the preferential margins have been eliminated or become insignificant, and those countries which have begun to export manufactured goods.

As regards tropical exports from ACP states, losses occur due to the elimination of MFN tariffs for coffee and cocoa and from preference erosion on cut flowers and plants, nuts and tropical fruits, spices and tobacco. These losses are particularly significant in the EU market as in other OECD markets these products already entered mainly duty free. ACP countries that are most affected by this erosion are Cameroon, Côte d'Ivoire, Ghana, Kenya, Malawi and Zimbabwe. Coffee- and cocoa-producing countries Burundi, Rwanda and Uganda, lose a relatively large proportion of their export earnings (around 5 per cent each) owing to their high dependency on these exports to the EU.

Among those countries which lose most as a result of the preference erosion on industrial products[7] are the ones that have been more advanced in processing and manufacturing or in other words have been able to take advantage of some of the Lomé preferences. In Africa the main losers are: Cameroon, Côte d'Ivoire, Gabon and Liberia, but Caribbean countries are most affected in this area, in particular the Bahamas, the Dominican Republic, Jamaica, Suriname and Trinidad and Tobago. In the Pacific only Papua New Guinea loses relatively significantly. The mere fact of losing margins of preference does not, of course, mean that these countries will not seek to develop new export markets in goods and services sectors which themselves are beneficiaries of liberalisation: in fact the past evidence that they have successfully exploited the preferences made available is an indication that they will be the countries performing better under a new, more liberal, trade regime.

Agricultural exports

Following the Agreement on Agriculture, non-tariff barriers such as quotas, controls and variable levies, imposed by the major trading partners for protection of their own suppliers, will be converted into tariffs and then reduced under binding agreements over the next ten years. The settlement further requires cuts in domestic and export subsidies and a reduction in the quantity of subsidised exports, although more than half the ACP countries are exempt from this requirement because they are classified as least developed countries. (ACP countries dominate this new 'preferential' category for WTO purposes.) The main effect the liberalisation of agricultural trade will have on ACP suppliers is through a likely increase in world market prices for agricultural exports caused by these changes. Within the EU, however, domestic prices for temperate exports, such as beef and sugar which come under the Common Agricultural Policy, are expected to fall.

The implications of these agricultural price changes vary among the ACP states. The net effects are most serious for those ACP countries which are food importers, such as Angola, Côte d'Ivoire, Senegal and Nigeria, and for those which currently enjoy preferential access to the EU market on an otherwise highly restricted product like sugar or beef, under one of the Lomé protocols, such as Botswana, Mauritius and Guyana. Overall, the Agreement on Agriculture is expected to cause a net deterioration of $227 million in the trade balance for ACP states.

Table 5.3 summarises those effects of the Uruguay Round on ACP states by region which can be quantified. It needs to be noted that these estimates

Table 5.3 Summary of the Uruguay Round settlement. Trade effects ($m and share of 1992 exports from the ACP to OECD countries)

	Change in net exports of temperate agricultural products	Change in revenue from exports of tropical products and fish	Change in revenue from exports of industrial products*	Total change in exports	1992 exports to the rest of the world	Total change as % of total exports
Africa	−173	−156.0	−175.8	−505.3	44,689	−1.1
Caribbean	−52	−11.0	−120.0	−183.1	6,109	−3.0
Pacific	−2	−9.0	−14.2	−25.0	2,390	−1.1
ACP	−227	−176.6	−317.0	−713.4	53,188	−1.3

Note: *excluding textiles and clothing

95

are based upon the assumption that the ACP states are fully benefiting from the Lomé trade provisions. They might therefore overestimate the losses.

Phasing out of the Multifibre Arrangement

The Multifibre Arrangement (MFA) was introduced to restrain developing country exports of textiles and clothing in order to protect developed country producers of garments and materials, supposedly while they adjusted to the new realities. As quotas were imposed on developing country exporters which were successful (mainly the large Asian countries), the MFA caused trade to disperse from the originally successful exporter to other suppliers with cheap labour until they too faced quotas. In effect, a market in quotas developed. Under the Lomé Convention, ACP states have been exempt from the MFA which stimulated some, though not many, ACP countries like Jamaica, Mauritius, Lesotho and Zimbabwe to develop these exports, even attracting inward – but often footloose – investment in the process. The phasing out of the MFA will lead to fiercer competition for those exporters once the preferences have been eroded. This could be as long as in ten years' time, since the textile provisions of the Uruguay Round settlement are heavily endloaded at present. Davenport and Page (1994) argue that this will have a major impact on export earnings of Mauritius and Jamaica, which are estimated to decrease by 16.5 per cent and 7.6 per cent (of 1992 exports) respectively, mainly because they are regarded as not having a natural advantage in producing clothing and textiles but are exploiting EU (and US) preferences in this sector instead. In general the ACP countries' loss of export earnings which can be quantified as a result of the phasing out of the MFA are expected to amount to only 0.2 per cent of export revenue. This does not seem much, but the change will further negatively affect ACP countries which are potential exporters of textiles and clothing (and are currently exporting raw materials) but have not yet taken advantage of EU market preferences. In particular, investment in the textiles and clothing sector is likely to be deterred due to the loss of its competitive advantage. This is important because this sector has, in the past, proved to be crucial to the process of industrialisation (Koning 1994).

Global liberalisation of trade in services

It is rather more difficult to estimate the impact of the liberalisation of trade services, especially because the individual country offers to the Round do not give an indication of the change in controls or the height of the barriers that remain, but only state the limits to protection of national service providers. Sectors in which ACP services are concentrated, in particular tourism, have not been subject to severe restrictions before, so gains from liberalisation will therefore be small for existing service suppliers. Offers of most ACP countries for liberalisation of their own service markets have been rather limited. Suppliers from outside are therefore not expected to overwhelm their markets in the near future, a risk which some fear if pressure on liberalisation of trade in services increases.

Overall impact of the Uruguay Round on ACP trade

In total the above effects show a negative effect on ACP export earnings, though a small impact (around 1.5 per cent), because the level of their trade and their involvement in the international economic system is too low to allow them to gain or lose much from the Round. Who wins or loses depends on the structure of the exports of the individual ACP country.

Countries which are net importers of agricultural goods and therefore have benefited from market distortions, leading to low world prices, will be hit particularly hard when food prices rise. A special committee within the World Trade Organization will examine the cost to net food-importing developing countries and will make recommendations concerning the possibility and appropriateness of food aid and/or compensatory finance from bilateral or multilateral sources. This will only be at best a recommendation since the WTO itself has no funds to provide compensation or to make up margins. On the other hand, the few food-exporting countries among the ACP states will be able to produce for a freer and more transparent world market where competitiveness, and not quotas, determines the trade pattern. For their exports to the EU there might be scope for increased preferential treatment in cases where quantitative barriers are being replaced by tariffs. Tariffs on CAP produce have generally been small, with the major trade barrier being the variable levies and other measures used to maintain the EU import price at an administered level, irrespective of world prices. Conversion of such non-trade barriers into tariffs would give the ACP states vastly improved preferential margins if they continue to enjoy tariff exemptions: the scale of the change could be so large as to encourage other ACP states to become exporters of food grains, legumes, fruits and other agricultural products.

The fact that the ACP states have been exempted from the highest trade barriers that are now being dismantled, on agricultural and MFA exports in particular, means that they will not gain from the Round to the same extent as other countries, whether developing or developed. In contrast, they lose out following the reduction of their preferential margin *vis-à-vis* other exporters. The effect of the erosion of their preferences is small, however, since the majority of their exports have duty-free access to the developed countries anyway – and would be even smaller if it is considered that preferences have not been fully exploited in the past. We have not been able to estimate the dynamic effects of the loss of preferences, but they are important, especially in sectors where preferences seem to have triggered a growth in exports and diversification in production.

On a more optimistic note the improved access to non-EU markets is expected to benefit ACP countries. In contrast to the preference erosion in Europe, ACP states will have more access to other markets where they currently have no preferential treatment. For Pacific islands and some countries in Eastern Africa in particular, the growing Asian markets offer obvious new opportunities. Tonga's seasonal squash exports to Japan are a leitmotif of this trade. Caribbean countries will, despite the erosion of their preferences under the Caribbean Basin Initiative, benefit from a more open US economy. Concern that they will be excluded from NAFTA arrangements, should they be extended, has stimulated many of them to develop a proactive strategy to be included. This is the kind of action that will be needed if ACP states are to exploit the opportunities in these and other non-EU markets. (It may be rather depressing to note that only one of the seventy ACP countries, Papua New Guinea, had by 1995 joined the APEC Pacific Rim group of fast-growing developed and developing countries, which together comprise by far the biggest market in the world – the USA and Japan are members.) Adequate preparation is essential to deal with fierce competition, to overcome structural problems, and to increase their competitiveness. In general, the Uruguay Round is likely to have a positive impact on the ACP states via the boost in world trade, investment and economic growth that the trade liberalisation generates, and optimists would say this far outweighs the preference erosion and other negative factors.

In addition to that, global income will be increased by improved access to the markets of trading partners and a more efficient use of resources, when trade barriers are reduced or removed, which will increase world demand. Studies by GATT, the World Bank, and the OECD predict an average annual increase of 1.05 per cent in world income by 2002 as a result of trade liberalisation. If these gains are combined with their losses occurring from the Round, the ACP states are still expected to lose approximately 0.3 per cent of their export earnings.[8] So it has to be stressed that some countries face a net loss rather than a net gain, which is why pressure for special treatment (possibly compensation) for the least developed countries has now built up.

Finally, although the ACP states might not be in a position to gain as much from improvements in the regulatory framework as other countries, since they have not been targeted for extra protectionist actions by the developed countries, the new World Trade Organization could have a positive impact on them. Most importantly it provides a 'certainty of what the rules are, of no arbitrary changes in market access [as has happened in the past for some of the more advanced ACP countries like Mauritius], of the criteria for actions like anti-dumping or the required standards on intellectual property, and in a last resort on dispute procedures' (ODI 1995). In fact, anti-dumping could turn out to be quite a venomous tool. Nonetheless, the improved transparency and organisation of the new trade regime give developing countries opportunities to become more integrated into the system, which is why so many have now joined GATT/WTO. Being part of it is better than being left out.

TRADE CHALLENGES FOR ACP STATES IN THE WTO

The results of the Uruguay Round clearly pose threats and some opportunities for ACP countries, most of which have not been able to establish a stable position in the EU markets (or other markets for that matter) utilising trade preferences. However, the future of Lomé preferences should be assessed not only in the light of the Uruguay Round Agreement but also in the current European and international trading environment.

Partly to compensate for the expected erosion of preferences in the EU market and partly because of the difficulties exporters have experienced in trying to exploit the Lomé trade provisions, the ACP insisted that trade policy and performance be raised as an issue for renegotiation in the Mid-term Review of the Lomé Convention (1994–5), requesting, among other things, improved market access for agricultural goods and a relaxation of the rules of origin. However, this has proved to be a controversial issue for the EU member states, which are increasingly under pressure from their domestic producers and fear the risk of growing unemployment arising from competition from successful 'cheap labour' countries – a categorisation which applies in fact to relatively few in the ACP Group – in times of recession in Europe. The negotiation of the Lomé trade provisions was left as one of the last issues to be decided on together with the size of the aid volume for ACP countries, the European Development Fund. Some EU member states were negotiating as if there was a trade-off between improved access or more aid,[9] though the ACP Group understandably felt they deserved both.

In the meantime, other pressures are pushing the EU to revise its approach to the Lomé Convention. Increasingly critical attitudes of the international trading community (especially the USA, but including some EU member states themselves) towards the ACP's special relationship with the EU, has created tension between the EU and its trading partners. A clear example of this was the banana dispute in which Latin American banana producers (and US multinationals) complained to GATT about the EU's banana protocol which favours ACP producers over others in the EU market, and which was subsequently condemned, resulting in increased quotas for non-ACP bananas. Although a waiver requested by the EU and ACP for continuation of the derogation from GATT for the Lomé preferences has again been accepted until 2000 with biannual revisions, the environment of progressive trade liberalisation under the WTO is not likely to have a lot of sympathy for non-reciprocal trading arrangements like the Lomé Convention.

The return of South Africa to the international community after the 1994 elections marked the watershed in this approach. Here at last was the opportunity for the one remaining sub-Saharan African country to join – and massively strengthen – the ACP group. But it rapidly became apparent that if the EU were to offer comprehensive trade discrimination in favour of a powerful (albeit dualistic) economy such as South Africa in the form of full membership of the Lomé Convention, that waiver would not be sustainable. An objection – likely at the very least from the USA – would have undermined all the special preferences accorded to the ACP for the rest of the decade. So it took a long time for the European Commission to deliberate and finally opt in March 1995 for a specially tailored approach for South Africa which recognises its special status and history.[10]

The Commission proposed that South Africa be given the special status of 'qualified' membership of the Lomé Convention. It will not be given the same duty-free access to the EU market as the ACP but will be offered a free trade agreement over ten years with product restrictions similar to those faced by the Central and Eastern European countries on agricultural and industrial products. South Africa will not, however, be obliged to give the EU reverse preferences.

Similarly, South Africa will not be given access to EDF aid; instead it has been offered a continuation of the EU's rather large country aid programme, totalling up to ECU 625m over the next five years. Nor will South Africa have any allocation under the special protocols on EU sensitive agricultural products (bananas, beef, veal and sugar) – or, put another way, the existing ACP states will not have to share their quota-like arrangements with the new state. It is not even clear what version of the Lomé Convention the Republic of South Africa will sign in order to obtain this 'qualified' membership, although the Commission insists that South Africa will be allowed to tender for EDF projects and will be permitted cumulation with other ACP states for rules of origin purposes. These last two concessions are likely to prove most valuable to South Africa's development. The rest is essentially a cosmetic change from the post-apartheid transitional arrangements, themselves a recognition by at least some EU member states that if a close association with Europe were not briskly formed, other major powers would fill the vacuum. The main change in trade relations with the EU in fact came earlier with the switch from a sanctions-bound economy to one trading on an MFN basis under President Mandela.

The new EU package was finally approved as a negotiating mandate by the EU Foreign Ministers on 12 June 1995, with the proviso that the aid arrangements be budgeted annually (i.e. in ECU 125m tranches rather than guaranteed over five years). The trade arrangements themselves – as well as any eventual free trade agreement – still have to be negotiated between the European Commission and the government of South Africa. The end result will resemble the new generation of EU trade arrangements with Mediterranean and Eastern European countries more than it will the Lomé Convention package deal.

This is a further sign that we are seeing the end of the era of special relations based on the colonial past. The Lomé Convention is unlikely to be renewed in its present exclusive form after 1999. A new EU approach focusing on the poorer ACP and other developing countries, as required by the Maastricht Treaty, after the fourth Lomé Convention comes to an end, is one of the possible routes that has been suggested. Although over half of the ACP countries belong to the 'least developed' group – a category now earmarked for special treatment under the WTO trading arrangements – it is sometimes argued that some of the other ACP members have reached a sufficient level of development and should be graduated out of the preferential trade agreement (as has been argued for some countries benefiting from the GSP in the past).

With these challenges in mind, it is clear that ACP and EU member states need to rethink their strategies for the development and promotion of trade between them. In the short run, ACP states still have great scope for making better use of existing preferences to strengthen their competitiveness in the EU market. As most effects of the Uruguay Round, in particular on agricultural products and clothing and textile exports, will only become apparent in the later stage of implementation of the agreement (i.e. at the beginning of the next century), this provides ACP states with opportunities in the EU market not yet exploited. The EU could help by taking away some of the remaining obstacles for ACP exporters wanting to enter the EU market (e.g. the restrictive rules of origin) and improving the coherence between its trade and aid provisions that are oriented towards trade development. The lack of awareness of the Lomé provisions could be countered by training in their utilisation in national and regional training centres in ACP countries – an idea already formally proposed by the joint assembly of EU and ACP members of parliament. At the same time, ACP states need to focus on their comparative advantage and now know they should rely less on preferences in the EU market. This means diversifying both the structure and the destinations of their exports and making trade a real priority.

NOTES

1 This chapter is based on research findings that are published in a Special Report by the Overseas Development Institute: *Europe's Preferred Partners? The Lomé Countries in World Trade*, by M. Davenport, A. Hewitt and A. Koning (1995).

2 The Convention also offers a large number of aid-financed instruments which are available for trade promotion, through development finance and technical assistance, in particular in areas of trade promotion and as risk-reducing mechanisms against fluctuations in the exports earnings of primary commodities (STABEX) and minerals (SYSMIN).

3 Figures for 1989, calculated by McQueen and Stevens (1989). Generally the Common External Tariff (CET) of the European Union becomes higher when more value is added to a product (i.e. when more processing or manufacturing

has taken place). This means that most benefits from duty-free access can be reaped from those kind of exports.'

4 Derogation procedures to obtain exemptions from the rules of origin exist but their use is complicated and the system fails to tackle the difficulty in proving that certain exports are impeded by the rules of origin.

5 The EU has extended preferences to certain countries in Central and Eastern Europe and republics of the former Soviet Union and improved access to four Andean Pact countries to stimulate exports other than drugs.

6 Research was undertaken by the ODI for the ACP Secretariat in Brussels in 1994. For more detailed information on the research see Davenport *et al.* 1995.

7 In our calculation this category includes processed metals and minerals; wood, pulp and paper; leather and footwear; chemicals; electrical equipment; non-electronic machinery and transport equipment. Clothing and textiles are excluded because they are dealt with separately.

8 These estimates consider an average elasticity of demand for ACP exports of 1; in an alternative case, of an elasticity of 3, they appear to gain 1.6 per cent of the current level of their export earnings.

9 The Mid-term Review was completed, belatedly, only on 30 June 1995 (at the time of writing this chapter), because of a breakdown in negotiations among the EU member states themselves on the size of the EDF (and the concomitant trade-off regarding market access).

10 This approach is not unlike that proposed three years earlier by ODI. See Page *et al.* (1992), *Trading with South Africa: The Policy Options for the EC*, London: Overseas Development Institute, Special Report.

BIBLIOGRAPHY

Agarwal, J., Dippl, M. and Langhammer R. (1985) *EC Trade Policies Towards Associated Developing Countries, Barriers to Success*, Kiel Study 193.

CEC (Commission of the European Communities) (1993) *European Economy 1993: The EC as a World Trade Partner*, Brussels: Commission of the European Communities

Cosgrove, C. (1994) 'Has the Lomé Convention Failed ACP Trade?', *Journal of International Affairs*, Vol. 48, No. 1.

Davenport, M. and Page, S. (1994) *World Trade Reform: Do Developing Countries Gain or Lose?*, London: Overseas Development Institute.

Davenport M., Hewitt A. and Koning A. (1995) *Europe's Preferred Partners? The Lomé Countries in World Trade*, London: Overseas Development Institute.

Koning, A. (1994) 'Challenges of ACP Trade with Europe after the Uruguay Round', *ECDPM Policy Management Brief, No.1*, Maastricht: European Centre for Development Policy Management.

McQueen, M. and Stevens, C. (1989) 'Trade Preferences and Lomé IV: Non-traditional ACP Exports to the EC', *Development Policy Review*, Vol. 7: 239–60.

ODI (Overseas Development Institute) (1995) *Developing Countries in the WTO*, Briefing Paper No. 3, May, London: Overseas Development Institute.

Part II

PERSPECTIVES AND POLICY OPTIONS FOR THE WORLD TRADING SYSTEM

6

THE FUTURE ROLE OF
THE WTO[1]

Jeffrey J. Schott

INTRODUCTION

On 1 January 1995, the Agreement Establishing the World Trade Organization (WTO) entered into force, and a new era of international trade relations began. In many respects, the 'new' trading institution is very much like the 'old' General Agreement on Tariffs and Trade (GATT) regime that has governed world trade since the late 1940s. The trading rules incorporate the results of the past eight rounds of GATT negotiations. The main difference is that the world's leading trading nations have now committed to strengthening the institutional foundation of the trading system, providing greater legal coherence among its wide-ranging rights and obligations, and establishing a permanent forum for consultations and negotiations on an ever-broadening agenda of issues affecting global trade and investment in goods and services.

This chapter summarises the main components of the WTO.[2] It then examines four challenges facing the trading system as it prepares to deal with the trade problems of the early twenty-first century.

THE WTO IN BRIEF

The Agreement Establishing the World Trade Organization establishes a legal framework that ties together the various trade pacts that have been negotiated under GATT auspices over the past four decades. The WTO Agreement encompasses the following trade pacts:

- the GATT 1994, including the agreement on Trade-Related Investment Measures (TRIMs) and the Tokyo Round codes (Annex 1A to the WTO Agreement);
- the General Agreement on Trade in Services (GATS) (Annex 1B);
- the agreement on Trade-Related Aspects of Intellectual Property Rights (TRIPs) (Annex 1C).

The WTO Agreement also consolidates the dispute settlement provisions of those different accords into one common dispute settlement mechanism

(Annex 2) and administers the trade policy review mechanism (TPRM) provided for in Annex 3. In addition, the WTO incorporates four plurilateral agreements (the civil aircraft agreement, the government procurement agreement, and the meat and dairy arrangements), the obligations of which apply only to their signatories, not to all WTO members (Annex 4).

The most significant aspect of the WTO Agreement is its 'single undertaking': member countries must adhere not only to GATT rules but (with a few exceptions) to the broad range of trade pacts that have been negotiated under GATT auspices during the past two decades. This single undertaking does not require much of countries like the United States that already adhere to almost all the existing pacts, but it ends the free ride of many GATT members that benefited from, but refused to join, new agreements negotiated in the GATT since the 1970s. Many countries, especially developing countries, will now have to undertake substantial new trade obligations that they had not adopted in previous GATT rounds. In this sense, the WTO Agreement entails a higher level of commitment than the existing GATT, which allowed countries to decline membership in new accords and maintained wide-ranging exemptions from other obligations.

However, the exception of the plurilateral agreements from the single undertaking of the WTO is a notable flaw, since it allows most countries to avoid obligations regarding key economic activities such as government procurement. Nonetheless, the existence of Annex 4 in the WTO Agreement does add flexibility to the WTO system by allowing trade pacts to be developed among a subset of countries as a way towards their future extension to the entire WTO membership. Indeed, the plurilateral accords in Annex 4 could provide a precedent for dealing with the new issues emerging on the WTO agenda (Jackson 1994).

In that regard, the new institutional structure of the WTO facilitates the conduct of continuing trade negotiations mandated in the Uruguay Round Final Act, as well as future talks in areas covered by the GATT 1994, the GATS and TRIPs agreements, and new issues affecting the trade relations of WTO members. For example, as evidenced by the creation of the new Committee on Trade and Environment, the WTO establishes an umbrella under which environmental issues can be added much more readily to the agenda of the world trading system.

The WTO also removes certain procedural relics of the GATT system, including the protocol of provisional application of the GATT and the so-called grandfather rights that exempted from GATT disciplines domestic legislation enacted prior to 1947 (or the date of accession for new GATT members) that violated multilateral trade obligations. Existing GATT Article XXV waivers that are not covered by the Uruguay Round accords, which are listed in Annex 1A of the WTO Agreement (e.g. the USA–Canada Auto Pact, the Caribbean Basin Economic Recovery Act and the Andean Trade Preference Act), must be terminated within two years of the entry into force of the WTO, unless extended pursuant to the provisions of Article IX of the WTO Agreement. In addition, a special provision in the general interpretative note to the WTO Agreement (Annex 1A, paragraph 1e) continues to exempt the US Jones Act (which restricts cabotage to US carriers) from WTO obligations.

As under the GATT, WTO decisions will normally be made by consensus (i.e. decisions become effective if no member officially objects). If a consensus cannot be reached, matters will be decided by majority vote.

However, important checks and balances were added to the voting rules that effectively institute a 'big power' block on all but the most mundane WTO decisions. The size of the blocking minority depends on the type of issue subject to the vote. For interpretations of any of the agreements, and for waivers of an obligation (which are subject to annual review), the rules require a three-fourths majority of the WTO members. Amendments generally require a two-thirds majority, but if an amendment would 'alter the rights and obligations of the members', it would be applied only to those countries that accept it.[3] Amendments to WTO Articles IX (on decision-making) and X (on amendments) and to the most favoured nation (MFN) provisions of the GATT 1994, the GATS, and the TRIPs agreement can only take effect upon acceptance by all members.

GATT signatories that deposit schedules of commitments for the revised agreement that emerged from the Uruguay Round (GATT 1994) and the GATS are eligible to become original members of the WTO. These countries have up to two years to deposit their schedules of commitments. However, if a country deposits its schedule after the entry into force of the WTO, the commitments must still be implemented counting from the date on which the WTO entered into force (WTO Article XIV:2).

The WTO will be directed by a Ministerial Conference, which will meet at least once every other year to guide the work of the trading system. In addition, a General Council (similar to the former GATT Council) will oversee the implementation and operation of the trade agreements, and establish subsidiary bodies such as a Goods Council, a Services Council and a TRIPs Council to administer agreements in those areas. Both the Ministerial Conference and the General Council will be composed of representatives of all members.

The WTO Secretariat will comprise most of the existing GATT staff, and the new WTO director general will be appointed by the Ministerial Conference. The GATT traditionally has placed tight restraints on secretariat functions and initiatives, forcefully implemented through tight budgets. Although the trade policy review mechanism has clearly enhanced secretariat responsibility for assessing member country trade policies, the WTO staff is likely to remain small compared with those of the World Bank, the International Monetary Fund (IMF) and the Organization for Economic Cooperation and Development (OECD) Secretariat.

Small can be beautiful (and efficient), but the size of the WTO staff will undoubtedly constrain activities in two areas. First, the added responsibilities imposed on the WTO Secretariat by the Uruguay Round accords, especially regarding dispute settlement and trade policy reviews, will strain the already lean resources for legal and economic analysis. Because WTO obligations encompass a broader range of trade and investment in goods and services than the GATT, and because of the ambiguity of numerous national liber- alisation commitments, one should expect a sharp increase in the incidence of trade disputes over time. The WTO legal office will have to be expanded accordingly to support the increased workload. Similarly, legal resources to administer and utilise the dispute settlement system will have to be upgraded within national governments (Hudec 1994).

Second, staffing constraints could limit the scope of joint activities that might be undertaken with other international economic institutions. In particular, the small number of economists in the WTO Secretariat could effectively undercut the intent of the hortatory, but nonetheless important, declaration in the Uruguay Round Final Act encouraging the director general of the WTO to review with the heads of the IMF and the World Bank possible cooperative efforts to help promote 'greater coherence in global economic policymaking'.

CHALLENGES FACING THE WTO

The Uruguay Round made great strides in strengthening the multilateral trading system, but much work remains to be done. Fortunately, the institu- tional reforms incorporated in the WTO Agreement establish a permanent forum for negotiations, and should facilitate the rapid return to the negoti- ating table. While negotiators may be exhausted from their long ordeal in Geneva, they need to get back to work right away, lest they repeat the mistakes of the past when a hiatus from negotiations allowed protectionist pressures – that had been held in abeyance lest they disrupt the ongoing talks – to resurface and attempt to reverse the reforms just negotiated.

The WTO faces major challenges that need to be addressed in its first few years to complement and reinforce the gains achieved in the recent negotiations. What needs to be done? To simplify the discussion, I analyse the WTO work programme under four broad headings: 'completing' the Uruguay Round; expanding the trade agenda; accommodating nego- tiations between regional trading areas; and finetuning WTO institutional reforms.

Completing the Uruguay Round

While the Uruguay Round achieved historic results, in many respects it is not yet over! Negotiations on financial services and a long list of other issues are continuing, and new talks on agriculture and services will be relaunched within five years.

Provisions of the various Uruguay Round accords establish an extensive work programme for WTO members, composed of three types of activities. First, WTO members need to complete the unfinished business of the Uruguay Round. In several service sectors, for example, negotiations were extended for up to eighteen months to attempt to resolve problems relating to financial services, basic telecommunications and maritime services. In addition, the GATS provides for continuing negotiation of emergency safeguards and provisions relating to the movement of natural persons.

Second, the Uruguay Round accords themselves require regular reviews of the operations of specific provisions of particular agreements and/or of the entire agreement itself. For example, the Committee on Subsidies and Countervailing Measures is charged with examining the operation of the provisions regarding research and development subsidies by July 1996, and all the provisions on nonactionable subsidies and serious prejudice by 1 January 2000; the TRIPs Committee is required to examine the effectiveness of the provisions on geographical indications by 1 January 1997; and WTO members must revisit by 1 January 1998 the provisions regarding the standard of review for panels judging disputes in the anti-dumping area, and consider whether comparable rules should apply in disputes involving countervailing duties.

Third, several WTO accords contain commitments to launch new negotiations after a set period of time to build on the results achieved in the Uruguay Round. These new negotiations must start as early as 1 January 1997 for the inclusion of government procurement contracts in the GATS and 1 January 1999 for new talks to update the recently revised Government Procurement Agreement. More importantly, new negotiations must be initiated by 1 January 2000 in two critical areas: to continue the agricultural reform process, and to promote the progressive liberalisation of trade in services.

Expanding the trade agenda

Trade negotiators always seem to be fighting the last war. By the end of the Kennedy Round (1967), they realised that new rules to govern unfair trade laws such as anti-dumping statutes were needed as much as tariff cuts; the Tokyo Round ended in 1979 with tentative first steps towards broadening the coverage of GATT rules to intellectual property issues; and the Uruguay Round concluded with a commitment to tackle the thorny interface of trade and environmental issues.

The WTO will be pressed to deal with an increasingly broad array of issues, many of which have not been traditionally associated with trade negotiations. At the top of this list is the issue of trade and the environment, on which the GATT has already issued some preliminary reports and held rudimentary discussions over the years. In addition, new issues are likely to be added to the negotiating agenda, including investment and competition policies, and social issues such as labour rights,[4] democratic reforms and human rights.

While environment and labour are not entirely new issues in the trade debate, there has been heightened concern that countries can gain unfair trade advantages through disregard for the environment or through unfair labour practices. Trade restrictions have been imposed as a stick to prompt acceptance of various environmental and social standards.[5] In some instances, however, trade measures designed to be environmentally friendly have also masked protectionist motives. Such actions raise the spectre of 'eco-protectionism' (in which countries charge that relatively higher environmental or labour standards implicitly favour domestic firms), or 'eco-dumping' (in which domestic production is allegedly injured by 'dirty' imports from un- or under-regulated foreign suppliers).

Finally, it is worth noting that global trade negotiations will have to focus more attention on government policies towards multinational corporations. Governments increasingly negotiate directly – at both the regional and global levels – with multinational enterprises over the location of their core operations. The objective is to secure industry commitments to conduct their value-added activities within the national borders. The purpose is clear: export unemployment (i.e. import jobs) and import tax revenues. The means are obvious as well: bribery via subsidies and public infrastructure investments; and coercion via threats of market closure through anti-dumping duties, domestic content requirements and other forms of administered protection.

The challenge to the trading system will be to forestall 'beggar-thy-neighbour' competition between countries that distorts international trade and investment flows. Efforts should concentrate on the development of comprehensive investment rules (the long-sought 'GATT for Investment'), including disciplines on the use of investment incentives and transfer pricing guidelines. The TRIMs agreement provided a tentative first step in this regard, but much more needs to be done. For example, the NAFTA provisions on investment could provide a useful model for a broader multilateral accord.

In addition, the WTO needs to promote the harmonisation of national and regional competition policies, so that predatory practices can be addressed at the source instead of through arbitrary anti-dumping proceedings. Most major industrialised countries have domestic competition policies – with common elements such as prohibition of cartels, price-fixing, market share allocation, and surveillance of mergers and acquisitions. However, they differ significantly in such areas as transparency, remedies against infringement and the extent of coverage.

Developing guidelines for inter-regional negotiations

The content and pace of multilateral trade negotiations will be determined in large part by the progress of regional integration efforts; global trade talks will focus more and more on harmonising the results of different regional integration schemes. The expansion of regionalism can be a healthy development for the multilateral system, if the regional accords accelerate the pace of trade reform and establish building blocks by which to extend the frontier of multilateral liberalisation.

Current GATT obligations seek to promote the complementarity of regional and multilateral trade objectives. GATT Article XXIV authorises derogations from the most favoured nation (MFN) obligation of Article I for FTAs and customs unions that meet two vague requirements: the accord covers 'substantially all' the trade among the partner countries; and the accord does not raise barriers to the trade of third-countries. No agreement has ever failed these tests!

Unfortunately, GATT Article XXIV reviews are lacklustre and provide little discipline on the preferences accorded under FTAs and customs unions. GATT obligations in this area are vague, and ignore practices that can have adverse effects on third-country trade. GATT rules suffer three main defects: they allow significant sectoral exceptions (e.g. agriculture); they skirt around problems caused by grey area measures such as voluntary export restraints, contingent protection measures (anti-dumping and countervailing duties), and rules of origin, that often significantly distort trade and investment flows between the region and third countries; and they fail to track regional pacts after they are signed, when transition provisions or rule changes can significantly affect market access for third-country suppliers.

The challenge is to close the loopholes in the trading rules to ensure that regional pacts do not compromise or undermine the commitment to the multilateral trading system. Efforts to bolster Article XXIV requirements produced feeble results in the Uruguay Round – except that comparably weak rules were added to the GATS so that WTO requirements now apply to a region's trade in goods and services. The proliferation of preferential trading arrangements in Europe, North America and Latin America make it increasingly important that GATT obligations under Article XXIV and WTO reviews of FTAs and customs unions be strengthened.

The first step that needs to be taken is to institute rigorous and continuous multilateral monitoring of all preferential trading arrangements. The means to do so already exist. The WTO's new trade policy review mechanism could be used both to analyse the schedule of trade liberalisation and the trade rules of each prospective agreement to guard against opaque protectionism hidden in the woodwork, and to monitor the implementation of the final agreement over time to ensure that it does not adversely affect the trading interests of third countries. Regional partners should welcome increased WTO surveillance of preferential trade pacts since it would provide external pressure to keep faith with the pace of liberalisation undertaken within the region. Other WTO members should demand it to ensure the consistency of these arrangements with the spirit as well as the letter of multilateral trade obligations.

Finetuning WTO institutional reforms

The Uruguay Round accords strengthened the institutional structure of the multilateral trading system. However, additional changes are needed in two areas to meet the growing demands that confront the WTO.

First, the WTO needs to adopt better procedures to accommodate the increasing number of new entrants seeking membership in the club. For most countries applying for WTO membership, technical assistance is needed both to understand the requirements of membership, and to develop and implement policies that will allow those countries to comply with WTO obligations over time. (In this regard, the WTO could usurp some of the responsibilities now handled by the UNCTAD.) More important, the WTO needs to be able to cope with the challenge of politically powerful new entrants such as China and Russia, whose standing in world trade is not yet commensurate with their political and military capabilities.

Second, the WTO must rethink and revise its management structure. Mirroring current GATT practice, WTO operations will be directed by a Council comprised of all current members. Like the GATT, the WTO will likely suffer from slow and cumbersome policy-making and management – an organisation with more than 120 member countries cannot be run by a 'Committee of the Whole'. Mass management simply does not lend itself to operational efficiency or serious policy discussion.

Both the IMF and the World Bank have an executive board to direct the executive officers of the organisation, with permanent participation by the major industrial countries and weighted voting. The WTO will require a comparable structure to operate efficiently. Attempts to form a small executive body, including proposals put forward in the Uruguay Round, were unsuccessful, and the political orientation of smaller WTO members remains strongly opposed to the concept.[6] These organisational challenges remain to be tested.

In the absence of WTO reforms, the United States and other major trading countries will continue to resort to ad hoc, extra-legal processes like the Quad (the USA, EU, Canada and Japan). Member countries must either delegate responsibility for WTO operations to a small steering group, or accept that countries that resist broadening WTO trade discussions or object to particular initiatives (such as new negotiations) will be able to continue to delay WTO decisions.

CONCLUSION

Overall, the Uruguay Round produced a rich array of accords that should open substantial new trading opportunities, strengthen world trading rules, and reinforce the institutional foundation of the world trading system. In the flush of victory, it would be a mistake, however, to ignore an important lesson of history: after each GATT round, protectionist pressures held in abeyance during the ongoing trade talks rapidly resurface to challenge and attempt to roll back the reforms just negotiated. To preempt a protectionist backlash, and to keep the 'bicycle' of trade liberalisation upright and moving forward, countries need to rededicate themselves to the remaining problems and to undertake new trade initiatives promptly.

What needs to be done to prevent a relapse? First, WTO members need to move quickly to implement the agreements concluded in the Uruguay Round, and to continue talks in areas mandated by the new accords. Second, WTO members should establish a new eminent persons' group, much like the one that was commissioned in the mid-1980s (Leutwiler *et al.* 1985) to recommend terms of reference for the Uruguay Round negotiations, to cover new issues such as trade and the environment, to lay the foundation for discussions of competition policy, to supplement the initial negotiations on investment issues (which to date have yielded rather meagre results), and to deal with other items left unresolved in the Uruguay Round. The group should submit their report within a year of its establishment, with the aim of launching a new round of negotiations before the end of the decade.

The reductions in trade barriers negotiated in the Uruguay Round create new opportunities to expand trade, but they do not guarantee increased sales. The Uruguay Round reforms must be complemented by domestic economic policies that promote greater efficiency in the production of goods and services, and higher labour productivity. Just as important as the removal of foreign trade barriers and unfair trade practices is the removal of domestic disincentives that constrain productivity growth, discourage efficiency, and thus undercut the global competitiveness of domestic firms.

In sum, the successful conclusion of the Uruguay Round should reinforce the market-oriented reforms that have been instituted in most GATT member countries over the past decade. At the same time, the Uruguay Round results should restore confidence in the multilateral trading rules and credibility in the multilateral negotiating process, and significantly mitigate concerns about the spread of unilateralism and discriminatory regional trading pacts. If indeed 'nothing succeeds like success', the new WTO should be able to build on the positive results of the Uruguay Round to reinforce and augment the important trade reforms already achieved.

However, success should not breed complacency, as has happened too often after previous GATT rounds. The trading system needs to keep pace with the changing nature and expanding scope of global trade in goods and services, not to mention the evolving national trade laws and regulations and the often innovative interpretations of those rules by trade bureaucrats. Fortunately, the Uruguay Round results already lay the groundwork for new negotiations, since the just-completed agreements mandate a host of new negotiations to be launched by the end of the decade. It is not too soon to start.

NOTES

1 Extracts from *The Uruguay Round: An Assessment*, Jeffrey J. Schott, Washington DC: Institute for International Economics. Copyright: Institute for International Economics, 1994. All rights reserved.
2 This chapter draws heavily on Schott (1994).
3 In rare instances, the Ministerial Conference can require, subject to a three-fourths majority vote, that a WTO member must accept an amendment or withdraw from the organisation.
4 In truth, the effects of labour standards and practices on trade is not a new issue, and has long been a subject of national and international debate. In 1890, the US Congress banned imports of prison-made goods. The Treaty of Versailles (1919) established the International Labour Organization (ILO) which to date has adopted 172 conventions on labour standards covering virtually every aspect of employment and labour relations. The stillborn ITO Charter (1948) also contained a chapter on labour and employment recognising that unfair labour conditions, particularly in the production for exports, could create difficulties in international trade, and committing countries to eliminate such conditions within their borders.
5 For example, trade sanctions have been levied against countries that have inadequate conservation practices (e.g. the US Marine Mammal Protection Act), or are not signatory to an international environmental treaty (e.g. discriminatory treatment under the Montreal Protocol). Import curbs have also been used as a means of safeguarding foreign and domestic workplace safety (e.g. 1905 Berne Convention banning production and imports of matches made with hazardous white and yellow phosphorus).
6 Past attempts to operate a GATT steering group, the CG-18, failed badly. The group was essentially a microcosm of the Committee of the Whole with all its warts and blemishes.

BIBLIOGRAPHY

Hudec, R.E. (1994) '"Dispute Settlement" in OECD Documents', *The New World Trading System: Readings*, Paris: OECD.
Jackson, J.H. (1994) 'Managing the Trading System: The World Trade Organization and the Post-Uruguay Round GATT Agenda', in P.B. Kenen (ed.) *Managing the World Economy: Fifty Years after Bretton Woods*, Washington DC: Institute for International Economics.
Leutwiler, F. *et al.* (1985) *Trade Policies for a Better Future: Proposals for Action*, Geneva: GATT.
Schott, J.J., assisted by J. W. Buurman (1994) *The Uruguay Round: An Assessment*, Washington DC: Institute for International Economics.

7

SOCIAL STANDARDS IN INTERNATIONAL TRADE

A new protectionist wave?

Harald Grossmann and Georg Koopmann

INTRODUCTION

Liberalisation of trade such as agreed in the Uruguay Round, in conjunction with technological and other structural change, leads to closer economic links between the countries concerned. Liberalisation also implies that inter-country differences, regarding the endowment with factors of production as well as the legal and regulatory framework and policy approaches, become more visible in international competition. The interface between different systems will, however, not only enhance global – and national – welfare but also create tension. In particular, it could render the achievement of certain national goals more difficult and therefore provoke defensive reactions aimed at correcting the resulting 'distortions' of competition. The policy response may basically assume two forms:

- Efforts to neutralise existing differences impinging on international competition. Instruments to this purpose are the available mechanisms of 'contingent' protection authorising the use of trade restrictions if certain conditions are met. This includes safeguard measures (contingent on import surges), anti-dumping measures (contingent on dumping practices) and countervailing measures (contingent on subsidies). Since in all these cases the interference with trade takes place at the border, the very structures, strategies and policies underlying the respective differences are not directly affected, nor is national sovereignty.
- Efforts to reduce the differences themselves. In this case an attempt is made to influence directly the national policy of trading partners in order to 'level the playing field'. In consequence, national policies with a major impact on international trade and competition would tend to converge and the scope for sovereign action narrow. The problem of competition would be tackled 'at the source'.

The question of 'social distortions' in international trade can be approached from the angle of both neutralising as well as reducing inter-country differences

115

which in the present case are differences in social conditions and regulation. With regard to the indirect, 'compensatory' way of bridging the differences, it has in particular been proposed to widen the range of anti-dumping measures to include action against 'social dumping'.[1] Unlike conventional dumping which means selling abroad below cost or at lower prices than charged in the home market, 'social dumping' refers to costs that are for their part artificially depressed below a 'natural' level by means of 'social oppression' facilitating 'unfair' pricing strategies against foreign competitors. Remedial action would either consist of the offending firms consenting to raise their prices accordingly or, failing that, imposing equivalent import restrictions.

As to the more direct, 'reductionary' method of coping with the competitive impact of internationally diverging social standards, the policy proposals seek to promote more protective and 'emancipatory' social legislation, and the establishment of appropriate enforcement mechanisms, in the countries concerned. The aim is to harmonise globally a number of basic social standards and to ensure the improvement of other working conditions as overall development proceeds. Trade sanctions would apply, as a means of last resort, in case trading partners should persistently fail to live up to the obligations they incurred beforehand.

It is, however, not at all self-evident that anti-social-dumping measures, or a multilateral agreement on social minimum standards, and on mechanisms to enforce them, in the framework of the newly established World Trade Organization (WTO), as a response to growing international competition, would promote economic welfare. It could, on the contrary, cause more economic harm than good by reducing the scope for mutually beneficial international division of labour and giving rise to plain protectionism in the guise of correcting 'social distortions'. With international labour standards in place, more protectionism might occur than would probably happen in their absence through recourse to the general safeguard clause (Article 19) or the 'non-violation' provision in Article 23 of the General Agreement on Tariffs and Trade (GATT).[2]

The present chapter discusses these possibilities in economic terms. It will first (pages 117–19) review definitions of social standards and substandards; the rationale underlying the demand for international social standards (pages 119–20); manifestations of social standards in trade policy and evidence on the experiences gained so far (pages 120–3). Second it will examine whether there is any good economic justification for regarding international differences in social standards as particularly harmful from the perspective of a country with relatively low standards, on the one hand (pages 123–4); or from the perspective of its trading partners, on the other hand (pages 125–8). Subsequently (pages 128–9), how far one can draw parallels to the setting of standards in the areas of intellectual property rights and environmental protection will be discussed. Finally (pages 129–30), countervailing measures against social dumping are compared with ordinary anti-dumping policies, and conclusions are drawn.

DEFINITION AND MEASUREMENT OF SOCIAL STANDARDS

In theory, social standards refer to the whole system of social security and equity ranging from various forms of social insurance (unemployment, health, disability, retirement) through labour market adjustment policies (e.g. training programmes) and the guarantee of a minimum wage to regulations concerning the rights of workers to determine their work environment (Ehrenberg 1994: 5). The actual political debate, though, concentrates on a limited number of 'core' standards. These concern both certain workers' rights and the conditions of labour and living. They are:

- the freedom of association and the right to organise and bargain collectively;
- wages and hours of work;
- occupational health and safety standards;
- non-discrimination of female labour;
- child, prison and forced labour.

Dating back to the first half of the nineteenth century, the early calls for international labour legislation emphasised the limitation of child and youth labour and hours of work as well as the abolition of dangerous work (such as the use of white phosphorus in the match industry) and night work by women and children. However, international agreement was only reached on the two latter, less contentious issues through the Berne Conventions of 1905 and 1906 on night work and white (and yellow) phosphorus, respectively. The convention on phosphorus called on each party to ban the production and importation of these toxic chemicals. It became the first international agreement to use import controls as a means of safeguarding foreign and domestic workplace safety (Charnovitz 1992: 339).

In 1919, the range of labour standards on which international conventions were to be concluded was substantially broadened in the Constitution of the International Labour Organization (ILO) to be established under Part XIII of the Treaty of Versailles. In particular, provision was made for 'adequate' wages to maintain 'a reasonable standard of life', for men and women receiving 'equal remuneration for work of equal value', for the equitable economic treatment of all workers 'lawfully resident' in a country, and for the right of association for 'all lawful purposes' including the forming of, and acting through, trade unions (Hansson 1981: 17). Activities of the latter had begun to be tolerated in North America and Western Europe in the second half of the nineteenth century before they were explicitly acknowledged by law in the industrialised countries in the beginning of the twentieth century.

In the course of time, the ILO (now with 179 member states) has adopted numerous Conventions (altogether 174) and Recommendations on labour and social questions. Of these, the proponents of social clauses in the multilateral trading system have selected seven conventions for incorporation into the World Trade Organization (WTO): Conventions 87 and 98 on freedom of association and the right to collective bargaining, respectively; Conventions 29 and 105 on the abolition of forced labour; Conventions 100 and 111 on the prevention of discrimination in employment and equal pay for work of equal value, and Convention 138 on the prohibition of child labour.[3] These 'key' conventions are held to constitute a floor level of social standards or basic social and human rights to be fully observed by all trading nations irrespective of their level of economic development, whereas other social standards would vary over time and from country to country. This would in particular apply to wages and related labour costs that would have to depend on productivity; a uniform international minimum wage obviously makes no sense. One basic social standard, the right to collective bargaining, would ensure that wages, and other conditions of work, move in line with productivity and economic development in general. However, the ILO has only limited power effectively to enforce its conventions. In particular, it does not provide explicitly for trade policy sanctions against countries that do not satisfy the conditions stated in the conventions.

After World War II, in 1953, the United States proposed to the other GATT signatories that working conditions (beyond prison labour the products of which were already subject to import restrictions allowed under Article 20 (General Exceptions) of the General Agreement) should be considered unfair, and hence 'actionable' under the GATT, if they fell short of a standard permitted by the level of productivity. Unfair standards, or 'substandards', were defined as the 'maintenance of labour conditions below those which the productivity of the industry and the economy at large would justify'.[4] No distinction was made between basic social standards applicable uniformly at any point of time to all countries, on the one hand, and dynamic labour conditions contingent on the state of development, on the other. In the final analysis, the proposed definition of social unfairness proved too broad and vague for a consensus to be reached among the GATT members.

Another, presumably more promising method, again originating in the USA, to identify social substandards has been to compare labour conditions and rights applying in different sectors of the same country or, more specifically, in export industries as against the rest of the economy. Accordingly, the determination of social dumping would rely, for instance, on wage differentials between the domestic and export production of similar goods (comparable with price differentials in conventional anti-dumping cases) rather than more elusive absolute standards like productivity.[5] Examples of double domestic/export standards, equivalent to an indirect export subsidy, would be national minimum wage legislation not applying in export processing zones in developing countries, or permission of 'union-free' enclaves, producing for export, in a country that generally permits collective bargaining.[6] Again, however, an official American proposal, offered in July 1979 after the conclusion of the

Tokyo Round, to insert a clause into the GATT prohibiting the maintenance of lower labour standards in production for export than in domestic production (along with defining maximum exposure levels for toxic substances in the workplace such as mercury and asbestos) was actively supported only by a few countries while meeting with open hostility from the majority of developing nations opposing the introduction of labour standards in international trade policy in the absence of other structural reforms.

THE MAJOR MOTIVES

The dominant motive behind the demand for international social minimum standards has traditionally been the intention to defend domestic social efforts and achievements, including wage levels, and the international competitiveness of domestic firms, against their erosion through low-standard competition from abroad creating an artificial and hence unfair comparative advantage. Basically, this is the classical pauper-labour argument for protection according to which the expansion of trade with labour-abundant economies causes (sectoral) unemployment and/or a reduction of wages in those countries where labour is the relatively scarce factor of production. Protection may then appear all the more justified when the labour cost advantage of foreign competitors derives from the exploitation of foreign workers with all the gains from international trade captured by a few owners of capital. Conversely, low-wage countries denounce the imposition of labour standards as pure protectionism and 'equivalent to removing our competitiveness'.[7]

The pioneers of labour standards for trade emphasised international rules as a means of making national labour legislation possible in the now advanced industrial nations. Industrial reform in these countries was to be preserved from the 'tyranny' of international competition cutting 'the throats of the workers' (Follows 1951: 43). The theme recurred, in 1919, in the Constitution of the ILO pointing to 'the failure of any nation to adopt human conditions of labour . . . [as] an obstacle in the way of other nations which desire to improve the conditions in their own country' (Hansson 1981: 9), as well as, in 1948, in the statutes of the International Trade Organisation (ITO) laid down in the Havana Charter where 'the Members recognize that unfair labour conditions, particularly in production for export, create difficulties in international trade, and accordingly, each Member shall take whatever action may be appropriate and feasible to eliminate such conditions within its territory'.[8] However, the ITO never came into being, and what remained from the Havana Charter (i.e. the GATT) did not deal with labour standards in any comprehensive way.

The early concern in Western countries, then still on their way to full industrialisation, about international trade undermining social progress has a modern counterpart in today's developing countries (DCs) seeking to outcompete each other on export markets by undercutting each other's social costs. Whereas, on the one hand, governments in many DCs denounce 'Northern' demands for international labour standards as hidden protectionism, it is on the other hand also realised, in particular by the trade unions and in the more advanced DCs, that free-for-all competition among DCs might frustrate policies aimed to ensure a more even and broadly based development process.

In Western countries, meanwhile, it is the established social welfare privileges built up over the years, even 'the whole of society ... its values, its traditions and its future' (Jacques Delors),[9] that are seen in danger in the face of competition from countries 'with levels of social protection infinitely smaller than ours' (Edouard Balladur).[10] A related argument refers to the exacerbation of social inequality in the advanced industrialised countries as higher and lower wage-earners drift apart, or lower skilled employees are more readily dismissed than their more highly skilled counterparts, under the pressure of imports produced below normal social standards. Unemployment, in particular for the unskilled, might also result in these countries, if low labour standards lead domestic companies to shift labour-intensive production abroad.

A second motive, not independent of the first, for the calls to introduce international labour legislation centres on social standards as 'facilitators' of a further liberalisation of trade. The latter would be easier to advance, the argument goes, if first the distortions of competition through inferior labour conditions were removed. Even though the benefits of trade liberalisation *per se*, regardless of social standards, are not denied, it is said to lack the necessary political backing if pursued in isolation. Attention to labour standards may, therefore, be a way to reduce opposition to new trade agreements (Charnovitz 1995: 168).[11] It has also been claimed in this context that the incorporation of labour standards in trade policy would protect the international trading system against an increased use of conventional trade barriers.

Finally, pushing for better social standards in developing countries is regarded as an act of international solidarity with people facing poor working and living conditions, and part of a development policy with social aims. In this case, the motive for promoting international labour legislation appears altruistic and strictly humanitarian, unrelated to the trade – and welfare – interests of the proponents' home countries. The solidarity aspect of incorporating labour standards in trade policy also includes the prevention of self-destructive, substandard competition between developing countries, as pointed to above.

SOCIAL STANDARDS IN TRADE POLICY

The country most active in legislating restrictive trade measures against 'unfair' foreign labour standards has been the United States. The first legislation came in 1890 when the USA prohibited the import of prison-made goods. In 1930, the law was extended to cover the products of forced labour. However, enforcement of these provisions has been lax. In 1912, the United States banned the import (as well as the domestic manufacture and export) of matches containing white phosphorus, as did a number of European nations (Germany, Great Britain, Denmark, France, Luxembourg, the Netherlands, Switzerland, Italy and Spain). This was the first time that trade legislation was rather altruistically employed to protect the health of foreign workers.[12]

Going beyond specific products and issues, foreign labour practices and working conditions were more comprehensively covered in the US Trade and Competitiveness Act of 1988. This legislation classifies the denial of certain worker rights in foreign countries as 'unreasonable' trade practices against which retaliatory measures like punitive tariffs or quantitative import restrictions might be imposed, if they cannot be eliminated by negotiation and if America's trade is impaired by the practices. Specifically listed are the right of association, the right to organise and bargain collectively, freedom from any form of forced or compulsory labour, establishment of a minimum age for the employment of children, and standards for minimum wages, hours of work, and occupational safety and health of workers.[13] So far, however, no use has been made in actual US trade policy of the broad legal authorisation to act against perceived social malpractices abroad. This may be explained by the fact that the law does not stipulate any definite need to take such action. Moreover, the trading partner's overall level of development must be taken into account and credit given for any progress already achieved in asserting employee rights.

The issue of social conditionality has won greater practical significance in preferential (as against most favoured nation) trade policies of the United States. For example, the inclusion of certain labour standards ('reasonable workplace conditions and . . . the right to organize and bargain collectively') in the Caribbean Basin Initiative (CBI) of 1983 has apparently led various countries in the region (Dominican Republic, El Salvador, Haiti, Honduras) to launch significant labour reforms in order to ensure duty-free access to the US market granted by the CBI for some of their major export products (Charnovitz 1986: 66).

In 1984, one year after the CBI went into force, social conditionality in preference policy was further strengthened through the introduction of a labour clause into the US General System of Preferences (GSP) for (eligible) developing countries.[14] Henceforth, a developing country failing to honour 'internationally recognised employee rights' would risk exclusion from the GSP. The selection criteria (specified in the same terms as for the 'unreasonable' trade practices referred to above) are expressly laid down in the legislation (not merely at the President's discretion as in the case of the CBI), so the President of the United States must refuse a country the granting of trade preferences, or rescind preferences already in operation, if he finds that the respective labour rights and working conditions are disregarded. A number of developing countries have lost their preferential status in the USA because of these requirements, while some of those have had them restored once they had initiated the necessary reforms (see Charnovitz 1992: 350).

A different approach to social standards was adopted in the North American Free Trade Agreement (NAFTA) between the United States, Canada and Mexico where labour issues are addressed in a supplementary 'Agreement on Labour Cooperation'. Abstaining from any intrusion into the sovereign labour legislation of its member states through imposing minimum standards, this agreement has been primarily designed to ensure compliance with the respective national laws. In theory, therefore, the parties to the agreement would even be free to introduce 'retrograde' legislation cutting into the acquis of existing labour standards (something that would not be possible with regard to the NAFTA core agreement). Adherence to the national labour regulations would be monitored on a trilateral basis. Should a member country persistently fail effectively to enforce its own standards, the agreement would permit trade sanctions (i.e. the suspension of NAFTA preferences) as a means of last resort. One of its major intentions is not to allow the signatory governments to attract direct investment from fellow members (and third countries) by means of permissive labour policies. Accordingly, the complaints that have been filed so far on the basis of the NAFTA side agreement on labour concentrate on the activities of multinational corporations such as General Electric, Honeywell and Sony. The chief accusation made against these companies is that they have blocked the establishment of independent trade unions (i.e. independent of the ruling party) in Mexico.[15]

In the European Union no legislation comparable to that enacted in the United States has been adopted so far in the field of foreign labour practices. However, after the attempt to place a binding social clause in the Lomé Agreement with the seventy African, Caribbean and Pacific (ACP) countries repeatedly failed, the EU has now unilaterally moved, in the framework of reforming the European GSP, to link the trade preferences for developing countries in general with these countries meeting a number of social requirements. Certain practices of social exploitation (such as slavery and prison labour, if the resulting products are exported) would be punished with the removal of preferences granted by the Union to the offending countries. In addition to this, and distinct from the American approach relying exclusively on the 'stick' of withdrawing trade preferences, the EU has devised a system of positive incentives ('carrots') to encourage social advance in beneficiary countries. Effective conformity in these countries to certain ILO Conventions (particularly regarding the right to organise in trade unions and bargain collectively, and the minimum age for child labour) would be rewarded by granting additional preferences – above and beyond the basic preferences, to help compensate for the additional costs associated with more progressive social regulations – for goods which have been demonstrably produced according to the respective norms.

Among the EU member states, France has been most outspoken about extending social conditionality also into the area of non-preferential trade policy. In particular, together with Austria, Sweden, Norway and Canada, it has joined the United States in calling for the anchoring of a social clause in the multilateral trading system (Adamy 1994: 269).[16] This, it is claimed, would substantially broaden the country coverage of 'core' ILO norms, support their effective enforcement and avoid the inefficiencies and trade-diversionary effects of uncoordinated unilateral approaches.

IMPACT ON THE DOMESTIC ECONOMY

In principle, levelling the international playing field by harmonising social standards is in apparent contradiction to the basic tenet of traditional trade theory, which tells us precisely that the gains from trade depend on there being differences among nations (i.e. the playing field being uneven), allowing them to make use of comparative advantages. This is not to say that the original social differences will be maintained over time. On the contrary, free trade will lead to a higher national income which in turn promotes economic development and social progress. Less developed countries will only be able to improve their populations' living and working conditions if they catch up economically by raising their productivity. Forcing poor countries to increase social standards irrespective of productivity would therefore look like putting the cart before the horse and killing the forward motion. Workers in these countries would either have to bear the costs of higher standards in the form of lower wages or, if wages do not fall (e.g. due to fixed minimum levels), unemployment would arise with lower national income and less social development in its wake.[17] Indeed, empirical evidence indicates that, by and large, economic development goes hand in hand with growing real wages.

It is true that traditional trade theory is based on several restrictive assumptions which do not always adequately reflect reality. For instance, the theory builds on perfect competition on factor markets such as the labour market. Accordingly, international differences in wages or working conditions are the result of disparities in labour productivity or individual preferences (e.g. for work as against leisure or wages versus working conditions). Such differences may, however, also derive from distortions on the labour market. A case in point would be a dominant monopsonistic firm, or a group of firms with some monopsony power, employing all the workers in an industry, which is in a position to hire less labour, pay lower wages and offer poorer working conditions than an industry that has to compete in the labour market would be able to do. In this case, the country's general interest would require action to stop the exploitation of workers and correct the general economic inefficiency involved.

Labour unions can be regarded as an instrument for reducing monopsony power and increasing economic efficiency by collective bargaining. However, granting workers the right to organise does not lead automatically to strong union activities. Illiteracy and lack of financial funds are important factors that usually weaken union power in less developed countries. Moreover, even strong labour unions would not necessarily improve the allocation of resources. Insider–outsider models, in particular, tell us that unions do not attach too much importance to the creation of employment for those who are currently unemployed (see Lindbeck and Snower 1988). They may just change the distribution of income in favour of insiders without increasing overall factor use and the income of outsiders. The granting of basic union rights will therefore hardly provide a panacea for the problems caused by labour market imperfections.

Labour unions could even create market distortions of their own by raising wages above competitive levels and thus producing unemployment. Korea or Taiwan, for example, which both suppressed independent labour unions until the mid- or late 1980s certainly performed better in economic terms than highly unionised India during that time. This would suggest a rather negative union influence on economic performance.[18] However, negative effects of trade unions on allocation and growth have to be weighed against their positive influence on productivity (e.g. through improving morale and cooperation among workers or inducing management to adopt more efficient policies). Moreover, legalising trade unions may promote political, social and economic stability of countries and improve their attractiveness for direct investment from abroad with favourable effects on growth, employment and labour conditions. Unionism can therefore reduce economic inefficiency and income inequality in some settings and increase them in others (Freeman 1989: 197). All depends on how the unions operate.

The economic implications of social standards other than the freedom of association and the right to organise and collective bargaining are ambiguous, too. Occupational health and safety regulations, for instance, will immediately raise costs for employers, but also tend to increase productivity. However, even with labour productivity gains more than compensating for higher labour costs in the long run, the short-term burden could be too high for the countries concerned to bear. In particular, workers might face present wage cuts which they cannot afford as a price for higher wages in the future. The same is basically true for restrictions on child labour while the positive impact on productivity seems less certain in this case. For the affected children the alternative to working could be even greater poverty and destitution instead of better education and schooling. Limitation of child labour entails economic benefits only if accompanied by programmes supporting the formation of human capital. Trade restrictions would hardly promote this aim. In sum, available evidence on the domestic economic impact of social standards is rather inconclusive. From a purely economic viewpoint, raising existing norms could therefore prove a mixed blessing in many countries, while it appears impossible to define ex ante the right social standards in individual cases.

IMPLICATIONS FOR INTERNATIONAL TRADE
AND INVESTMENT

Labour standards will also affect international trade flows, but their external significance appears less pervasive than their influence on internal transactions. The incidence of child labour, for instance, is typically higher in domestic industries such as small-scale farming, retail trade and services than in the export sector. According to ILO estimates, there are 100 to 200 million child workers today worldwide, but less than 5 per cent of these children are employed in export sectors, such as manufacturing and mining (US Department of Labor 1994). Export earnings derived from forced and prison labour are also small in most cases. Even in Chinese exports to the United States, their share is less than 1 per cent. In export processing zones (EPZs) of developing countries, basic worker rights, including the equal treatment of female labour, are often disregarded, but there is also plenty of evidence of better labour conditions concerning wages, health and safety in EPZs, particularly with subsidiaries of multinational corporations, than outside the zones (Brand and Hoffmann 1994; Edgren 1979: 525; Sautter 1995). However, no systematic survey is available of how much low-standard production is actually traded internationally (Schöppenthau 1994: 254).

Even where low labour standards matter in international trade, they will not necessarily put trading partners at a disadvantage. On the contrary, other countries are more likely to benefit from inferior labour conditions abroad, as their terms of trade would tend to improve (i.e. import prices fall in relation to export prices). This is obvious in the case of industrial countries importing labour-intensive products from developing countries which would become cheaper in relation to capital-intensive goods. Distortions of trade flows arising from social substandards abroad look rather like a gift for the importing economy as a whole, albeit possibly causing problems for individual industries. In a longer run perspective, however, the overall economic interest of industrial countries would also call for a removal of social distortions in developing countries (which must not be identical with raising social standards), in order to promote the process of capital accumulation in the world.

Low social standards are often held to entail an 'unfair' locational advantage for developing countries squeezing out industrial countries' production. International differences in social standards may indeed, like labour cost differences, induce companies to shift labour-intensive production abroad and re-export part of the output. With perfect competition on product and factor markets, capital movements of this kind would increase global as well as national welfare. However, if investment flows arise from imperfections on foreign labour markets, for example, too much capital could be exported from industrial countries with the gains accruing to capital owners not offsetting the losses through decreased domestic production. The negative impact of a reduced labour productivity following from a lower capital labour ratio could be more significant than a further improvement of the terms of trade in conjunction with outward investment.

In actual fact, capital has not flown strongly to less developed countries in the more recent past. In the 1980s, new foreign direct investment (FDI) in developing countries was lower in real terms than it had been in the 1970s. In the 1990s, more capital has again been exported from industrial to developing countries, but the amounts are still minor compared with the overall level of investment. It has been estimated that the entire emerging market investment boom since 1990 has reduced the rich world's capital stock by only about 0.5 per cent from what it otherwise might have been (Krugman 1994: 119).[19] Moreover, the bulk of FDI is not driven by labour cost differentials but the search for natural resources and markets (UNCTAD 1994). This is largely due to the fact that direct investment abroad is a long-run decision. Investors will therefore relocate labour-intensive manufacturing to low-cost sites not because labour costs are presently low, but only if they expect them to remain at a low level in the future. With social substandards, this will frequently not be the case as they may change over time. As a result, standard-related FDI would appear rather insignificant in quantitative terms with very limited, if any, negative impact on domestic production and employment in industrial countries.

PRESSURE ON LESS SKILLED WORKERS

More important than capital diversion to low-standard countries could be the implications of trade with these countries for domestic income distribution. Competitive pressure due to low labour costs in less developed countries will, of course, not leave everyone a winner in the advanced economies. In particular, the fear is that less skilled workers would either have to accept lower pay or, if wages are not sufficiently flexible, might lose their jobs. This kind of effect is quite plausible in theoretical terms. The Stolper–Samuelson theorem predicts that a reduction in trade barriers will reduce the income earned by the relatively scarce factor of production, which effectively becomes more abundant as a result of trade; factor prices will tend to balance out internationally. Applying this prediction to trade between industrial and developing countries and to the factor labour – viewed for the sake of simplicity in terms of a skilled and unskilled component – one would expect the earnings of unskilled workers in the industrial countries to approach the level prevailing in developing countries and decline further in relation to the income of better trained employees.

Empirical studies to test this hypothesis have led to differing conclusions. For the United States, one study finds, contrary to expectations, that the relative prices of internationally traded goods involving a relatively large input of unskilled labour have not fallen but, if anything, have tended to increase. From this the conclusion is drawn that foreign trade can hardly explain the

126

growing spread in wage earnings which is observed in that country (Lawrence and Slaughter 1993). A stronger though not precisely definable influence of foreign trade on wage inequality in the USA is detected in another study based on a disaggregated analysis covering 131 different industries and more than 150 trading partners (Sachs and Shatz 1994).[20] Both of these studies draw attention to the crucial role of technological change. Apparently, technology, not trade, is the main driving force behind the increasing differential between skilled and unskilled labour.[21]

However, technological change may itself have been partly caused by import pressure. This aspect ('defensive innovations') is stressed in a third study which also includes industrial countries other than the United States. According to the study, North–South trade is the main cause of social decline among less skilled workers in the old industrial countries. To cope with the problem, however, it is not recommending the erection of trade barriers but instituting a policy of improved education and training (Wood 1994). This would also be the better strategy with regard to social distortions (as against mere social differences in comparison with trading partners) in developing economies in order to neutralise their (presumably small) autonomous influence on the distribution of income in advanced countries.

SOCIAL STANDARDS AND STRATEGIC TRADE THEORY

So far, economic analysis does not support the view that industrial countries will seriously suffer from low social standards abroad. It would rather be in the developing countries' own interests to take action to correct any distortions on their labour markets. A different conclusion may be reached in the context of strategic trade theory. Under conditions of oligopolistic instead of perfect competition prevailing on world markets, it could be attractive for governments to create artificially a competitive advantage for domestic industries, either by intervention or omission, and thus increase national welfare at the expense of trading partners. Applying the theory to the context under examination here, it can be shown, for example in the framework of an international duopoly (with Cournot competition where two suppliers decide autonomously on their output while leaving price formation to the market), that the institutional structure of labour markets may importantly affect the nature of rivalry between firms (Brander and Spencer 1988). For example, weak labour unions could mean a strategic advantage for a country's industry, enabling domestic firms to keep labour costs low, capture market shares of foreign rivals and increase profits through 'rent-shifting'.

Despite these theoretical possibilities, strategic trade analysis hardly provides a convincing practical case for low social standards as a suitable means of improving domestic welfare through international trade. For one, all the objections raised against strategic trade policy in general also apply to strategic social dumping.[22] Moreover, in most industries where developing countries are internationally competitive the number of firms is large enough for strategic interactions to be negligible. Finally, those sectors in which international competitiveness mainly depends on labour costs are unlikely to yield high profits. It is therefore hard to believe that countries seriously risk suffering overall economic damage due to lost rents caused by low social standards abroad.[23] Conversely, it would also not pay for countries to enforce (too) high social standards in other countries for strategic reasons. Raising the costs of foreign rivals in order to defend market shares of domestic firms in troubled industries might be tempting for politicians not guided by the general economic interest. Seen from an overall economic viewpoint, the strategy would certainly backfire.

COMPARING SOCIAL STANDARDS WITH PROPERTY RIGHTS AND ECO-PROTECTION

Demands for social minimum standards are often based on a notion saying that what is right for the protection of intellectual property cannot be wrong with regard to fundamental human rights. It is largely undisputed that missing or non-binding standards for intellectual property protection have a negative effect on the international division of labour as well as on the creation and transfer of technology. Trade in counterfeit goods weakens quality competition and may even represent a danger to the health and security of consumers. In order to remove the incentives for countries to profit by free-riding from investment in research and development abroad, harmonisation of standards is urgently necessary in this field. However, the interest in the extent of intellectual property protection may differ between countries. Particularly for the developing countries, higher standards not only mean advantages but also entail costs due to higher prices and limited trade in counterfeit goods. An indulgent application of intellectual property rights, however, is probably even more harmful to the developing countries since it may cause the separation from technical progress and international division of labour. Therefore, all countries will be better off if they meet certain standards.

A similar conclusion is reached in the case of environmental protection provided transborder externalities are involved.[24] If pollution spreads beyond national frontiers, it is quite feasible that countries pass the costs of environmental protection on to their trading partners in order to profit from other countries' stringent environmental policy. Since free flows of trade and investment undermine national sovereignty, harmonisation of standards may prove to be appropriate for avoiding trade conflicts in this context. Yet, from an economic point of view market solutions (like compensation mechanism or trade in certificates) taking the different environmental interests of individual countries into account should be preferred.

In contrast to the protection of intellectual property rights and global environmental problems, there is no compelling need for a social clause within the WTO. For one thing, countries cannot expect to benefit from low standards at the disadvantage of their trading partners. Essentially, social dumping is a problem of national income distribution. Since there are no negative spillover effects there is also no room for reasoning that domestic standards will be threatened by low social standards abroad. In order to defend high social standards, countries should not cling on to the manufacture of products that can be made more cheaply in other countries. Demands for social minimum standards as well as trade policy measures for enforcing them are therefore hardly justified on economic grounds.

Of course, if markets are not functioning well, the situation cannot be optimal for the world as a whole. While there are little objections that ideally designed actions would improve world economic welfare, it is highly doubtful whether the imposition of international social standards would eliminate existing distortions. As it is almost impossible to forecast in detail which social standards would lead to an optimal resource allocation, the fear must rather be that if minimum standards are set too high this will impede the developing countries in their bid to catch up economically. This could ultimately also have an adverse effect on prosperity in the industrial countries. One part of the problem is that it would probably be impossible to lay down operational criteria and threshold values. Another is that not all of the intentions that underly the calls for adherence to social standards are good ones. They may represent an attempt to restrict imports from countries with lower labour costs under a humanitarian pretext. In this sense, there is danger that the use of trade sanctions to enforce minimum standards may do more harm than good.

CONCLUSIONS

The calls for import restrictions to be imposed on countries providing low social standards seem to have more in common with anti-dumping policy. If import competing domestic industries and their employees are injured by low-priced imports, trade policy is given the task of achieving equal and 'fair' competitive conditions, even in those cases where domestic enterprises have actually got into trouble due to their own shortcomings. While it is true that the profits of domestic industries competing with the imports fall, consumers will benefit from lower prices. If the economy-wide impact is taken into account, the economic arguments for linking social standards with trade policy are even less convincing than anti-dumping measures, because 'predatory' dumping is rather unlikely in the case of social standards. Moreover, experience with ordinary anti-dumping policy demonstrates how easily blurred rules and procedures can be transformed into a mere protectionist instrument. Therefore, widening the range of anti-dumping policy to include action against 'social dumping' would indeed provoke the danger of a new protectionist wave in international trade.

The conclusions drawn here from an economic point of view do not mean at all that blatant violations of fundamental human rights should be tolerated. From an ethical point of view trade sanctions aimed at enforcing basic human rights are generally acceptable. However, the WTO is hardly the appropriate forum for such matters. It can neither bind its member states to uniform action nor are trade sanctions the only instrument available. In order to address these issues, a broader framework is needed including development cooperation, the International Labour Organization and the United Nations as well as the 'triad' of multilateral economic institutions (i.e. WTO, IMF and World Bank) working together. An exclusive option within the WTO to erect trade restrictions against other countries which violate basic human rights would more likely tend to close home markets than to improve social conditions abroad. Under the WTO the cause of social progress in developing countries would be served better by further liberalisation of trade, thereby increasing export opportunities, rather than social conditionality entailing the risk of deliberalisation. Resistance to market opening offered by protectionist forces in advanced countries can hardly be 'bought off' with social standards. On balance, higher rather than lower barriers to market access would result.

NOTES

1 Social dumping was considered a problem in international trade as early as 1927, when the World Economic Conference, convened by the League of Nations, urged governments to encourage producers to apply methods of remuneration giving the worker 'a fair share in the increase of output'. An early example of extending the range of anti-dumping measures to cover social dumping is provided by Spain. In 1934 the country included in its definition of dumping lower prices caused by the fact that 'international regulations in respect of social matters and especially as regards wages and working conditions have not been observed' (both quotes from Charnovitz 1987: 566, 573).

2 The non-violation clause in Article 23 GATT allows member countries to invoke the multilateral dispute settlement procedure (which has been significantly strengthened in the Uruguay Round), and eventually take retaliatory measures, even in cases where actions (or non-actions) of trading partners do not explicitly violate GATT provisions as long as they are found to harm the trade interests of the defending country.

3 Occasionally, Convention 135 on the protection of workers' representatives at their place of work is also listed (Adamy 1994: 271).

4 Cf. US Commission on Foreign Economic Policy: Staff Papers, February 1954: 437–8, quoted in Charnovitz (1987: 574).

5 In 1954, the US Commission on Foreign Economic Policy defined substandard wages as wages for a particular commodity that are 'well below accepted standards in the exporting country' (quoted in Charnovitz 1987: 572).

6 Charnovitz (1992: 343), with reference to an analysis by the US Department of Labour, points to the government of Malaysia prohibiting national unions in the

two industries, electronics and textiles, that account for most of its export zone employment.

7 Statement by the Foreign Minister of Singapore, quoted in International Trade Reporter, 3 August 1994: 1214.

8 Cf. Havana Charter for an International Trade Organization, Article 7 (Fair Labour Standards).

9 Quoted in Steil (1994: 18).

10 Quoted in *Financial Times*, 'EU action over "unfair" trade urged by Balladur', 31 October 1993.

11 In this context, the Group of Experts examining the social aspects of European economic integration (chaired by Bertil Ohlin) suggested, in 1956, that preventing labour standards 'from falling below an internationally accepted level might eliminate abnormal competition and thus facilitate the establishment and preservation of a regime of freer international trade' (ILO 1956: para. 180). In 1980, the Brandt Commission endorsed international action on 'fair labor standards' for the same reason (Charnovitz 1995: 183).

12 The danger to the user of the matches was relatively minor compared to the risks borne by the workers, and there was no substantial import-competing domestic production to be protected.

13 For details on the controversial debate of the issue in the US Congress see Hippler-Bello and Holmer (1988: 18–22).

14 The GSP amendment with the new social conditionality was part of the GSP Renewal Act, included in the Trade and Tariff Act of 1984, which added new criteria for the President to consider in designating eligible developing countries. For details see Pellegrini (1985).

15 See *Financial Times*, 'US unions bring first charges under NAFTA', 5 August 1994; *Financial Times*, 'Unions accuse Sony under NAFTA accord', 17 August 1994.

16 The main argument put forward by France is to prevent countries from enjoying unfair competitive advantages through lower labour costs due to inadequate labour standards. The French position is challenged within the European Union mainly by the British government which resists any attempt to impose social standards on developing countries, since they would raise costs in those countries and thereby 'deny them market access, condemning the world's poor to perpetual poverty' (Employment Secretary Michael Portillo, quoted in *Financial Times*, 'France to push worker's rights in WTO', 2 February 1995).

17 Ehrenberg (1994: 6–10) considers the provision and financing of unemployment insurance benefits through an employer-based payroll tax as an example to demonstrate that at least much of the cost is shifted on to workers. Nickell (1994: 104) even goes so far as to assert that 'significant *permanent* tax wedge effects on labour costs do not seem plausible unless there is a fixed floor to wages'.

18 See also OECD (1995: 22): 'Those countries in the Far East that have relied on indirect methods of pulling wages and employment opportunities up through supply and demand have progressed much more rapidly than have countries in other parts of the world that have attempted to push labour standards up through minimum wages, government pay policy, support of trade unions, extensive labour codes, and the like.' However, this does not mean that economic growth is tantamount to greater social satisfaction in the population. Lee and Lindauer (1991), for instance, report high levels of dissatisfaction among Korean workers despite increases in real wages and falling inequality. See also Freeman (1993). There is also evidence that freedom of association promotes economic growth. Charnovitz (1995: 169) quotes Hong Kong and Japan as examples to show that countries need not repress unions to achieve high economic growth.

19 In 1994 – a record year for capital flows to developing countries – there was a net capital flow of $60 billion to newly industrialising economies. This compares with net domestic investment in the OECD of $3.5 trillion and an OECD capital stock of $50 trillion (Paul Krugman quoted in *IMF Survey*, 23 January 1995: 25).

20 This study, contrary to the first one, finds that the prices of wage-intensive goods have indeed fallen relative to those of technology-intensive goods.

21 Krugman points to a shift–share analysis showing that employment in skilled labour intensive industries is not growing faster than employment in unskilled sectors. Almost all of the shift in labour demand is happening within sectors indicating the importance of technology as against trade (Krugman quoted in *IMF Survey*, 23 January 1995: 26).

22 For a review of the general difficulties that arise in applying strategic trade theory in practice, see, for example, Grossman (1986).

23 For similar reasons, competition among developing countries by means of low social standards would hardly earn the 'first mover' economic advantages. It would be a rather shortsighted policy as it totally neglects the positive impact of right social standards on productivity in the long run.

24 While there are some examples of global environmental problems like depletion of the stratospheric ozone layer, greenhouse gas emissions which affect the world's climate, atmospheric testing of nuclear weapons or the use of pesticides which pollute international waters, it should not be overlooked that most environmental externalities are local in nature (Cooper 1994: 38). In cases where environmental externalities remain strictly within each nation, convergence of international environmental standards is neither necessary nor desirable.

BIBLIOGRAPHY

Adamy, W. (1994) 'International Trade and Social Standards', *Intereconomics*, 29, 6: 269–77.

Brand, D. and Hoffmann, R. (1994) '"Sozial-Dumping" oder Protektionismus? – Zur Kontroverse über eine Sozialklausel im internationalen Handelssystem', *IFO-Schnelldienst*, 47: 25–6.

Brander, J.A. and Spencer, B.J. (1988) 'Unionized Oligopoly and International Trade Policy', *Journal of International Economics*, 24, 217–34.

Charnovitz, S. (1986) 'Fair Labour Standards and International Trade', *Journal of World Trade*, 20, 1: 61–78.

—— (1987) 'The Influence of International Labour Standards on the World Trading Regime. A Historical Overview', *International Labour Review*, 126, 5: 565–84.

—— (1992) 'Environmental and Labour Standards in Trade', *The World Economy*, 15, 3: 335–56.

—— (1995) 'Promoting Higher Labor Standards', *The Washington Quarterly*, 18, 3, 167–90.

Cooper, R.N. (1994) *Environmental and Resource Policies for the World Economy*, Washington DC: The Brookings Institution.

Edgren, G. (1979) 'Fair Labour Standards and Trade Liberalization', *International Labour Review*, 118, 5: 523–35.

Ehrenberg, R.G. (1994) *Labor Markets and Integrating National Economies*, Washington DC: The Brookings Institution.

Follows, J.W. (1951) *Antecedents of the International Labour Organization*, Oxford: Clarendon Press.

Freeman, R.B. (1989) *Labour Markets in Action. Essays in Empirical Economics*, New York: Harvester Wheatsheaf.

—— (1993) 'Labour Markets and Institutions in Economic Development', *American Economic Review*, Papers and Proceedings 83, 2: 403–8.

Grossman, G.M. (1986) 'Strategic Export Promotion: A Critique', in P.R. Krugman (ed.) *Strategic Trade Policy and the New International Economics*, Cambridge MA: MIT Press.

Hansson, G. (1981) *Social Clauses and International Trade. An Economic Analysis of Labour Standards in Trade Policy*, Lund: Lund University.

Hippler-Bello, J. and Holmer, A.F. (1988) 'The Heart of the 1988 Trade Act: A Legislative History of the Amendments to Section 301', *Stanford Journal of International Law*, 25, 1: 1–44.

ILO (1956) *Social Aspects of European Economic Co-operation*, Geneva: International Labour Organization.

IMF Survey (1995) *Assessing European and U.S. Employment Trends*, Washington DC: International Monetary Fund, 23 January.

Krugman, P.R. (1994) 'Does Third World Growth Hurt First World Prosperity?', *Harvard Business Review*, July–August: 113–21.

Lawrence, R.Z. and Slaughter, M.J. (1993) 'International Trade and American Wages in the 1980s: Giant Sucking Sound or Small Hiccup?', *Brookings Papers on Economic Activity, Microeconomics* 2: 161–226.

Lee, J.-W. and Lindauer, D.L. (1991) 'The Quality of Working Life', in D.L. Lindauer *et al.* (eds) *Korea: The Strains of Economic Growth*, Cambridge MA: Harvard Institute for International Development.

Lindbeck, A. and Snower, D.J. (1988) 'Cooperation, Harassment, and Involuntary Unemployment: An Insider–Outsider Approach', *American Economic Review*, 78, 1: 167–88.

Nickell, S. (1994) 'Comments', in R.G. Ehrenberg, R.G. *Labor Markets and Integrating National Economies*, Washington DC: The Brookings Institution.

OECD (1995) *Trade and Labour Standards. A Review of the Issues*, Paris: Organization for Economic Cooperation and Development.

Pellegrini, V.J. (1985) 'GSP: A System of Preferences, not a Bargaining Lever', *Law and Policy in International Business*, 17, 14: 879–906.

Sachs, J.D. and Shatz, H.J. (1994) 'Trade and Jobs in U.S. Manufacturing', *Brookings Papers on Economic Activity*, 1: 1–84.

Sautter, H. (1995) 'Sozialklauseln für den Welthandel – wirtschaftsethisch betrachtet', *Hamburger Jahrbuch für Wirtschafts- und Gesellschaftspolitik*, 40: 227–45.

Schöppenthau, P. von (1994) 'Sozialklauseln: die falsche Waffe im Kampf um Menschenrechte und soziale Standards', *Internationale Politik und Gesellschaft*, 3: 240–56.

Steil, B. (1994) '"Social Correctness" is the New Protectionism', *Foreign Affairs*, January/February, 14–20.

UNCTAD (1994) *World Investment Report* (Transnational corporations, employment and the workplace), New York and Geneva: United Nations Conference on Trade and Development.

US Department of Labor (1994) *By the Sweat and Toil of Children: The Use of Child Labour in American Imports*, Washington DC: US Department of Labor.

Wood, A. (1994) *North–South Trade, Employment and Inequality. Changing Fortunes in a Skill-driven World*, Oxford: Oxford University Press.

8

LINKING TRADE AND ENVIRONMENT TO PROMOTE SUSTAINABLE DEVELOPMENT

Nevin Shaw and Arthur J. Hanson

INTRODUCTION

The World Trade Organization (WTO) was established on 1 January 1995, to oversee the administration of improved or new trade rules which resulted from the Uruguay Round of Multilateral Trade Negotiations. It is more global in membership than the General Agreement on Tariffs and Trade (GATT) and much wider in scope of commercial activities covered. It will begin to reverse protectionism in textiles and clothing, agriculture, services and other sectors. In this context, it is asserted by many governments and business that the Uruguay Round will significantly improve future prospects and policy alternatives to promote a transition to sustainable development, including protection of the environment. However, detailed analyses and implications, positive as well as negative, remain to be carried out in light of the actual manner of implementation of trade commitments made.

The optimistic forecasts of the impact of the Uruguay Round immediately face at least two kinds of reactions. First, this will not bring about an equitable distribution of income. Second, it will not result in an efficient allocation of resources as there are imperfections in various markets. In particular, markets fail to allocate resources in keeping with social goals where social interests fail to coincide with those of individuals. For example, the cost of harm to the environment is not incorporated in the private cost of production, consumption and disposal of a product. Such a cost is increasingly claimed to be significant, but related practical and ethical issues have yet to be resolved.

The 1992 United Nations Conference on Environment and Development tried to address these issues through a statement of principles in the Rio Declaration and to give effect to the principles through an integrated programme of domestic and international action, Agenda 21. Chapter 2 of Agenda 21 concluded that domestic policies must be supported by a dynamic international economy and an open, equitable, secure, non-discriminatory and predictable multilateral trading system. In particular, there must be better market access for exports of developing and transition economies, a provision of adequate financial resources, acceleration of the development and diffusion of environmentally friendly technologies and promotion of patterns of consumption and production which reduce environmental stress as well as meet the basic needs of the poor.

The purpose of this chapter is to consider perspectives and policy options for the world trading system in this context of continuing struggle to integrate environment and economy to promote sustainable development worldwide. Pages 135–6 describe changes in trade and trade policy. Changes in environment and environmental policy are covered on pages 136–8. Pages 138–42 deal with links between trade and environment, and highlight some of the substantive differences over the relationships between economic growth, trade and environment. Pages 142–5 describe the relevance of trade rules to the achievement of environmental objectives. Pages 145–7 sketch a composite perspective of environmental coalitions in rich countries who favour a proactive use of trade measures to protect the environment. The penultimate section (pages 147–9) then presents a perspective of those who react to such a policy approach, especially in developing countries. The final section (pages 149–53) responds to these differences with a consideration of some general and exemplary rules of conduct within which policy development might take place.

CHANGES IN TRADE AND TRADE POLICY

Many businesses and workers experienced the painful effects of the growing and pervasive use of tariffs, quantitative restrictions, import bans, exchange controls and other trade measures during the 1930s. Governments engaged in the rhetoric of freer trade but adopted such measures to protect domestic industry from foreign competition to increase their well-being. They ended up undermining human welfare worldwide, as trade collapsed.

The general public was then willing to accept a different approach resulting from public policy formulation processes (i.e. more open trade regimes) which facilitated a very significant expansion in trade and income. It recognised the need to adjust to changing patterns of industry specialisation and trade, including rise and fall of different industries domestically and internationally. Complementary public policies to ease the burden of adjustment played an important role in making trade-based economic development possible. Simply, we learned to work with, not against, markets, at least until recently.

Business today is becoming more global and its activities more knowledge driven. It is restructuring various activities domestically and internationally, with 'networks' of financing, investment, research and development, production, sourcing, marketing, and distribution spread around the world. What matters is to find a variety of new ways to improve efficiency and penetrate new markets. These include greater flows of goods, services, investment, technology and skilled people. Innovations in communications and transportation relentlessly drive this process of globalisation of industry, as does progressive trade liberalisation.

Consequently, the pace of change in the nature and composition of trade also has accelerated. An increasing number of firms are no longer nationally organised and identified businesses which totally design, engineer, fund, make, market and service product lines – with miniature replicas of themselves abroad as subsidiaries and affiliates. Instead, they are specialising with the purpose of carrying out each separate operation in a production chain in the most skilled and efficient location. This could be in their own facilities or in facilities owned by independent suppliers or subcontractors. Joint production, research and development, licensing, contracting out and brokering among local, state, national, regional, continental and global firms and networks are proliferating.

This means increased trade in parts, components and semifinished goods, in addition to trade in resources and final goods. It also means significant foreign investment, which has been facilitated by the rapid liberalisation of investment regimes worldwide, coupled with transfers of proprietary and non-proprietary technology. Globalisation also allows more intra-firm trade as single global ventures move specialised components and partly finished goods rather than final products from their facilities in one country to another.

Changes in the ways in which domestic and global economies work have made a number of trade agreements outdated. It is no longer enough to secure foreign market access by obtaining obligations to reduce tariffs and quotas. It is becoming clear that trade effects are caused not only by such border measures but also by government and business conduct, inside the border, such as more stringent environmental standards applied to domestically produced and imported goods. Growing pressures to resist change are triggering new forms of protectionism through such conduct, putting the benefits of post-war trade liberalisation and standards of living at risk. This is becoming apparent where governments are unable to generate socially desirable outcomes in the interests of those they represent. The results of the Uruguay Round go some way to contain protectionism, as they open markets, make or improve rules and build the World Trade Organization as well as provide for a dynamic process of positive adaptation to an acceleration of globalisation of industry and international economic interdependence. They need to be secured.

CHANGES IN ENVIRONMENT AND ENVIRONMENTAL POLICY

The Earth Summit faced the challenge of what to do about the damage being done to the planet. Heightened concerns over the environment cover the atmosphere, general air and water quality, depletion of the ozone layer, climate change, oceans, lakes, land use and soil protection, outer space, diversity of biological resources, health of ecosystems, pollution, toxic substance control, conservation, waste management, species protection, and so on. Since we inhabit the Earth, management of the Earth's environment and its health and life-supporting quality take on pervasive meanings and expressions of concern, with broad economic impacts.

A wide range of measures is taken to achieve results with respect to so many concerns. Prohibitions, emission standards, environmental quality standards, product and process standards, environmental impact assessment requirements, monitoring and reporting, testing, packaging, labelling are components of an environmental policy. The so-called market-based or economic instruments and definition and enforcement of property rights now also form part of such a policy. This is a tentative shift to address market and government policy failures of the past in new ways.

A growing array of formal and less formal trade impacting international agreements, arrangements and understandings deal with environmental issues, as awareness and concern grow about transboundary, regional and global environmental problems. They also continue to be contested within and between countries as well as regions, on efficiency and equity grounds. For example, the use of a ban on ivory trade under the Convention on International Trade in Endangered Species (CITES) to ensure that international trade in elephant products does not threaten the preservation of the elephant places a disproportionate burden on African countries. The international competitiveness of recycling industries in developing and transition economies may be preempted by the ban under the Basel Convention on exports of hazardous but recyclable waste from rich to poor countries. The Montreal Protocol on phasing out the use of ozone depleting CFCs incorporates discriminatory trade provisions, such as targeted use of a ban on imports associated with ozone-depleting substances, which is not applied against imports from all WTO members who are or are not also members of the Protocol.

These are designed to limit the relocation from signatory to non-signatory countries of industries producing or using CFCs and to force non-signatories to accede to the Protocol. International organisations such as the World Health Organization and Food and Agricultural Organization address particular environmental issues under their mandates. Still others such as the International Standards Organization are producing voluntary environmental management systems that can influence choice of suppliers based on certifications. Consumers are encouraged to boycott sales of objectionable products such as furs from animals caught in leghold traps or wood products not produced from sustainably managed forests. Domestic efforts designed to increase liability for environmental damage and to use trade measures against imports perceived not to meet environmental standards create international tensions. While well intentioned, such a vast array of efforts to protect the environment could have wider, possibly negative, effects.

As the litany of poverty and environmental problems grow, and their solutions prove unsatisfactory, public concerns mount. Daly and Cobb (1994) and Goodland and Daly (1995) argue that current modes of production prevailing in most parts of the world economy deplete natural capital such as top soil, ground water, tropical forests, fisheries and biodiversity. They argue that the accelerated loss of these natural resources, coupled with degradation of land and atmospheric quality, are reducing future potential bio-physical carrying capacities. Such conclusions cause them to object to current patterns of development, including trade. These local and regional concerns lead them to link trade to local and regional ecosystemic changes as well as to global environmental degradation.

Governments that negotiated in the Uruguay Round did not seem to reflect seriously enough the future trade implications of the growing array of international environmental regimes that they have also been constructing over the past decade in particular. The international environmental law agenda is still relatively new and struggling with uncertainties, surprises and significant differences in views among negotiating blocs. It may not always lend itself to international agreements based on differing shares of benefit and cost of corrective measures, in particular as both rich and poor countries try to avoid or minimise costs. In addition, such an agenda may run counter to national trends to reduce costly impacts of government interventions, where it depends on a larger role for governments in terms of definition and enforcement of property rights, regulation and perhaps market-based economic instruments to account for unpaid environmental costs. The potential for politicisation of sciences is large. It is also significant for misallocating scarce resources in integrating environment and economy. Human and financial costs of wrong choices are also high. Therefore, a highly accountable process of assessing and balancing to establish priorities and to choose the most effective and, possibly, differentiated and equitable ways to meet them is badly needed.

LINKS BETWEEN TRADE AND THE ENVIRONMENT

There have been demands by environmentalists especially from those in rich countries that governments establish open processes to examine the relationship between trade and the environment. The debate came to a head during the negotiations and ratifications of the North American Free Trade Agreement (NAFTA) and Uruguay Round. But it is clearly an issue now influencing all major trade agreements. It has involved people and organisations with different goals, attitudes, preconceptions, cultures, ideologies, academic disciplines, assessment methods and policy priorities. Their expectations and allegations have been magnified in the media, giving the impression of trade and environment in conflict. At the extreme, environmentalists are represented as spawning non-tariff barriers, or hindering the acceptance of valuable trade agreements or derailing freer trade through threat of trade sanctions.

This has produced a number of highly contested generalisations, even within the context of increasing bridge-building efforts by governments and international organisations such as the Organization for Economic Cooperation and Development (OECD), United Nations Conference on Trade and Development, United Nations Environment Programme, Commission on Sustainable Development and what is now the World Trade Organization. It is claimed, for example, that an expansion of trade as a result of progressive trade liberalisation would lead to levels and kinds of greater production and consumption which would damage the environment. It is argued that additional negotiated commitments to liberalise trade would further limit domestic policy flexibility to use punitive trade restrictions to protect the environment, even if this must change the basic contractual undertakings of the GATT/WTO for this purpose. It is also argued that such commitments would in fact protect the weak against abuse of such restrictions by the strong. An argument promulgated from the time of the 1972 Stockholm Conference on Environment is that trade liberalisation without harmonisation of environmental standards would cause rich country business to move to 'pollution havens' in poor country jurisdictions. Stronger environmental measures would thereby lead to an unfair loss of competitiveness, market shares, income, jobs and future investment. Many in poor countries believe they would lose in this way from increased cost and uncertainty of exporting to rich countries with higher standards. Others assert that actual trade-related environmental measures would be influenced more by professional industry protectionists, not fund-and-staff-short environmental organisations and a downsized public service. Conversely, others point to alliances between rich country environmental interests and domestic industry protectionists. It is also asserted that a widespread use of punitive trade restrictions to achieve environmental goals will undermine the trading system.

These kinds of generalisations need to be viewed from the perspective that it is economic growth – of which trade can be a part – that is held accountable for the particular levels and patterns of production and consumption which may cause environmental degradation. Even if this assertion was true, trade is largely an indirect cause and trade policy is one of a spectrum of macro and micro policies which impact economic growth. Indeed, the actual effects of economic growth are likely to be mixed (i.e. make more resources available to alleviate poverty), for example, thereby help the poor not to cause deforestation in order to obtain firewood, and pay for environmental remediations as well as lead to more pollution, natural resource depletion and environmental degradation. The particular mix of effects is likely to vary, depending on the country, its stage of development and markets, and policies. Policy adjustment to address negative effects therefore has to be context specific.

The overall competitiveness effects of generally high environmental standards have not yet played the major role feared by environmentalists. As costs of compliance are borne by individual firms, increased costs related to environmental standards are claimed to impact adversely competitiveness of firms in countries where such standards are higher or more strictly enforced than in other countries. Studies by Repetto (1995), Benedickson *et al.* (1994), Globerman (1993), Pearce (1995) and OTA (1992) indicate costs are relatively small and do not appear to have resulted in a significant loss of overall competitiveness or relocation of industries to other countries with lower standards. Competitiveness and investment depend on a variety of factors. Fears of a high standard country losing market shares, income, jobs and future investment have yet to find an empirical base. In this regard, the effects on competitiveness and market access of developing and transition economies also needs to be systematically analysed. Likewise, the competitiveness effect of high environmental standards in terms of developing comparative advantages in 'green technologies' needs to be better investigated, as it is too readily alleged to be positive.

Freer trade should promote a more efficient allocation and use of resources by permitting countries to specialise in production of goods and services in which they possess a competitive advantage. This should result in a maximum level of output for a given level of energy and materials, with trade enabling greater consumption and economic welfare. It should reduce price distortions typical in oligopolistic markets and managed economies. It should also make more green technology available, provide markets for green products and allow diversification which reduces dependence on environmentally unsustainable exports of commodities. However, continued existence of trade-distorting subsidies as well as tariff and non-tariff trade barriers, and perhaps intra-firm trade which does not face disciplines of competitive markets, can act as obstacles to such an outcome. Other obstacles are failures to assign appropriate market values to the use of environmental resources, since these will determine the intensity of their use as factors of production.

It is argued that, through its contribution to greater economic welfare, progressive trade liberalisation can support environmental protection in several ways. Poverty and underdevelopment can harm the environment where desperate people have to overuse natural resources for fuel or food or other basic needs, and are unable to give the environment a greater priority. Economic growth and development supported by trade can provide countries with larger incomes as well as ability and willingness to commit more resources to improve the environment and reduce poverty together with the environmental harm that goes with it. Since there are hardly ready market demands for such environmental improvements or automatic efforts to alleviate poverty, specific efforts are required to do so in order not to incur larger, trade-magnified, social and economic costs and limitations in the future. Focused effort is also essential to ensure that technologies to reduce environmental harm are appropriate to identified needs.

Those who worry about environmental and social costs of export-led growth need to compare this approach with the estimates of overall benefits and costs that would need to be incurred through a less trade-intensive, import-substituting, pattern of development. For both more and less trade may have impacts on local and regional environments as well as poverty. They should reflect further on the root of their concern and what to do about it, and the consequences of developing and transition economies imitating the patterns of economic development of the rich countries, including concerns over new threats to consumer health and safety posed by imports from new sources. Countries and regions with different preferences, endowments, income and understanding about how various private activities affect the environment have different assessments of the most appropriate domestic and international environment and resource management priorities and practices. There is much uncertainty about how uniform standards should be throughout the world.

As already suggested, gone are the traditional forms of industry protection – transportation and communication costs, tariffs, quotas – which prevented the inflow of foreign goods, services, information and capital. The resulting experience of much fierce foreign competition due to trade liberalisation has caused business to scrutinise domestic policies which could have impacts on their competitiveness, including more stringent environmental standards. Business may go along with such standards as long as it is subsidised or protected from foreign competitors to compensate for possible loss of competitiveness due to relatively higher cost of compliance. Subsidies to those producing environmentally damaging output only increase societal costs. This kind of debate has caused advocates of more stringent domestic environmental standards to try and impose their preferences on foreign producers. The means to do so are import restrictions on like products objected to, either directly or through international environmental agreements. Such trade protection to level the costs of compliance with one country's policies violates other countries' rights as well as equity concerns. It could also encourage advocacy to extend this approach to cover differences in wages, healthcare, pension and other costs to business competing internationally. It also opens up the risk of protectionism.

Governments, especially in OECD, have created multi-stakeholder processes to explore a host of trade and environment linkages, analyse the differences over them and improve understanding and policy coordination at home and in various international organisations. These include efforts to be more transparent, assess reciprocal effects of the policies involved, develop country positions and cooperate internationally. It has also led to linkages in agreements such as the North American Free Trade Agreement, Maastricht Treaty and World Trade Organization. The linkages are in terms of inclusion of environmental issues, agencies, and groups in the negotiating process. They are also in terms of provisions such as inclusion of environmental goals, transparency, conditions regarding choice and enforcement of environmental standards, and screening and arbitration of disputes. These are perceived to be crucial to advocate and implement policies which anticipate and avoid conflicts, if not mutually support one another.

TRADE RULES AND THE ENVIRONMENT

Trade rules do allow governments to use many different measures to protect and improve the environment under its jurisdiction, for example, sales tax on products that can generate pollution (e.g. those containing chlorofluro-carbons), deposit refund schemes for recyclable waste (e.g. bottles) or favourable tax treatment of environmentally friendly products (e.g. lead-free gasoline) and establishment and enforcement of product standards (e.g. residue levels in food). They also permit a government to tax or regulate domestic producers who engage in polluting activities. They enable a government to regulate or ban the consumption of domestically produced or imported products.

There are some limitations on a government's right to select specific measures to protect health or the environment under its jurisdiction. For example, any environmentally motivated trade restriction should be implemented only when they complement parallel measures regarding domestically produced goods. Since tariffs are lowered and bound through mutually beneficial commitments flowing from rounds of negotiations, they cannot be raised even for environmental reasons except through an elaborate process of renegotiation between affected countries. Quantitative trade restrictions for similar reasons are also prohibited. A country can override these limitations if this is necessary for the protection of human, animal or plant life or if this primarily relates to the conservation of natural resources that are within the territory of the importer. However, such special efforts must be transparent and justifiable multilaterally, especially in the light of the provision in trade rules to treat developing countries more favourably than others (i.e. not less favourably).

Trade rules also permit the banning of imports of goods contributing to transborder, regional or global environmental problems as long as such bans apply to all countries and are complementary to parallel domestic measures. However, a problem may arise when trade provisions in the kinds of international environmental agreements mentioned earlier require signatories to apply more punitive trade measures to non-signatories than to signatories, for the same non-compliance. These provisions can be challenged. They require governments collectively to clarify the rules further. International disputes arise because domestic industry almost always succeeds in unduly influencing a purely domestic standard setting process to the disadvantage of foreign competitors. They are likely to proliferate as more domestic policies are implemented in ways indirectly to protect domestic industry.

Such trade tensions increase in magnitude when a country unilaterally makes access to its market conditional on competitors in other countries using the same or comparable production methods or emission levels to those imposed on domestic producers through particular 'environmentally-motivated' measures – even when this has no impact on final characteristics of the good used by customers. For example, many rich country environmentalists exploded in anger when a GATT (1991) dispute settlement panel ruled that a United States ban on Mexican tuna was inconsistent with its international trade obligations. The USA imposed the ban because it claimed that too many dolphins were caught by Mexican tuna-fishing techniques. The ban was to stay until the United States determined that Mexico had submitted acceptable evidence of compliance with its production standards concerning the incidental killing of dolphins in the fishing process. The US measure set a prospective absolute yearly ceiling for the number of dolphins killed by domestic tuna producers, but required that Mexican tuna producers meet a retroactive and varying ceiling for each period based on actual dolphin kill by the US tuna fleet in the same period. The GATT panel noted that the manner and content of the US measure to protect the dolphin raised questions of unilaterally setting conservation objectives, and applying them to a production method rather than a product, with little international agreement on scientific evidence about the nature of the threat to the dolphin or on policy options to take corrective measures. It also noted that the US action was directed at conserving a resource outside national jurisdiction, without showing how Mexico's conduct significantly impinged on the US conservation programme. Targeting Mexico in a discriminatory fashion and favouring domestic producers were also objectionable. The Mexicans lost much of their market in the United States, with loss of income and human well-being. While it may on occasion be desirable to change a method of production in a particular country, an exemplary use of trade measures to do so has not yet emerged and specifics of such a use may be contested for some time to come.

As initial response to these concerns, the preamble to the agreement establishing the World Trade Organization refers to the objective of expanding production and trade in goods and services, while bringing optimal uses of the world's resources in line with the objective of sustainable development. The considerable dilemma and burden is both to protect and preserve the environment at various levels of economic development. In addition, the 1994 Technical Barriers to Trade Agreement aims to ensure that the use of non-discriminatory mandatory technical regulations concerning products, voluntary standards and conformity assessment procedures does not create unnecessary barriers to trade. It recognises that countries should not be prevented from taking measures necessary to protect human, animal or plant life or health or the environment. It also recognises that each country has the right to set the level of standards it chooses, although the use of science, transparency and advanced notification are considered important safeguards against abuse in cases where such a choice is not based on international standards. None of the nearly 400 measures notified since 1980 has been challenged as unnecessary trade restrictions subject to dispute settlement procedures. Moreover, the 1994 Agreement on Sanitary and Phytosanitary Measures provides even more flexibility to deal with measures which protect human, animal and plant life or health, including that of flora and fauna. Such measures are designed to control the spread or importation of plant- or animal-borne pests or diseases and to control the presence of additives (e.g. food colourings), contaminants (e.g. pesticide residues), toxins or disease-causing organisms in foods, beverages or foodstuffs. Since this Agreement allows particular countries to be targeted on a discriminatory and precautionary basis, measures have to be substantively based on scientific principles as well as evidence, and must not arbitrarily or unjustifiably restrict trade.

Participation by more developing and transition economies in making government purchases increasingly open to international competition would improve market efficiency and access to new technology and equipment to overcome environmental problems where this is only available abroad. Similarly, improved market access and reduced domestic and export subsidies to agriculture could make agriculture more sustainable, although the manner of implementation of obligations by the European Union and others could undermine the benefits. The Agreement on Trade-related Aspects of Intellectual Property Rights will protect intellectual property rights, now over-whelmingly concentrated in favour of the rich – but with perhaps hopes of encouraging more research and access to innovations as well as foreign investment, at least for some of the less poor countries. It also provides for the exclusion of applications for patents, if preventing their commercial exploitation is deemed essential to protect the environment. In addition, there is a carve-out for the environment in the Agreement on Subsidies and Countervailing Measures. Government assistance provided for industrial research relating to the environment or the precompetitive development of new, modified or improved environmental products, processes or services within certain limits will not be subject to countervailing duties. Similarly, assistance for adapting existing facilities to new environmental regulations is also allowed. However, the Agreement specifies conditions to prevent industry protection. Finally, the new General Agreement on Trade in Services will begin to facilitate major transformations in many countries. This is due to greater access to foreign environmental, consulting, engineering, scientific and other best 'solutions' services. The efficiency and environmental integrity of projects should improve over time.

Governments have chosen to date to keep WTO as a trade organisation to oversee many closely related agreements which support increased globalisation and interdependence, subject to negotiated interpretations and changes in its 'constitution', including 'balancing' criteria, monitoring the use of trade measures for environmental purposes and relationships to international environmental agreements. Governments have recognised the need to identify and build a positive interrelationship between trade and the environment. They have agreed and established a WTO Committee on Trade and Environment to look fully into such matters, in addition to acknowledging and clarifying the extent to which existing trade rules already allow the use of trade measures for environmental purposes. The Committee is 'to identify the relationship between trade measures and environmental measures in order to promote sustainable development' and 'to make appropriate recommendations on whether any modifications of the provisions of the multilateral trading system are required, compatible with the open, equitable and non-discriminatory nature of the system' (TNC 1994). Such a broad mandate has already permitted considerations of the relationship between trade rules and charges and taxes for environmental purposes as well as requirements for environmental purposes relating to products, including standards and regulations, packaging, labelling and recycling. There has been a focus on the relationship between trade rules and trade measures for environmental purposes, including those pursuant to international environmental agreements. The effects of environmental measures on market access and the environmental benefits of removing trade restrictions and distortions have also been reviewed, as has been the issue of exports of domestically prohibited hazardous goods. More issues will be considered in the future (e.g. adequacy of transparency measures and dispute settlement procedures, and intellectual property rights).

THE PERSPECTIVE OF ENVIRONMENTAL COALITIONS IN RICH COUNTRIES

It is not surprising that environmentalists are so angry and frustrated. They have been identifying fundamental market and government policy failures to account for the accelerated abuse of the environment for decades! Lack of adequate responsiveness by governments and international organisations, lack of desired results and worry about trade rules nullifying environmental gains have produced escalating demands under the rubric of trade and environment, for example, encouragement of consumer boycotts of products from other countries because products are perceived to have been made in environmentally harmful ways.

The pro-environment coalitions demand that non-governmental organisations be allowed to observe WTO committee meetings. The WTO should expand timely public access to all documents prepared in connection with the dispute resolution cases, as well as panel reports, official reports, negotiating texts, institutional matters and notices of dispute challenges, with exceptions allowed only for business confidentiality or national security reasons. It should include the perspectives of citizens and non-governmental organisations in all stages of dispute resolution (e.g. allow amicus interventions), create an autonomous office modelled along the lines of the Advocate General in the European Court of Justice to evaluate and publicise a synthesis of all arguments made in a case, and include experts in environmental law and policy in panel rosters. It should also recommend in-depth minimum level environmental impact guidelines for trade policies and agreements, reflecting recent OECD work.

These coalitions demand that the WTO formulates legal provisions to make the trading system more consistent with, and supportive of, policies that account for the full cost of environmental impacts, for example, at least make polluter-or-user pays and precautionary principles essential terms of reference and requisite considerations in the settlement of disputes involving environmental or sustainable development issues. The WTO should recommend consistent rules incorporating common minimum production and process requirements which should be developed under outside competent institutions (to enforce regulations for pollution control or protection of public and occupational health within industrial processes or harvest natural resources sustainably), with special consideration for developing countries in terms of late implementation, financial and technical resources. It should recommend a strategy and schedule by which countries would phase out trade distorting subsidies for unsustainable natural resource development and for agriculture, and reward careful stewardship (energy efficiency and pollution prevention). It should also forbid countries from weakening environmental regulations to entice new investment and even develop measures such as adherence to strong codes of environmental conduct for international investment.

The WTO is expected more clearly to support domestic and international efforts to internalise environmental costs, for example, trade-neutral taxes imposed on products in support of environmental or conservation objectives, and border adjustment fees to compensate for energy or pollution taxes imposed on domestic industries worried about competitiveness. It is also expected to recognise the appropriate role of 'unilateral' actions to restrict trade in some cases. The WTO rules should not prevent or impede countries from employing trade restrictions to implement or enforce existing or future international environmental agreements. It ought to conduct intellectual property rights analysis and formulate recommendations on several key themes, for example how incentives under the Agreement on Trade-related Aspects of Intellectual Property Rights for development and international transmission of new technology might be targeted to prevent pollution or conserve natural resources, how to compensate indigenous people who help fuel multibillion dollar industries, and how to improve institutional relationships to protect international biodiversity and conserve genetic resources.

The pro-environment coalitions want the WTO to recommend ways to direct new revenues derived from expanded trade into initiatives for environmental protection and sustainable development. An example would be to charge a fee on all trade to fund the Global Environmental Facility and 'losers' from trade liberalisation. They want the WTO to conduct analysis and to develop recommendations which would allow countries to take a full range of measures to alleviate impacts of transportation services on the environment. They also wish to ensure that any process to promote international equivalence of product standards as a means of reducing non-tariff barriers is open and deferential to standards more stringent than international norms and strict on trade in domestically prohibited goods. These proponents want to establish a multi-stakeholder intergovernmental panel to provide the WTO and others with factual and analytic foundation for constructive reforms linking trade, environment (and sustainable development). Finally, they insist that the WTO be guided by the United Nations Commission on Sustainable Development (CSD) to incorporate the results of the Earth Summit.

DEVELOPMENT PERSPECTIVES

As people in developing and transition economies listen to these kinds of demands, many become increasingly apprehensive and angry. First, they see how the most rich and competitive respond to continuous pressure for structural adjustments in the patterns of investment, production and trade associated with accelerating globalisation and interdependence – as if they were less rich and competitive than the poorest and weakest elements of global society, and therefore could not afford investment in poverty allevia-tion, environment improvements and open trade promised in Agenda 21.

Second, they wonder how this would also affect their abilities to under-stand and promote linkages between trade, environment and development. They question press releases from the World Trade Organization, and other international organisations, based on flexible number crunching which predict the expected benefits of the Uruguay Round to them, but which cannot deal well with the growing use of various trade protection measures as well as trade-related environmental measures to reduce such benefits. Instead of more favourable treatment promised thirty years ago, poor countries have continued to face a raft of barriers as their export or export prospects improve. Increased and more rapid assumption of obligations under the Uruguay Round preclude the poor from pursuing the economic development paths of the rich and force them to search for options based on more secure and enhanced foreign market access. The kind of advocacy described in the previous section has become a constraint on trade, rather than an essential component of sustainable development.

Third, these people see patent injustice in any effort to promote legally binding trade obligations to deal with environmental priorities of the rich in return for soft and uncertain promises to deal with issues of poverty, inequity, distribution and lack of capacity over time, on an issue by issue basis. This will further foreclose a development path that the rich largely refuse to give up, let alone meaningfully share the benefits resulting from that course.

Fourth, they are furious that the rich continue largely to ignore how the pressures on the poor to earn foreign exchange were forcing disproportionate

147

reliance on increasing commodity exports to the point of long-term unsustainability.

Finally, they wonder if green industries in OECD are trying to impose higher standards on other countries because they can then sell them green goods, services and technologies and dominate future markets worldwide.

These concerns lead to a search for balance. The poor and the vulnerable want a review of environmental measures which have a significant trade effect with a view to determining and ensuring their consistency with a more open trading system. They demand an improvement of mechanisms to ensure that transparency and notification requirements in the formulation and implementation of trade-related environmental measures such as eco-labelling, packaging and recycling are met. They advocate a ban on unilateral extraterritorial imposition of trade measures to achieve environmental goals and respect for existing trade rules in the use of trade measures against non-parties to international environmental agreements. In particular, there must be justification of measures adopted for environmental protection on grounds of legitimacy, objectivity and least trade restrictiveness. There has to be an avoidance of trade measures to address alleged competitiveness concerns and to force participation in international environmental agreements.

Most of those with wider concerns seek effective cooperation within WTO and between WTO and major intergovernmental organisations. They seek analysis of recent cases of trade–environment friction to assess trends and soundness/fairness of measures used. They want to develop an organisational structure and delivery system which respects these and other commitments in Agenda 21. Such an approach should lead to an expansion and enhancement of public and private sector mechanisms for technology transfer, beyond stronger intellectual property rights and more liberal rules for foreign investors. It should improve market access for commodity products in primary and processed forms currently or potentially of interest to poor countries. There ought to be a more substantial and more progressive reduction in subsidies which induce inefficient industrialised country production (e.g. agriculture, mining, textiles). Certainly, there have to be capacity building measures, and financial assistance in the form of grants, loans and debt relief. Developing and transition economies challenge the use of discriminatory and unilateral extra-jurisdictional trade measures to influence their behaviour. They get upset at attempts to conduct trade-offs between development (trade) and environment which impose disproportionate burdens of adjustment on them. They find the prospects of a more open WTO, without effective ability to argue their case internationally, to be playing into the agenda of rich environmentalists and industrialists and their 'funded subsidiaries' abroad in poor countries.

Increasingly rich country business and governments do agree with parts of such perspectives and argue that effective environmental protection is unlikely to grow out of weak, debt-ridden and high unemployment economies. They

148

view efficient and dynamic economic growth, induced by liberalised clearer rules on trade and investment with predictable consequences, as a helpful means for enhanced environmental protection. A portion of the wealth generated by trade, in this view, must be used to support and restore environmental quality. To do so will require clarifying the intent and scope of the kinds of changes proposed in this section, while observing and strengthening codified multilateral trade principles. It also means developing mechanisms to resolve disputes arising from such clarifications and changes. There is real worry about industry protectionists capturing the environmental policy process and a very strong desire to build in public accountability procedures, such as openness, non-discrimination, justification or proportionality, objectivity, cost effectiveness and so on. Illegal, unilateral and distortive use of trade measures as environmental enforcement tools is not acceptable, although there is willingness to explore such issues within the specified disciplines of genuine international environmental agreements.

TOWARDS SUSTAINABLE DEVELOPMENT

It would appear that the relationship between trade and the environment is neither simple nor clear. The linkages are often indirect and the use of trade policy to solve environmental problems is viewed in many policy analyses as second-best, as well as not all that effective. The range of assumptions underlying claims of inherent conflict, specific effects, and effectiveness of alternative remedies need to be further sorted out, together with the future role of technology in global sustainable development. The very effectiveness of current expenditures to improve the environment has to be assessed. More importantly, the interests of the majority of the people of the world must be accommodated both efficiently and equitably. The greater the number of trade restrictive international environmental agreements we have, the more the prospects of using punitive trade policy as an instrument to coerce others against their preferences and even ability to go along. Such occurrences also risk being captured by the professional industry protectionist for narrow benefits, and certain to increase the use of dispute settlement procedures. The wider effects on sustainable development deserve scrutiny, for example, inflationary effects of measures to add environmental costs to prices and their impacts on pensioners and unemployed.

It is far from clear what the WTO should do, and how to accommodate environmental concerns. It is necessary to review this issue in the wider context of the future agenda concerning remaining high tariffs and other barriers to trade, foreign investment, services, competition and anti-dumping policies, subsidies and countervail, waivers and exceptions to trade rules, movement of service providers and so on. It is also important to assess such a review in terms of setting precedents to address other pressing claims involving inter-country differences in costs of pensions, taxes, healthcare, wages, and so on. The scope of the WTO is very broad indeed and its trade policy reviews, now permanent institutional structures and rule-based trade regime should be deployed to make globalisation and sustainable development more compatible. Issues of the use of waivers and reinterpretations as well as of amendments to the 'constitution' of the WTO to resolve trade and environment conflicts need to mature before appropriate decision-making and possibly negotiation could be recommended.

These kinds of fundamental assessments must be better done at home, not only or firstly in international organisations. Mutually beneficial trade has been based on existing inter-country differences of all kinds. Such a trade has been also based on the recognition that individual and collective welfare is a function of choice of consumption, leisure, health, environmental quality and so on and differing weights in this choice are legitimate. Internationally, each country naturally has a different set of competing priorities and goals. The issue is therefore to develop a system which adapts and responds to a spectrum of competing values and interests, both of the rich and the poor. What this suggests is a need to devise some general and exemplary rules of conduct within which policy ought to operate in the first instance, unless different behaviours can be justified multilaterally.

We need proactive and rule-based, bilateral, trilateral, regional, plurilateral and multilateral institutions to promote sustainable development – development which meets the needs of the present without compromising the ability of future generations to meet their own needs in their varying contexts. Such a development would preserve the Earth's basic environmental and resource capital, ensure a sustainable level of population, reduce the energy and resource content of growth, integrate environment and economics in decision-making, ensure a more equitable distribution of the benefits of growth, in addition to reviving growth to meet basic human needs. Sustainable development provides a common framework for discussion among trade, environment and development constituencies. It can move the discussion by providing the opportunity to identify common concerns, goals, and courses of action. Institutions which constitute our system of global governance can be strengthened in the light of such debates. The quality of coordination of such institutions is reflected in the quality with which the world community deals with sustainable development issues. Therefore, there is a need to conduct reform in a way which enables government and international institutions more easily to adapt to a more coordinated view of an increasingly integrated economy and environment.

It is to promote a more cohesive approach or framework to trade, environment and development that the International Institute for Sustainable Development (IISD) broke new ground in 1994 by proposing Trade and Sustainable Development Principles or Winnipeg Principles. To facilitate and stimulate the process, the Institute convened a distinguished international working group to develop a concise set of agreed, interdependent and mutually reinforcing Trade and Sustainable Development Principles. The nine members of the trade, environment and development communities spent a year actively listening to each other to overcome the kind of confusion described above and drafting the Winnipeg Principles as well as consulting on them with numerous contacts. The principles provide a mechanism that is flexible and responsible in addressing many issues. They address the complexity and uncertainty of trade and environment interlinkages and the unacceptable tendencies of some to choose certain actions while ignoring others. The principles seek to enhance the ability of different countries to negotiate and adhere to trade/environment agreements as they promote wider concerns among governments. What follows is a brief description of each principle and how it applies to the trade/environment debate.

Efficiency/cost internalisation

Efficiency entails the progressive and predictable reflection of unpaid environmental costs in the prices of products so as to minimise input of environmental services per unit of output, and progressive trade liberalisation. Environmental costs must be internalised through the combined use of economic instruments and various forms of environmental regulation. They can also be reduced through the elimination of environmentally damaging subsidies and escalating tariffs. Resources must be allocated and used more efficiently because the expected surges in population will very significantly increase demand for food, energy and industrial output.

Equity

Further trade liberalisation and sharing of capital, knowledge and technology is needed to promote greater equity today and tomorrow (within and between countries, as well as groups of countries) given past, present and expected use of the environment and distribution of related benefits. As standards of living outside the OECD are far too low (as indicated earlier, poverty is a key source and victim of environmental degradation), future policy must build in much greater equity considerations.

Environmental integrity

This refers to measures which respect and help maintain environmental integrity where cost internalisation cannot capture environmental values (e.g. where irreversible depletion of fish stocks or forests are involved, or irreplaceable losses such as extinction of animal populations and species). Where such efforts require the use of GATT-inconsistent trade measures, they should be within the context of multilaterally agreed criteria (e.g. CITES and the Montreal Protocol).

151

Subsidiarity

Where there are significant transborder, regional or global impacts, there should be international cooperative responses. Subsidiarity is the implementation of environmental measures (and development) at a jurisdictional level appropriate to the source and scope of the problem and appropriate to effectiveness in achieving objectives. There will be legitimate differences in standards between countries, reflecting environmental and social conditions, preferences and priorities.

International cooperation

More aggressive and innovative efforts should be made to develop common understanding and approaches as to how our multilateral system should evolve and how questions relating to a variety of linked issues could be addressed, including more open, equitable, effective and alternative dispute settlement processes where disputes are unavoidable. Agenda 21 illustrates some of the new dimensions and relationships necessary. Unilateral sanctions are a matter of last resort, signifying failure by all concerned.

Science and precaution

We should encourage a precautionary approach to the adoption of environmental policies which would allow governments to deal collectively with serious threats of environmental harm in advance of conclusive scientific evidence concerning that harm. It is recognised that environmental changes inherently involve scientific uncertainty (e.g. climate change and ozone depletion). There must be transparent efforts to identify and clarify the changing risks, and to relate the risks to costs and benefits of corrective measures. Therefore, institutions and legal regimes should be structured to be responsive to environmental changes and evolving scientific knowledge.

Openness

There should be timely, easy and full access to information by all affected or interested parties, and public participation and accountability in the decision-making process informed by considerations of feasibility. This is critical to local, national, regional and global governance in support of sustainable development.

Conclusion

At present many deficit and debt-ridden governments do not share the environmental priorities of the United States and the European Union, nor views on how these priorities are to be given effect. This is reflected in their positions in Geneva's trade rule-making processes and the subsequent results. The principles serve as a bridge because they give legitimacy not only to improved environmental protection, but also to the related issues of equity and cooperation in ways that cannot be ignored by major governmental powers. Indeed, it is hoped that the principles will influence the creation of new coalitions for change, publicly linking expected change in behaviour to incentives as well as creating pressure on laggards, including pressures to avoid the use of trade measures, while at the same time addressing the demands of global equity.

The Winnipeg Principles also provide a basis for negotiations and account-ability in a variety of activities that support trade and sustainable development. They can improve the quality of International Environmental Agreements. They require information sharing and regular interactions between affected parties on issues of common interest, thus making commitments more credible. Indeed, in this regard they would support notification measures, trade policy reviews and the dispute settlement processes of the World Trade Organisation. They accommodate minimum international standards and agreements, eco-labelling and packaging, and even the use of trade measures within the larger context of achieving progress towards sustainable develop-ment. There is also a need to build capacity to negotiate environmental commitments which respond to stakeholder concerns domestically and inter-nationally. Information, research, analytical, political, legal, administrative and technical competencies will be the keys to integrating policy in this way. In this regard, non-governmental and governmental organisations must find more creative means of helping the vast majority of poorer nations. Increased or redirected bilateral and multilateral assistance, increased market access on a preferential basis, technology transfer, debt relief, concessionary export credits, greater flows of private foreign investment and better commodity agreements are examples of what is required. The lending programmes of the World Bank and other international financial institutions should also be made more accessible. Other institutions should look to funding transfers of technology, research and development, as well as shared implementation of projects in particular countries. Policy coherence is badly needed to promote sustainable development. The IISD expects the various institutions involved in trade and environment interlinkages to adapt and work together in a pluralistic approach to future problem solving.

BIBLIOGRAPHY

Benedickson, J., Doern, G.B. and Olewiler, N. (1994) *Getting the Green Light: Environmental Regulation and Investment in Canada*, Toronto: C.D. Howe Institute, Policy Study 22.

Daly, H.E. and Cobb, J.B. (1994) *For the Common Good*, Boston: Beacon Press.

General Agreement on Tariffs and Trade (1991) *United States – Restrictions on Imports of Tuna, Report of the Panel*, Geneva: GATT, 3 September.

Globerman, S. (1993) 'Trade Liberalization and the Environment', in *Assessing NAFTA: A Trinational Analysis*, Vancouver BC: Fraser Institute.

Goodland, R. and Daly, H. (1995) 'Poverty Alleviation is Essential for Environmental Sustainability', *International Journal of Sustainable Development*, 2, December: 31–48.

International Institute for Sustainable Development (1994) *Trade and Sustainable Development Principles*, Winnipeg: IISD.

Natural Resources Defence Council and Foundation for International Environmental Law and Development (1995) *Environmental Priorities for the World Trading System*, Washington and London: January.

OTA (Office of Technology Assessment, US Congress) (1992) *Trade and Environment: Conflicts and Opportunities*, Washington DC: Office of Technology Assessment.

Pearce, D. (1995) 'The Greening of the GATT: Some Economic Considerations', in J. Cameron, P. Demaret and D. Geradin (eds) (1995) *Trade and the Environment: The Search for Balance*, London: Cameron May.

Repetto, R. (1995) *Jobs, Competitiveness, and Environmental Regulation: What Are the Real Issues?*, Washington DC: World Resources Institute.

Shaw, N. and Cosbey, A. (1994) *GATT, the WTO and Sustainable Development*, Winnipeg: IISD.

TNC (Trade Negotiations Committee) (1994) *Decision on Trade and Environment*, MTN.TNC/W/141, Geneva: 29 March.

9

CENTRAL AND EASTERN EUROPE'S INTEGRATION INTO THE WORLD TRADING SYSTEMS

András Inotai and Judit Kiss

INTRODUCTION

Following the political and economic transformation in Central and Eastern Europe (CEECs),[1] the 'trade geography' of the old continent has changed fundamentally. While abolishing the CMEA trade bloc, the transforming economies have institutionalised their trade relations within Europe in three directions. Key importance was attached to the European Union (EU) with which association agreements (AA) were signed. Free trade treaties created the framework of trade relations with EFTA countries. In addition, the Central European transforming countries established their own free trade area (CEFTA). As a result, the agreements are set to create a large free trade area including most European countries by 2001.

At the same time, substantial changes have also been characterising the development of the global trading system.

On the one hand, a new pattern of continental (or even transcontinental) regionalism started to emerge as a result of the creation of large trading blocs (see Chapter 1). In Europe, the single internal market, the European economic space and, most recently, the enlargement of the EU to three EFTA countries, as well as political and economic discussion about future (Eastern) enlargement exacerbates this trend. In the Western hemisphere, the Initiative of the Americas, NAFTA and Mercosur, as well as a number of regional cooperation agreements indicate similar developments. Also in Asia, mainly in and among the Pacific Rim countries, different patterns of regional cooperation have been elaborated in the last years.

On the other hand, growing regionalism has been accompanied by efforts of global trade liberalisation, featured by the successful conclusion of the GATT's Uruguay Round negotiations and the creation of a new institution, the World Trade Organization (WTO).

The integration of Central and Eastern Europe into the global trading system is mainly conditioned by two external factors, namely the development of the EU, its major (dominant) trading partner, and the shaping of the global framework according to the GATT agreement. Moreover, the pattern of the transforming countries' integration will also depend on the 'liberalisation heritage' of the last years and the internal resources that can (or cannot) be mobilised for strengthening global competitiveness.

This chapter is divided into three major sections. First, the unique heritage of liberalisation will be outlined in order to understand both the short-term achievements and the not unlikely medium- to long-term consequences of the trade policy of Central and Eastern Europe. The second section deals with the likely impacts of the implementation of the GATT agreement. Finally, some key issues of the trade relations with Europe, both with the EU as the undisputed 'external anchor' of the transforming economies and the CEFTA, will be addressed.

UNIQUE FEATURES OF TRADE LIBERALISATION

The process of liberalisation of foreign trade in the CEECs, partly preceding the institutional framework of trade relations, partly as a consequence of valid agreements, was embedded into the general economic liberalisation which characterised the systemic change. Trade liberalisation consisted of two key elements: institutional changes in the transforming economies (elimination of state-owned foreign trade monopolies, freedom of firms to carry out export–import deals), and the opening up of domestic markets.

According to international experience, small developed and semi-developed economies used to rely heavily on foreign trade and considered it to be a major factor of growth, efficiency and international competitiveness. This also holds true for the transforming economies. Before the start of the transformation, and based partly on heavily distorted exchange rates and GDP figures, exports accounted for 25 to 45 per cent of national GDP.

At the same time, trade liberalisation, as implemented in Central and Eastern Europe, reveals several unique features:

- Successfully modernising economies, mainly in Asia, have clearly separated export-oriented economic policies from import liberalisation. The opening up of their domestic market started several years after their export position in international trade had become well established. The transforming countries opened up their markets not only before but, more importantly, without a clear and already successful (or successfully sustainable) export-oriented strategy.
- Slow growth and particularly recession have never favoured trade liberalisation. In this situation, policy-makers and domestic pressure groups used to concentrate on maintaining or increasing their share of the domestic market by protecting it against external competitors. In contrast, all transforming economies implemented substantial trade liberalisation only during the years of unprecedented output decline.

- The collapse of the CMEA and of the Soviet Union, the main market for all Central and Eastern European countries until the late 1980s, has seriously exacerbated the output decline and the 'transformation crisis'. One can only guess what kind of trade (and overall) policies would have followed Western European countries if they had lost 30 to 60 per cent of their external markets almost overnight (e.g. Austria losing the German market). Rapid trade liberalisation would hardly have been among the policy measures to be suggested.

- Liberalisation of imports was mainly a one-sided, unilateral action, also a step not very common in the history of trade liberalisation practice of developed countries. As a consequence, some transforming countries have substantially reduced their tariff levels (and their bargaining power) well before trade negotiations with the EU and the EFTA started.

- In addition, compared with the situation before 1989, import liberalisation happened extremely quickly. In about three years the transforming economies became almost as open as the more developed and stronger Western European economies which had evolved only gradually over several decades.

- Probably the most striking difference between the import liberalisation carried out in the developed countries and that carried out in the transforming European countries is that opening up has not been accompanied by the establishment of 'secondary protection' (non-tariff and non-quota barriers). Because tariffs and other market protecting instruments had never played a role in intra-CMEA trade, there was no need to introduce such measures. The history of global trade liberalisation clearly shows that almost every tariff reduction has generated non-tariff trade policy steps in order to maintain the effective level of protection or, at least, to mitigate the impact of tariff reduction on domestic producers.

IMPLICATIONS OF THE GATT AGREEMENT

As the Central and Eastern European countries (Czech Republic, Hungary, Poland, Slovakia, Bulgaria and Romania) are highly reliant on their foreign trade turnover, the future development of these countries also depends on the impact of the GATT Agreement concluded in April 1994. With the exception of Bulgaria, all five countries are signatory parties to the GATT,[2] their foreign trade is conducted under GATT rules and some of them (like Hungary) have already ratified the Uruguay Round.

The overall impact of the GATT Agreement

One of the greatest merits of the Uruguay Round, which is also the greatest benefit for the Central and Eastern European countries (CEECs), is that the present complicated and discriminatory world trade system, causing severe market distortions, will be replaced by a more transparent, stable and predictable trade regulation system dominated by the elements of quasi free trade *vis-à-vis* protectionist tendencies.

The other merit is that the Uruguay Round covered not only foreign trade in industrial goods, but also agricultural products, services, intellectual property rights and trade-related investments. As current CEEC foreign trade is dominated by the turnover of commodities, the regulations concerning industrial and agricultural goods are more important than those relating to services and intellectual property rights. However, in coming years the foreign trade in services and investments will probably also gain momentum for the CEECs.

According to preliminary estimates by the OECD and the World Bank, world trade is expected to expand by an annual US$200–300 billion by the year 2000, compared to 1994, as a result of the implementation of the GATT Agreement.[3] World trade is expected to expand both from the demand and the supply side. As a consequence of the tariff reductions and minimum market access, new markets will be opened up, while the reduction of domestic farm support and export subsidies will lead to a decrease in the role of non-competitive, previously over-subsidised agricultural producers and exporters, and to the appearance of new competitive producers and exporters.

The expansion of world trade, the opening up of new markets and the emergence of new producers and exporters on the world market will promote investments, boost production and create new jobs. GATT, OECD and World Bank studies suggest that the Uruguay Round will eventually bring about an annual 1 per cent gain in world income over the next ten years, ranging from US$200 billion to US$300 billion per year (in 1992 dollars). In addition, there will be important dynamic gains arising from externalities generated by increased competition, economies of scale and greater innovation.

However, the main issue for the CEECs is whether and if so to what extent they would benefit from the overall welfare effect of the GATT Agreement. In other words, will they be among the new exporters emerging on the world markets? If this happens depends on whether their market access would improve, whether they would be in a position to make use of that better market access and whether market protection would change in their favour. In order to draw the overall balance of the GATT Agreement on the CEECs, one must analyse these issues.

Improved market access for the CEECs?

As far as the markets for industrial goods are concerned, currently the most important obstacle to market access for the CEECs is not so much the different tariff and non-tariff barriers as the lack of or weak competitiveness of their products. Tariffs on industrial goods were negligible, even prior to the conclusion of the Uruguay Round.[4] These tariffs will be further lowered as a consequence of the GATT Agreement: the developed countries' tariffs will be cut by an average of 38 per cent, lowering their average tariff to 3.9 per cent, the developing countries' tariffs by an average of 20 per cent and that of the economies in transition by 30 per cent (leaving these countries with a 6.0 per cent average tariff level for industrial goods).

Above average tariff cuts are taking place in six product groups (metals, mineral products, precious stones and metals; electric machinery; woods, pulps, paper and furniture; non-electric machinery; chemical and other manufactured articles), while below average cuts have been made in four product groups (textiles and apparel; leather, rubbers, footwear and travel goods; fish and fish products; and transport equipment).

In some specified product groups, the main industrialised countries have gone beyond the average cuts in industrial tariffs and reduced their tariffs to zero.

One of the main results of the Uruguay Round was to reduce uncertainty about future tariff levels by increasing the number of bound tariff rates: the Uruguay Round ensures that virtually all imports of developed countries (99 per cent) will enter under bound rates, as well as almost 60 per cent of the imports of the developing countries. In addition, the share of imports of industrial goods being granted duty-free treatment by developed countries will more than double as a result of the Uruguay Round, from 20 per cent to 44 per cent.

According to certain views (Sorsa 1994) the largest gains for the transition economies are expected to arise from the removal of non-tariff barriers in clothing, textiles, agricultural, forestry and fishery products, and processed food and beverages.

However, in order to get a real picture of the impact of tariff cuts, zero-for-zero commitment, peak tariffs, tariff bindings, duty-free trade, tariff escalation and tariff harmonisation on the market access of the CEECs, one should take into consideration the fact that all six CEECs have signed an Association Agreement with the EC and a free trade agreement with EFTA, so a free trade of industrial goods has been or is being created among the three groups of countries.

With regard to foreign trade in agricultural goods, the market access possibilities are changing in a less ambiguous way. As a consequence of the tariffication process, that is the conversion of all non-tariff trade barriers (including quantitative restrictions, quotas, licences, variable levies, etc.) into tariff equivalents, the average customs level will be significantly increased. This sudden and significant customs increment might prevent in certain cases – and especially in the first years – the further expansion of agricultural exports from the CEECs.

This negative impact is expected to be felt especially in the case of agricultural trade with the EU, due to the fact that certain trade concessions granted in the framework of the Association Agreements (like the levy reductions) will disappear, while others (like customs reductions) will become eroded, unless compensation is provided. It is self-evident that under the conditions of increased tariffs, the same percentage of tariff reduction would imply a higher market protection on the side of the EU.[5] According to estimates deriving from EU experts, the cereals, cattle and poultry exporters of the CEECs would be handicapped on the EU market due to the introduction of the GATT Agreement.

On the other hand, the customs on agricultural goods will be decreased by 36 per cent from their 1986–8 levels in the coming six years. In principle, this could provide better market access for exporters, but it should be borne in mind that the 36 per cent customs reduction obligation is an average. Countries have flexibility in structuring the cuts for individual products: tariffs may be cut by much more than the average for some products and by much less for others as long as each tariff is reduced by at least 15 per cent. Consequently, all importing countries have the right to modify their customs reduction policy according to their market protection objectives, implying that the level of protection remains high for products currently subject to non-tariff measures.

Another possibility for improved market access is provided by the so-called minimum market access, meaning that 3 per cent of the domestic consumption of the base period (the average of the 1986–8 years) should be taken as a minimum import requirement. However, it is doubtful whether the CEECs would be in a position to make use of the minimum market access, due to their weak competitiveness.

In connection with the so-called current market access, the CEECs are potential losers, as the preferences granted to the CEECs in the framework of the Association Agreements are not included in the current market access in contrast to the preferences given to the developing countries and other nations prior to the base period of 1986–8.

In principle, market access will generally become easier, simpler and will improve as the customs will remain the only trade barriers and their level will decrease with time. Furthermore, as a consequence of the minimum market access, new markets will be opened up. However, the main issue is how the CEECs could make use of the market access possibilities, especially as certain possibilities will remain for importers to protect and to counterbalance the opening up of their markets.

One of the possibilities is the introduction of import surcharges in the case of significant import increase or low import prices. The other possibility is provided by the fact that the tariff reduction obligation relates to unweighted averages, so it is up to the importer how to calculate: in which product group should the market be opened to a greater degree and where it should be protected to a greater extent. The third opportunity is given by the different sanitary and phytosanitary measures aimed at imposing trade controls to protect human, animal or plant life or health.

Who benefits from the domestic farm support and the export subsidy cut?

Until now, world trade in agriculture has been distorted not only by the different non-tariff barriers but also by domestic support and export subsidies. In this context, the agreement on reducing both domestic farm support and export subsidies has been a significant achievement of the Uruguay Round. Domestic farm support – expressed by the Aggregate Measurement of Support (AMS) indicator – should be decreased by 20 per cent in the developed countries, compared to the base period of 1986–8, while the value of export subsidies should be cut by 36 per cent and the volume of subsidised exports by 21 per cent in the coming six years, from 1986–90 levels.

One of the positive outcomes of the above-mentioned regulation is that some elements of market distortion will be eliminated. Primarily, competitiveness based mainly on the comparative advantages and efficiency differences, rather than subsidies and state budgets, will compete on the world markets. This change is in favour of those countries that were not able to enter the escalating subsidy wars due to financial constraints and which are able to compete on the basis of comparative advantages. Fortunately, many of the CEECs belong to this group, especially in the field of agricultural trade.

Consequently, in principle the relative competitiveness of many of the CEECs could improve in the world market, especially as most of them have already cut their domestic farm support[6] and export subsidies prior to acceptance of the GATT Agreement to such an extent[7] that no further decrease is necessary to meet its requirements (see Table 9.1). In addition, countries with high inflation (like many of the CEECs) have the right to adjust their subsidy cut with their inflation, that is even a slight subsidy increase is allowed for them.[8] The only limiting factor is the budget constraint. Another possibility available for the CEECs is to restructure their subsidies from the 'red box' to the 'green box', that is to apply those

Table 9.1 Agricultural subsidies in the CEECs

	Country	1990	1991	1992	1993	1994
In the % of estimated budget expenditure	Poland	4.7	4.5	3.5	2.7	2.4
	Hungary	9.1	3.7	3.3	3.6	3.7
	Slovakia	18.4	8.2	7.8	6.4	5.7
GDP	Poland	1.3	1.3	0.9	0.8	0.8
	Hungary	3.0	1.6	1.4	1.4	2.1
	Slovakia	8.6	3.6	2.8	2.5	2.1

Source: *Népszabadság*, 18 March 1994: 18

forms of domestic support and export subsidies which are allowed by the GATT Agreement.

It would also be a positive outcome that as a consequence of the farm support and export subsidy decrease, the agricultural production of the over-subsidised countries (like the EU) will probably show a decreasing tendency, which will lead to smaller world supply and increasing agricultural prices. This change would be favourable for the CEECs with significant agro-potential and agricultural export possibilities (like Hungary, Poland, Bulgaria, Romania), while it would be unfavourable for the agricultural importers of the region (like the Czech Republic, Russia).

However, one should not forget that in spite of the farm support and export subsidy cuts, there will remain certain possibilities (contained in the so-called green box) for supporting agricultural production and promoting agricultural exports. For instance, the US deficiency and the EU set-aside compensatory payments, the structural funds, the food aid programmes, the expenditures on environmental, regional and infrastructural development, R&D, educational and marketing purposes, export credits, credit guarantees and insurance programmes are all exempt from the farm support obligation to cut. This implies that the highly developed countries will find a way to keep on supporting their agricultural production and exports by indirect forms, while the CEECs will be deprived of these methods, due mainly to financial constraints.

What kind of market protection is left for the CEECs?

Presently most of the Central and Eastern European markets are over-liberalised, especially as far as their import regime is concerned. In Hungary, for instance, the rate of import liberalisation is higher than 90 per cent. The markets of the CEECs are too open compared to their level of development, and also if we consider their GDP decline and market loss.

The main issues deriving from the GATT Agreement, concerning the market protection of the CEECs, are as follows:

- whether the process of tariffication will protect the markets of the CEECs better than the present trade regimes in the initial period of the functioning of the GATT Agreement;
- what will happen to the market protection in the ensuing six years when the tariff reductions have to take place;
- what will be the ratio of market protection between the CEECs and the highly developed countries;
- what measures will be left for the CEECs to protect their markets?

It is expected that, as a consequence of the tariffication process, due to the increment of customs, the level of border protection for the CEECs will be increased or at least be strengthened for the initial period of the functioning of the GATT Agreement. In the case of Hungary, for instance, the agricultural tariff rate of 20–22 per cent has been increased to an average of some 45 per cent since 1 January 1995 due to converting the import quotas and licences into tariffs.

However, the increased tariffs will be decreased in the coming six years by 36 per cent, resulting in a 29–30 per cent average agricultural tariff rate in the case of Hungary, which is above the average agricultural tariff rate prior to the introduction of the GATT Agreement. Though the system excludes the possibility of applying other trade restrictions (like quantitative restrictions, licences, quotas, etc.), this would have the effect of protecting the domestic market, reducing imports and increasing budget revenues.

However, in the case of industrial goods, the average tariffs of the economies in transition will be cut from 8.6 per cent to 6.0 per cent due to the average tariff cut of 30 per cent. Furthermore, the percentage of tariffs bound will be increased from the pre-Uruguay Round of 74 per cent to 96 per cent and the percentage of duty-free trade from 13 per cent to 16 per cent. Consequently, the industrial markets of the CEECs will be left less protected than prior to concluding the Uruguay Round.

As regards the ratio of market protection between the CEECs and the highly developed countries, the gap between their level of protection will probably still remain significant, despite the fact that the degree of market protection will also decrease in the highly developed countries. This gap will prevent the CEECs from easily entering the markets of the highly developed countries and will leave the markets of the CEECs unprotected against the inflow of still subsidised goods.

Better world trade situation – also for the CEECs?

Having analysed the impact of the GATT Agreement on the foreign trade of the CEECs, one should conclude that:

- though in principle market access for the CEECs will improve, it will depend on the economic conditions and on the commodity structure of the exports by these countries whether they can make use of the available possibilities;
- the agreed market access improvement could be curbed by different safeguard measures;
- though the domestic support and the export subsidy of the highly developed countries will be decreased, there will be a great number of possibilities to distort the principle of free trade and fair competition;
- as the CEECs are also obliged to accomplish the tariffication process and the tariff reduction, their market protection will be very fragile, due to the low level of their development and the high level of their foreign trade liberalisation.

In spite of the fact that the world trade situation will improve in the coming years – due to the expansion of world trade, the opening up of new markets, the increasing demand for investments and the disappearance of oversupply in agricultural products – it is not sure whether the CEECs would be among the beneficiaries.[9] Due to their domestic problems (lack of exportable commodities, poor quality, inefficient marketing, packaging, advertising, etc.), it is uncertain whether they will manage to make use of the improved market access, increasing agricultural prices and seemingly less protectionist international environment.

According to certain estimates (Nguyen *et al.* 1993) the net welfare gains of the Uruguay Round for the former centrally planned economies of Eastern Europe, the former Soviet Union and China would be around US$37.4 billion, that is 17.6 per cent of the projected global net welfare gains. US$19.9 billion out of the US$37.4 billion net welfare gains will be due to the liberalisation of the Multifibre Arrangement, US$13.2 billion to the liberalisation of services, while US$1.6 billion only to the liberalisation of agricultural trade. This distribution of the net welfare gain can be explained by the significance of the transition economies of Eastern Europe and the former Soviet Union (and of course, China) as producers of textiles and clothing, the opening up of their markets for services and their low level of agricultural protection.

On the basis of data from the World Bank and the OECD the net gain by Eastern Europe and the former Soviet Union would be US$2.2 billion only, while the net gain for China would be around US$37 billion (Madden and Madeley 1993).

According to preliminary estimates – which sound very optimistic – as a result of the implementation of the Uruguay agreement, the Hungarian export revenues are expected to increase by US$200–250 million yearly, the agricultural export revenues by US$100–150 million yearly. This growth will be the consequence of making use of the improved market access and of converting the Hungarian comparative advantages into competitive ones.

However, the welfare impact of the GATT Agreement will be limited in the Central European region, as not all the CEECs are signatory parties. Furthermore, the association and free trade agreements that they signed with the EU and the EFTA, plus the CEFTA – covering around 70 per cent of their foreign trade turnover – will determine their foreign trade relations to a higher extent than the GATT. It can happen that in some trade matters the authorities of the CEECs consider their EU obligations prior to their GATT commitments, that is the EU acquires a significance that surpasses that of the GATT.[10] This phenomenon is unfavourable as the GATT represents a constructive and liberal standard for the CEECs while the EU offers a somewhat less liberal standard.

Moreover, the value of concessions granted in the framework of these international agreements will lessen and the CEECs can nonetheless suffer market losses because barriers to third countries in general will be reduced.

Furthermore, one cannot exclude the possibility that those actors of the world economy (like the EU) which would lose their international competitiveness – due to opening up their markets, lowering the tariffs, cutting domestic farm support and export subsidies – will try to compensate themselves on the markets of the CEECs, and crowd them out of third countries, while they will make efforts to exclude the newly emerging competitors from their own market.

MAIN FRAMEWORKS OF EUROPEAN INTEGRATION

Traditionally, CEECs had been strongly relying on European trading partners. Of their total trade 80 to 90 per cent was carried out with European countries. Nevertheless, within this European framework, a drastic reorientation of their institutionalised trade contacts took place. The collapsed CMEA, disrupting Soviet Union and illiquid successor states of the USSR, once the main trading partners, were replaced by association agreements with the EU. In parallel, trade from Eastern to Western markets has shifted rapidly in the last five years. In the Czech Republic, Hungary and Poland the share of trade with the OECD grew from 25 to 40 per cent in 1989 to 70 to 80 per cent in 1994. Exports to the EU reached 60 per cent of total exports in Poland, 51 per cent in Hungary, 46 per cent in the Czech Republic and 30 per cent in Slovakia.[11] The corresponding import figures are somewhat lower, but the key position of the EU (and within it, that of Germany) in the foreign trade of the transforming economies is evident.

In 1989, the general view regarding likely developments in the foreign trade of the transforming countries started from three, at least partly wrong conclusions. It was emphasised that:

- No rapid geographic reorientation from the East to the West is likely due to the fundamental links established within the CMEA and mainly with the Soviet Union.
- Most products sold on Eastern markets cannot be sold in Western Europe, and the transforming countries will require a long period to become competitive in EU and EFTA markets.
- The only exception to this rule are sensitive products (steel, textile-clothing and agriculture) which enjoy limited access to Western markets. While policy-makers in Brussels used this assessment as an argument against more liberal trade regimes *vis-à-vis* the transforming economies, other experts, including most of those in Central and Eastern Europe, emphasised the need for market opening just in these sectors, as a major factor of rapid export growth.

The first years of institutionalised contacts with the EU only partially support the above expectations:

- Trade reorientation was dramatic, even if a number of factors other than better market access to the EU had an impact on this shift. It has to be noted that the EU's main positive impact on Central and Eastern European exports was generated by the GSP treatment, and only to a much smaller extent by the AA.

- Although starting from an extremely low share, particularly the Visegrád countries could substantially improve their market position in almost all non-sensitive product groups. In five years, the·Visegrád group's share in total extra-EU imports rose from 2 to 4 per cent. This growth was almost entirely generated by industrial products (in SITC 6+8, mainly clothing, footwear, steel and metal manufactures, the share rose from 2.8 to 5.6 per cent; in SITC 7, mainly specialised machinery, electrotechnical goods and transport equipment, from 0.9 to 2.5 per cent). Their share in the agricultural market declined. Between 1989 and 1993, the EU's total machinery imports from non-EU countries grew by 19 per cent, while from the Visegrád countries they trebled. In 1989, 39 per cent of Central European exports consisted of different manufactured goods (SITC 6+8), 18 per cent of agricultural products (SITC 0+1) and only 12.9 per cent of machinery. By 1993, with a share of 22 per cent, machinery became the second most important product group after other manufactured products (51 per cent), and almost two-and-a-half times higher value than agricultural exports to the EU.

  In international comparison, only China was able to increase its market share in the EU more dynamically than the Visegrád countries. While in 1989 Canada, Brazil, Taiwan or the ACP group exported more to the EU than the Visegrád group, in 1993 the latter's exports were substantially higher than those of their competitors. In 1989, Korea and Taiwan together exported 76 per cent more to the EU than the Visegrád group, in 1993 the exports of both groups were on the same level.

- Sensitive products, except for clothing, did not play the role of export engine, and could not achieve trade surplus. Nevertheless, there were substantial differences among the exporting countries (steel from Czechoslovakia). Agriculture deserves special attention. Here, due to various factors, the Central European market share could not be increased.

It has to be stressed that differences in the export pattern of the individual Visegrád countries are becoming manifest. It would be another mistake to consider these countries as exporters of the same or similar goods. In the last years, a rather clear specialisation pattern has been emerging. While Czechoslovak exports, fuelled by huge devaluation, grew across the board, with a rather high share of energy and material intensive products, Hungarian exports clearly concentrated on higher value-added goods (UNECE 1994). Of Hungary's export growth from 1989 to 1993 to Germany, 40 per cent is covered by machinery products, in comparison with 30 per cent for Czechoslovakia and less than 20 per cent for Poland. Regarding exports to

Austria in the same period, 76 per cent of the Hungarian export growth is due to machinery products, as compared with 49 per cent for Poland and less than 25 per cent for Czechoslovakia.

Trade with former CMEA members was reduced to critically low levels, with particularly adverse impacts on higher value-added industrial consumer goods and machinery. Therefore, rapidly declining shares of intra-regional trade were accompanied by a 'naturalisation' of the still remaining trade flows (growing share of raw materials and semi-manufactured products). The share of the successor states of the Soviet Union, once the leading trading partner, decreased from above 30 to 50 per cent to less than 10 per cent in several cases. It is interesting to note that Hungary was the only country in the exports and imports of which the successor states of the Soviet Union could maintain a relatively high share of above 10 per cent in exports and 15 per cent in imports. The latter is due to the high level of energy dependence; the former can be attributed to the microeconomic (firm level) trade relations established well before the collapse of the CMEA.

Trade with Eastern Germany, once the second largest CMEA partner, was almost completely eliminated after the reunification of Germany. Also trade relations among the small CEECs, mainly among the Central European economies, have suffered substantially. It is characteristic that discussions about renewed institutionalised contacts among the Central European trans-forming economies fundamentally started because of external factors. Two of them are related to the EU. First, from 1990, indirect but evident political pressure has been exerted by Brussels on the to-be-associated countries in order to strengthen their (sub)regional contacts, and not only to look at Western Europe. Rightly or wrongly, this attempt was interpreted in all coun-tries as an instrument to slow down the dynamic approach to the West and reorient part of the Central European export capacities towards this region instead of the EU markets. Second, after the signing of the AA, the threat of further trade diversion from Central Europe to the EU became manifest.

With the purpose of avoiding this threat and trying to treat Central European exports and imports on equal footing with those to and from the EU, a free trade agreement had to be signed. The initial stage of imple-mentation of this agreement fell into a stage where first adverse consequences of the overhasty trade liberalisation became manifest and also trade with the EU started to reveal unexpected problems (protectionist measures almost immediately after the signing of the Association Agreement in the agricultural and steel sectors). Under these conditions, it was very difficult to negotiate on further mutual concessions. In addition, the similar development level, similar problems of transformation and similar production patterns have further hindered a major breakthrough.

Provided with the political will, it would have been easier first to agree on the liberalisation of regional trade, accounting for about 5 per cent of the Visegrád countries' total trade, and, in a subsequent round, to negotiate with

Brussels on the Association Agreements. As the other sequencing was chosen, it is understandable why each Visegrád country was ready to make much larger concessions to the economically much stronger (dominant) EU which accounts for about half of its total trade, than to agree on the liberalisation of 5 per cent of trade among non-dominant partners.

The original CEFTA document, although following the pattern of the trade section of the AA, opted for a more limited scope of immediate liberalisation. Most products were either put on the 'normal' or on the 'sensitive' list, and very modest concessions have been made in agricultural trade. Even so, various unilateral trade measures have been applied by all member countries (quotas, import surcharges, higher tariffs, etc.). Also the separation of Czechoslovakia has produced uncertainties and trade barriers, although, statistically, it has resulted in a visible increase of intra-regional trade.

In the spring of 1994, once again, not without external influence, the member countries could agree on the acceleration of the tariff dismantling process, resulting in free trade for most industrial goods by 1998. In addition, on a bilateral level, Hungary and Poland agreed on substantial liberalisation of their agricultural trade (while agricultural trade liberalisation follows the original track with regard to the Czech and Slovak Republics).

It has to be stressed that, even if intra-regional trade would keep on developing dynamically, there is no reason for accepting the rather widespread EU argument that more intense regional trade should precede integration into the EU, and, even less, that this factor should be considered as an important element of 'EU maturity' of the associated countries.

First, considering the qualitative difference of the CEFTA countries' trade with the EU and among themselves, the latter cannot become an engine of growth and export-oriented development.

Second, global, and partly also EU, experience indicates that the sequencing should be not from (sub)regional to European (global) integration, but in the inverse direction. (See the experience of the export-oriented development of Far Eastern economies or Spanish–Portuguese trade relations before membership.) This obviously does not mean that the Central and Eastern European countries should not strive for more and a higher level of economic cooperation until they may become members of the EU. However, they should not become prisoners of an illusion.

Third, more intra-regional trade is not a precondition for membership but a consequence of membership, which can already be predicted with rather high certainty. It is higher growth based on EU membership and changing output and export patterns generated by integration into the EU production (subcontracting) network which will create higher domestic demand and an increasing scale of production complementarities among CEFTA countries. On these two pillars, intra-CEFTA trade is likely to grow well above average after accession to the EU.

The next years, however, raise other trade policy priorities. It goes without saying that the success of transformation badly needs export-oriented strategies which are affected by external and internal developments.

On the external side, relations with the EU bear the utmost importance. Unfortunately, the Association Agreements have several shortcomings. While together with other factors they have supported spectacular trade reorientation, they have proved unable to act as an efficient anti-recessionary instrument during the economic decline in Western Europe or to be in a position to support sustainable export-led growth and economic modernisation in CEECs. On the contrary, several well-founded concerns can be formulated.

First, asymmetrical trade liberalisation did not eliminate historical reversed 'development asymmetries'. On the contrary, in the last years, more important asymmetries have been working in favour of the EU. These asymmetries are likely to be growing in the coming period, as the CEECs have to liberalise trade more rapidly than the EU.

Second, trade in agriculture has become a key problem for most countries. Barriers to exports have been accompanied by rapidly rising imports of highly subsidised EU products. As a result, at present all transforming economies except Hungary have deficits in their agricultural trade with the EU. Although the CEECs have clear comparative advantage in agricultural trade, they are unable to win a subsidisation competition.

Third, and partly originating from agricultural trade, the CEECs' trade with the EU indicates an increasing and preoccupying deficit. Only with the CEFTA countries has the EU registered a cumulative trade surplus of more than ECU 7bn between 1989 and 1993. Apart from trade with the Mediterranean region, this was the only EU surplus trade relation. It is obvious that the transformation and modernisation process of the CEECs urgently needs additional external resources. However, substantial trade deficits with the EU, their major 'external modernisation anchor', can only support this process if trade relations are more balanced and based on real comparative advantages, and, in addition, non-trade financial flows more than compensate for this outflow of hard currency. Currently, there is no EU strategy on how to finance the unavoidable and emerging medium-term 'modernisation gap' in trade relations with the CEECs.

Turning to domestic policy issues, it is an open question to what extent the transforming economies are prepared for the import liberalisation as stipulated in the AA. All of them still struggle with serious transformation problems, the competitiveness of the domestic producers is at least uneven, and high imports have already caused serious trade (and current account) imbalances. In addition, in all countries a growing pressure is developing on governments to curb imports and limit import competition. Various main sources of this pressure can be identified. First, there are domestic producers who either fear growing competition due to scheduled import liberalisation, or, mainly for financial (liquidity) problems, cannot keep pace with much stronger foreign

169

competitors. Second, to an increasing extent, foreign companies (both fully foreign owned and joint ventures) try to limit competition in order to build up (quasi-)monopolistic positions on generally small domestic markets. Third, economic policy-makers may also tend to accept arguments for import restrictions, as trade deficit widens and the inflow of external resources is not in a position to cover the trade (and current account) deficit.

In this context, the serious consequences of an overhasty trade liberalisation are becoming manifest. Obviously, the raising of tariffs and/or reintroduction of quotas would not only violate the spirit of the AA, but would seriously question the EU maturity of any transforming economy.[12] The implementation of temporary safeguard measures for balance-of-payments reasons can be considered. However, it might have adverse effects on the international financial standing of the given transforming economy. Unfortunately, in any country an efficient mechanism of secondary protection could be established after 1989. Thus, the exchange rate policy seems to remain the last but a very delicate resort. First, stabilisation (anti-inflationary) priorities are likely to clash with a higher level of protection for domestic production. Second, and not less importantly, devaluations would be necessary not in order to increase exports but in order to decrease imports.

However, at present, there is a large gap between higher consumer price and lower producer price inflation. Devaluation as an export incentive should be adjusted to the difference in domestic and international producer price inflation rates. This, however, would substantially fall short of the difference between domestic and international consumer price inflation rates. Therefore, small devaluations are unlikely to protect the domestic market, while large devaluations, in open economies, have strong inflationary pressures.

There is a general understanding that prospects for free trade in the transforming economies are fundamentally influenced by the success of an investment-led and export-oriented growth, which requires domestic policy measures and international support.

In the domestic context, savings have to be generated and used for investment purposes. Also the overdue restructuring of the budget has to set free resources for investments.[13] After years of passive (if any) trade policy, an active, export-supporting strategy, making use of all devices allowed by valid international treaties (mainly the GATT agreement and the AA) has to be implemented.

In the international context, free market access, clear timetable of EU membership and at least medium-term resources to finance the modernisation process are needed. It has to be recognised that the trade liberalisation process and its ultimate goal, free trade, can only be sustained if, in the next years, the transforming economies can achieve substantial economic growth fuelled by exports. The latter, however, are crucially dependent on new investments. Unfortunately, the present production and export capacities are hardly sufficient to support a sustainable export-led growth. The collapse of the CMEA, the significant decline of domestic demand, high and partially avoidable costs of transformation, as well as the untimely and overhasty import liberalisation have substantially reduced the available and competitive production and export capacities in the transforming economies.

Given their relatively high level of openness, there are modest gains in further opening exclusively. The share of exports and imports in the GDP of Hungary, the Czech Republic and Slovakia is about 25 per cent,[14] which is not very far from the level of some smaller Western European economies. In turn, there is a wide gap in the comparison of per capita export and import figures. Hungarian, Czech and Slovak figures of about US$1,000 to US$1,400 are one-fourth of the EU average and one-sixth of the old EFTA average. The conclusion is straightforward: there is enormous room for intensifying foreign trade relations, but mainly as a result of high rates of export growth.

NOTES

1 Countries of the former Soviet Union are not included. This chapter concentrates on the experience and prospects of CEFTA countries. The terms Visegrád group or Central Europe are alternatively used, and mean the Czech Republic, Hungary, Poland and Slovakia.

2 Poland joined the GATT in 1966, Hungary in 1973 and Romania in 1976 on the basis of a special status. To become full members, they need to renegotiate the GATT protocol and comply with the Uruguay Round commitments. The Czech Republic and Slovakia are regular members because Czechoslovakia, one of the GATT founders in 1947, formally kept its membership during the Communist era. When both countries rejoined in 1992 they were given *carte blanche*, and did not need to renegotiate any protocols.

   Other transition economies have observer status (Azerbaijan, Estonia, Lithuania, Kazakhstan, Kyrgyzstan and Turkmenistan), or as observers are already negotiating to join the GATT (Albania, Armenia, Belarus, Bulgaria, Croatia, Latvia, Moldova, Russia and Ukraine). A few countries have no ties yet (Georgia, Tajigistan and Uzbekistan).

3 On the estimates of computable general equilibrium models of the impact of the Uruguay Round agreement on income and trade see Schott (1994: 17).

4 The pre-Uruguay Round trade-weighted average tariff rate for industrial goods equalled 6.3 per cent in the case of the developed countries, 15.3 per cent for the developing countries and 8.6 per cent for economies in transition (Schott, 1994: 61).

5 If a 100 per cent tariff rate is increased to 200 per cent, and the concession on tariff reduction remains the same (let us say 60 per cent), then the level of market protection will increase from 40 per cent to 80 per cent.

6 In the case of Hungary, during the base period of 1986–8 the domestic farm support and the market price support taken together equalled HUF42.3 billion, while in 1992 it amounted to HUF5.0 billion, in 1993 HUF18.4 billion and in 1994 HUF37.1 billion. In 1995 the budget support and the market price support taken together are projected to equal HUF54.3 billion. Out of this sum HUF43.1 billion is supposed to be decreased to HUF40.9 billion in 1995 according to the GATT obligation.

7 In three out of the six countries of Central and Eastern Europe (Hungary, Poland and Slovakia) the agricultural subsidies – compared both to the budget expenditures and the GDP – decreased by between one-half and two-thirds during the period of 1990–3. In the case of the Czech Republic the level of agricultural subsidies declined from 40 per cent in 1989, to 29 per cent in 1990, to 13.5 per cent in 1991 and to 10 per cent in 1992. (See Table 9.1.)
8 In Hungary, during the base period of 1986–90 the value of agricultural export subsidies equalled HUF43.9 billion, while in 1992 and 1993 it amounted to HUF26 billion, in 1994 HUF23 billion, and in 1995 it is expected to increase to HUF35 billion. Consequently the agricultural export subsidy cut obligation is over-fulfilled in Hungary; moreover there is a chance for further increase. The same is true for the share of subsidised exports, which has decreased from 40 per cent in the base period of 1986–90 to 29 per cent in 1991 and 1992, and to 17 per cent in 1993 (Mészáros and Orbánné 1994).
9 According to certain estimates 80 per cent of the welfare effect of the GATT Agreement will be enjoyed by the OECD countries.
10 A good example for this is provided by Hungary which has introduced the GATT Agreement since 1 January 1995, with the exception of foreign trade relations with the EU, where GATT regulations are expected to be introduced from 1 July 1995.
11 The falling but still high share of bilateral trade between the Czech and Slovak Republic is responsible for the relatively lower share of the EU in their exports.
12 According to experience, membership in the EU requires (almost) full adjustment in two key areas: trade policy and the *acquis communautaire*.
13 In economic policy discussions, two basic views can be identified. One is emphasising the reduction of budget deficit at any price, while the other can live with budget deficit, if it finances investment activities and not consumption.
14 This is somewhat lower than before 1989. However, one has to consider that previously higher figures were partly due to distorted exchange rates and, of course, to the existence of the CMEA. A relevant reduction of the exports/GDP ratio can be observed in the case of Poland only (from 23 per cent in 1990 to 13.7 per cent in 1993).

BIBLIOGRAPHY

Anderson, K. (1991) *Global Effects of Liberalising Trade in Farm Products*, New York: Harvester Wheatsheaf for the Trade Policy Research Centre, London.
Karp, L. and Stefanou, S. (1993) 'Domestic and Trade Policy for Central and East European Countries', Centre for Economic Policy Research, Discussion Paper No. 814.
Kiss, J. (1995) *Fordulóponton a világkereskedelem (A GATT Uruguay-i Fordulójának hatása)* [The world trade at a turning point. The impact of the GATT Uruguay Round], in Hungarian.
Madden, P. and Madeley, J. (1993) *Winners and Losers: The Impact of the GATT Uruguay Round on Developing Countries*, Christian Aid.
Mészáros, S. and Orbánné, N.M. (1993) 'Importszabályozás és piacvédelem az agrárágazatban' [Import regulation and market protection in the Hungarian agriculture], *Európa Fórum*, July, No. 2: 67–80, in Hungarian.
—— (1994) 'A GATT-egyezmény következményei a magyar agrártámogatási rendszere' [Consequences of the GATT agreement for the Hungarian agricultural support system], *Gazdálkodás*, No. 6: 1–17, in Hungarian.
Nguyen, T., Perroni, C. and Wigle, R. (1991) 'The Value of the Uruguay Round Success', *The World Economy*, Vol. 14: 359–74.

—— (1993) 'An Evaluation of the Draft Final Act', *Economic Journal*, Vol. 103.

Roberts, I., Kottegé, J. and Graeme, T. (1993) 'Eastern Europe, The Former Soviet Union and World Agricultural Markets', *ABARE Research Report*, 93.18, Canberra.

Schott, J. J. (1994) *The Uruguay Round. An Assessment*, Washington, DC: Institute for International Economics.

Somai, M. (1994) 'A GATT-egyezmény és az EU agrárpolitikája (magyar tanulságokkal)' [The GATT agreement and the agricultural policy of the EU – lessons for Hungary], manuscript, in Hungarian.

Sorsa, P. (1994) 'The Uruguay Round and the Transition Economies: the Attractiveness of GATTing', *Transition*, February–March: 10–12.

Tracy, Michael (ed.) (1994) *East–West European Agricultural Trade: The Impact of the Association Agreements*, Brussels: Agricultural Policy Studies (APS).

UNECE (United Nations Economic Commission for Europe) (1994) *Economic Bulletin for Europe*, Vol. 46, New York and Geneva: United Nations.

10

THE FUTURE REPRESENTATION OF THE SOUTH IN THE INTERNATIONAL SYSTEM

Murray Gibbs

THE SEARCH FOR A DEVELOPMENT-ORIENTED TRADING SYSTEM

Shifting perspectives

Over the last three decades, the international trade debate has been strongly influenced by the efforts of developing countries to reform the trading system so as to make it more responsive to their needs and aspirations. Those efforts reflected their perception that they had inherited a system in the design of which they had played little or no part, and which was intrinsically biased against their interests. The major policy thrust, embodied in the establishment of UNCTAD and the Group of 77, was the realisation of the need for and the possibility of achieving reform of the system through coordinated negotiating initiatives and solidarity.

In the trade field it was envisaged that such corrective action should take the form of initiatives by developed countries to grant generalised preferential, non-reciprocal and non-discriminatory treatment to developing countries in all areas of international economic cooperation where it might be feasible. The principle of non-reciprocity was incorporated into GATT (in Part IV) in the early 1960s but the first concrete achievement in this regard was the generalised system of preferences (GSP), negotiated in UNCTAD and implemented in 1971. The Tokyo Declaration of 1973 recognised the principles of differential and more favourable treatment in favour of developing countries, and provisions to this effect were incorporated in several of the instruments emerging from the Tokyo Round, including the 'Enabling Clause' which legitimised such deviations from MFN treatment in the GATT context. The Punta del Este Declaration reaffirmed the principle of differential and more favourable treatment in respect of the Uruguay Round. Other resolutions, such as the Charter of Economic Rights and Duties of States dealt with a wider range of issues, particularly investment.

However, during the early 1980s, it became increasingly evident to developing countries that a parallel process was under way through which, rather than receiving more favourable treatment, they were encountering increasing discrimination against their trade, evidenced in such measures as:

- voluntary export restraints and other 'grey area' measures directed against their most competitive exports;
- bilateral pressures by major importing countries aimed at obtaining trade concessions through the threat of trade sanctions rather than the offer of reciprocal benefits;
- the extension of free-trade agreements and customs unions among developed countries;
- higher MFN tariffs on products of export interest to developing countries compared to those of interest to developed countries after seven rounds of multilateral trade negotiations;
- the proliferation of restraints on textiles and clothing exports under the Multifibre Arrangement;
- the diminishing effectiveness of any GATT disciplines governing trade in agricultural products.

In addition, the GSP was beginning to be applied in a conditional and discriminatory fashion, frequently being used by some preference-giving countries as a means of leverage to influence the policies of the beneficiary countries, including in areas outside trade. The Tokyo Round codes, with their limited membership, appeared to represent a major step towards the 'GATT plus' approach, advocated in developed country circles in the early 1970s, according to which those countries would create an inner system of rights and obligations encompassing areas of mutual interest among themselves. These approaches not only tended to introduce fragmentation into the system of multilateral rights and obligations but also led to active consideration of the resurrection of the so-called 'conditional' MFN clause, which had constituted a major impediment to past efforts to construct a viable multilateral trading system. In addition, as the system evolved, differential and more favourable treatment came to be reflected in greater degrees of flexibility for developing countries in the application of trade measures, rather than any binding commitments by developed countries in favour of their exports.

As a consequence, the thrust of the developing countries' initiatives shifted in that, while seeking to preserve the preferential commitments made in their favour, they began to concentrate on defending the integrity of the unconditional MFN clause, obtaining MFN tariff reductions, and strengthening the disciplines of GATT (particularly in the product sectors mentioned above) so as to prevent the restriction and harassment of their trade. Particular emphasis was laid on the dispute settlement mechanism, as a means of defence against bilateral pressures from their major trading partners. At UNCTAD

VI (Belgrade 1983), all countries recognised the need to strengthen the international trading system based on the MFN principle.[1]

Meanwhile, the acceptance by many developing countries of IMF structural adjustment programmes led to their adoption of an export-oriented development model and unilateral trade liberalisation through the elimination of quantitative import restrictions and reduction of tariffs. This stimulated an enhanced interest by developing countries in export markets. The Uruguay Round was consequently viewed as a means of obtaining improved and more secure access for their exports, consolidating the liberalisation undertaken unilaterally and demanding 'negotiating credit' from the countries that were benefiting from this unilateral liberalisation. The Uruguay Round (unlike the Tokyo Round) was open only to GATT contracting parties or to countries that committed themselves to negotiate accession to GATT during the Round; a large number of developing countries followed this course of action.[2]

The disciplines of the Multilateral Trade Agreement

As a result of the intensification and extension of multilateral commitments[3] in the Uruguay Round, all countries will have less flexibility in their use of both trade and domestic policy instruments. However, in relative terms, this acceptance of higher levels of obligations has been much more dramatic for developing countries. The outcome of the tariff negotiations, including by those developing countries which had been contracting parties for many decades, has been an extensive binding of tariffs, up to 100 per cent by many developing countries, which has served to consolidate the tariff reductions undertaken by developing countries as part of their autonomous trade liberalisation measures under their economic reform programmes and constitute the 'entry fee' paid by those countries that acceded to the GATT during the Uruguay Round. Furthermore, the conversion of the revised Tokyo Round codes (which had previously been accepted by a limited number of developing countries) into Multilateral Trade Agreements has resulted in a major increase in the level of multilateral obligations for most developing countries. While the balance-of-payments provisions of GATT have not been substantially modified by the Understanding on Article XVIII, many developing countries had, in any case, disinvoked Article XVIII:B during the negotiations.

The extension of multilateral disciplines into areas traditionally viewed as pertaining to domestic policy, such as subsidies, investment measures, intellectual property rights, and access to domestic telecommunication networks has also limited developing countries' options with respect to policy measures aimed at increasing the competitiveness of their exports or achieving other development goals. In recent decades, a number of developing countries have successfully deployed a wide range of policy measures to strengthen their international competitiveness and export performance, enabling them to 'catch up' with developed countries. The multilateral disciplines emerging from the

Uruguay Round, which reflect the evolution of legislation and trade and economic policy in the developed countries, reduce the scope of available policy options in this regard. On the other hand, some of the key policy areas of interest to developed countries in the areas of agricultural support, research and development and regional development were left virtually untouched. Thus, the disciplines of the Uruguay Round Agreements may deprive late-comers (including countries in transition) of the opportunity of emulating the successful strategies of those countries and cause them to turn to different development strategies, the success of which will depend largely on the more secure and liberal market access achieved in the Uruguay Round, and on continuation of the momentum toward further multilateral liberalisation.

Before the Uruguay Round, differential and more favourable treatment had been embodied mostly in instruments of an autonomous nature, such as the GSP, or in the form of 'best endeavour' clauses, time-bound exceptions for obligations and longer periods for implementing them, flexibility in procedures and access to technical assistance and advice. Such provisions exist in many Agreements. However, in certain Agreements, differential and more favourable treatment has been given a contractual character, particularly in the form of numerical thresholds for undertaking certain commitments.

The least developed countries

In launching the Uruguay Round, the Punta del Este Ministerial Declaration recognised the need for 'positive measures to facilitate the expansion of trading opportunities' for the least developed countries. At Marrakesh, Ministers adopted a Decision on Measures in Favour of Least Developed Countries which, in the main, exhorts members to give prompt effect to the provisions in favour of these countries contained in the various Agreements. These provisions include advance implementation of MFN concessions on tariff and non-tariff measures for products of export interest to the least developed countries (LDCs). Apart from these provisions, participants in the Round gave an undertaking to consider further improving their GSP and other schemes in respect of products of interest to LDCs. In addition, there is a recognition of the weak export base and undiversified nature of their exports and thus a commitment substantially to increase technical assistance in the development, strengthening and diversification of their production and export bases, including those of services. It should be noted that where the various Agreements provide for differential and more favourable treatment for developing countries, the treatment extended to the LDCs is more favourable than for other developing countries, generally according them longer or indefinite periods for compliance with and implementation of obligations. Other than the above provision, the Uruguay Round results did not, however, include anything that could be considered as a 'positive measure' to facilitate the expansion of trading opportunities of least developed countries.

177

The LDCs and net food-importing countries were successful in negotiating a Ministerial Decision intended primarily as a political message to mobilise the support of governments, through technical and financial assistance for food aid, as well as of the multilateral financial institutions, to take action to mitigate the impact of the higher food prices that were expected to result from the new multilateral disciplines on agricultural export subsidies.

Developing country solidarity

During the Uruguay Round, effective joint action by developing countries took the form of common proposals on specific issues, supported by groups of like-minded developing countries, often widely dispersed geographically. The impact of these joint initiatives, which in most cases were not confined to seeking the inclusion of provisions on differential and more favourable treatment, can be witnessed in many provisions of the Agreements. At the beginning of the Round, it appeared that the traditional developing country coordination mechanism might well be abandoned in favour of mixed groups of like-minded developed and developing countries, such as the Cairns group of agricultural exporters. However, such alliances did not stand up well under pressure, and as the negotiations progressed on some crucial issues developing countries were able to formulate and pursue proposals that were eventually incorporated into the final results. While the formal Group of 77 mechanism could not be effectively applied in cases where there was a high degree of technical complexity and where the interests of different groups of developing countries clearly conflicted, there was a strong tendency for ad hoc groups of developing countries to meet to pursue specific common goals. Areas of particular concentration by developing countries in this respect included trade in services (movement of persons, telecommunications, the structure of GATS), TRIMs, TRIPs and textiles and clothing (where the International Textiles and Clothing Bureau played a major role) and the impact of the Round on net food-importing countries.[4] In addition, the Informal Group of Developing Countries met throughout the Round and the developing countries spoke with a common voice on key issues at crucial points.

THE CHALLENGES OF THE POST-URUGUAY ROUND SYSTEM

The WTO has thus resulted in important concessions by developing countries to reduce tariffs, eliminate non-tariff measures and has reduced their flexibility with respect to a range of other policy measures (notably in the areas of subsidies, investment measures, intellectual property protection and services). In return, they received improved access to markets, differential treatment of a contractual and specific character and, above all, stricter multilateral disciplines that were to provide more secure access to markets and eliminate bilateral pressures and unilateral actions by the major trading countries.

The challenges facing the developing countries in the post-Uruguay Round trading system are twofold:

1 They must protect the gains they have achieved and ensure that their rights are respected in practice.
2 They must strive to regain the initiative in the establishment of the future trade agenda.

Defending acquired rights

The immediate challenge facing developing countries will be to ensure that the Uruguay Round commitments are fully respected. This will involve their acquiring the ability effectively to defend their interests both in the context of the Committees established to administer the individual multilateral agreements and to make effective use of the integrated dispute settlement system. The WTO 'Understanding' on dispute settlement contains a number of improvements over the previous system, the most important being that no country, no matter how large, can block the establishment of a panel or impede its proceedings. There are also a number of more technical details, many of which will work in favour of developing countries, for example, that the dispute settlement panels can take the initiative of obtaining relevant information, thus compensating to a certain extent the weaker position of developing countries in obtaining and analysing information relevant to the case. However, the 'bottom line' remains the same as in GATT, that the ultimate recourse of an offended party, even though found to be 'in the right' under the rules, is to implement 'compensatory withdrawals of concessions' (i.e. retaliate). It is hoped, however, that an 'ambience' of greater moral suasion will develop so that even the largest trading powers will feel obliged to conform to the decisions of the dispute settlement mechanism.

The WTO Understanding also commits members not to make a determination to the effect that a violation of obligations has occurred except through recourse to the mechanism. This should protect developing countries against intimidation by threat of unilateral action by developed countries (such as Section 301 action by the United States). However, resistance to bilateral pressures will require confidence in the system and in the government's ability effectively to defend itself in the dispute settlement mechanism. It has been frequently stated that as a result of their active participation in the Uruguay Round and the dramatic increase in their multilateral trade obligations, the developing countries have become 'major stockholders' in the WTO system.[5] As such they will have to ensure that they are confident in their ability to make the system work for them.

The increased complexity and detail of the WTO multilateral agreements has increased the need for new skills in developing countries' governments, to assure a full understanding of the rights and obligations contained in the agreements and in the implementing legislation of trading partners. It is likely that many developing countries will find themselves targets of dispute settlement action in the first years of the WTO, as the major developed countries attempt to set the limits of these obligations by establishing precedents. It is also possible that these countries will make use of this mechanism to exert pressure to place new items on the future negotiating agenda.

Administratively and technically, many developing countries are poorly equipped effectively to assert their rights in the WTO framework, which calls into question their ability to derive concrete benefits from the strengthened multilateral disciplines. There is a need not only for training and technical assistance in the traditional sense, but for the creation of a new 'milieu' of persons in both the public and private sectors, conversant with the multiple facets of multilateral and regional trade agreements, as well as domestic trade laws and those of major trading partners.

Setting the future agenda

The developing countries' ability to 'hold their own' in the WTO system will be tested in the drawing up of the future negotiating agenda. Article III:2 of the Agreement Establishing the World Trade Organization states that 'the WTO may also provide a forum for further negotiations among its Members concerning their multilateral trade negotiations, and a framework for the implementation of the results of such negotiations, as may be decided by the Ministerial Conference'. This provision has been seen as permitting an eventual further extension of multilateral trade rights and obligations into new areas, in the manner in which this was accomplished during the Uruguay Round.

The future negotiating agenda has, to a large extent, been set out in the Multilateral Trade Agreements themselves. Provisions have been included in the various agreements for decisions to be taken related to future negotiations at specific times in the future, such as the continuation of the reform process in agriculture and a new round of negotiations on trade in services. Parallel negotiations on investment policy and competition policy are foreseen in the context of the TRIMs Agreement, as are negotiations with respect to particular aspects of Anti-dumping, Subsidies, Rules of Origin, State Trading Enterprises, etc.[6]

However, in the final stages of the Uruguay Round, initiatives were taken by major trading countries to establish, as part of the final package, a new agenda for the WTO. Such initiatives were successful in obtaining agreement to deal with the issue of trade and environment; a Ministerial Decision established a Committee on Trade and Environment which is to make recommendations as to the 'need for rules to enhance positive interaction between trade and environmental measures'. The issue of labour rights was raised in the period between the conclusion of the negotiations in December 1993 and the adoption of the results in April 1994, primarily by the United States and France. This initiative did not obtain the support of all developed countries and was firmly opposed by most developing countries. The compromise solution was to include in the 'concluding remarks' of the Chairman of the Ministerial Meeting of the Trade Negotiations Committee at Marrakesh, a list of all the issues which had been suggested for future consideration in the course of the Ministerial Meeting. The key statement was to the effect that:

> Ministers representing a number of delegations stressed the importance they attached to their requests for an examination of the relationship between the trading system and internationally recognised labour standards; between immigration policies and international trade; trade and competition policy, including rules on export financing and restrictive business practices; trade and investment; regionalism; the interaction between trade policies and policies relating to financial and monetary matters, including debt, and commodity markets; international trade and company law; the establishment of a mechanism to compensate for the erosion of preferences; the link between trade, development, political stability and the alleviation of poverty; and unilateral or extraterritorial trade measures.[7]

The WTO Preparatory Committee did not discuss these issues and forwarded this matter to the General Council of the WTO for further consideration and action as appropriate.[8] There is obviously the concern that any agreement to discuss these items in the WTO context would represent an irreversible step toward their inclusion in the overall package of issues for future negotiation.

The Marrakesh Chairman's Concluding Remarks represent the only comprehensive indication of what governments consider to be 'new and emerging issues' expressed at the Ministerial level. More closer examination of these issues reveals considerable common features, in that they would seem to derive from perceptions that the future trade agenda should address the interrelated issues of (a) policy harmonisation; (b) coherence among global policy objectives; and (c) ensuring that weaker countries and populations are not marginalised by the process of trade liberalisation and globalisation.

Previous experience with trade liberalisation, especially in the context of regional economic integration arrangements has shown that as frontier trade barriers are removed and progressively tighter disciplines imposed on the use of trade policy measures, remaining differences in policies, even those addressed to primarily domestic issues, become to be perceived as distortions to the conditions of free competition that the liberalisation and disciplines were intended to ensure. Differences in national policies or in the degree of application of international norms are perceived to create unfair competitive opportunities in trade or in attracting investment, or to frustrate multilateral disciplines.

The increasing globalisation of production and marketing exacerbates concerns that differences in national policies can distort the flow of trade and investment, by influencing decisions of transnational corporations as to the location of production tasks (i.e. different parts of the production process to be performed by subsidiaries or subcontractors in different countries), which is determined by a host of factors such as labour costs, availability of expertise and skills, environmental regulations, cost of energy and proximity to markets. Many of these factors are influenced by specific domestic policies. They are also affected by problems of access to information networks and distribution channels. The effective integration of the world economy is creating the same challenges that have been faced in the regional context, particularly in Europe. These call for policy measures to ensure that while the overall process is encouraged, its benefits are distributed in an equitable fashion.

Policy harmonisation

These factors combine to create political pressures for a harmonisation of policy measures among countries and for the continuous extension of multilateral trade disciplines into new areas, in pursuit of what has been termed the 'level playing field'. Such pressures can have as their objective the establishment of stricter and wider ranging multilateral disciplines over those actions by governments which could adversely affect the ability of firms to execute global strategies for competing on the world market.[9] Pressures for such 'policy harmonisation' also arise from concerns that globalisation and liberalisation can lead to the erosion of social welfare programmes, resulting from the increased ability of private enterprises to seek to locate in those jurisdictions where they find the regulatory and fiscal structure less constraining. Trade liberalisation and more stringent multilateral disciplines are viewed as being in conflict with domestic economic and social policy objectives and impinge on the ability of governments to pursue goals such as poverty alleviation and to channel investment into priority sectors. Policy harmonisation is seen as necessary to prevent a 'race to the bottom' in which governments will lower or maintain sub-optimal standards in order to attract or retain investment.[10] There is the increasing perception that the process of globalisation tends to exacerbate inequalities both as between regions, countries and groups within countries, and that corrective action is necessary.[11]

The proponents of multilateral rules to govern foreign investment now view it as a policy harmonisation issue to establish common 'rules of the game' to permit TNCs to carry out global production and marketing strategies, and thus to maximise efficiency without these being distorted by special conditions imposed by governments. While it has proved possible to negotiate general principles and guidelines to govern foreign investment at the regional and sub-regional levels, the negotiation of multilateral disciplines to govern foreign direct investment has been complicated by a number of factors, particularly in finding common ground between the interests of the few 'home' countries and the many 'host', mainly developing countries, as well as between the many 'interested' countries, which compete to attract foreign investment and few 'interesting' countries which are able to impose conditions on the foreign investors for the 'right' of investing in their countries. As a result of the opposition from developing countries to moves to broaden the mandate of the TRIMs negotiations, the WTO TRIMs Agreement does not deal with investment policy other than specifically to prohibit (permitting a phase-out period for developing and least developed countries) investment measures that result in conflict with GATT obligations. The fact that many of the conditions imposed on foreign investors are designed to preempt resort to restrictive business practices, and that excessive investment incentives could be seen as distorting competition has led to provisions in the TRIMs Agreement for possible parallel negotiations on competition and investment policy in 1999.

On the other hand, GATS establishes a framework for negotiating commitments to liberalise foreign direct investment in the services sector, through granting national treatment or 'rights' of establishment on a sectoral or subsectoral basis, but in return for reciprocal commitments in other services sectors, or with respect to other 'modes of supply' or access for trade in goods. This could facilitate future concessions with respect to investment as these could be traded off for reciprocal action in other sectors or modes of delivery of export interest to developing countries, and form part of a broader 'package'.

Policy harmonisation is thus seen both as a means of promoting globalisation and world economic integration as well as a means for mitigating its effects. Domestic political pressures for such policy harmonisation become even more acute when moral considerations are introduced into the discussion so that countries are portrayed as achieving competitive advantages through immoral, irresponsible or unfair behaviour. The pressure for policy harmonisation in the areas of labour rights, environmental protection, and competition policy, can be seen in this context. The proponents for the incorporation of such items within the WTO framework argue that differing policies in these areas can have a distortive effect in international trade and that the links to trade obligations within the integrated dispute settlement mechanism of the WTO are necessary to ensure the effective enforcement of any obligations negotiated. Their model is most likely the approach used in the Uruguay Round TRIPs negotiations to incorporate intellectual property rights within the system of multilateral trade rights and obligations. Developing countries have generally considered that if disciplines with respect to these issues were to be incorporated in multilateral trade agreements, their inability to meet the norms established by the developed countries could open the door to a whole new generation of trade remedies which could be applied with protectionist intent, as well as exposing them to dispute settlement cases and possible trade sanctions. There is the added concern that overloading the trade policy instrument to serve too many diverse objectives, particularly those of a socio-economic or political character that may arise from changes in the size and direction of trade flows, could place severe strains on the multilateral trading system and undermine the efficacy of its primary function of ensuring the respect of the multilateral rules.

Coherence in the international system

Multilateral trade disciplines can also be frustrated by action and policy measures which are not covered by comparable levels of discipline. Most evident are the distortions caused by imbalances in the stringency in multilateral disciplines governing different areas of economic policy. The much more stringent constraints on national trade policies resulting from the disciplines of the Multilateral Agreements negotiated in the Uruguay Round contrast sharply with the virtual absence of discipline over national monetary policies. Developing countries and countries in transition which have opened up their economies to pursue market-oriented policies, are particularly vulnerable to the effects of interest rate and exchange rate instability. Their predicament in this respect is compounded by the failure to deal adequately at the multilateral level with the problems arising from heavy commodity dependence and external debt burdens. The importance of the trade/monetary link had been emphasised in both the Tokyo and Punta del Este Declarations but the only result to emerge from the Uruguay Round was the Ministerial Declaration on the contribution of the WTO to Achieving Greater Coherence in Global Economic Policy-making, which called for cooperation between the WTO and the IMF and World Bank.

The globalisation process is leading to a much freer movement of goods, capital and information, even when not facilitated by multilateral or regional agreements. On the other hand, migratory pressures are leading countries to impose even greater restrictions on the movement of persons across national frontiers. This asymmetry of treatment of the movement of factors of production creates the perception that there is a significant imbalance in the benefits which labour-rich and capital-rich countries derive from the trading system. This has led to the proposals to discuss the trade/immigration link in the future WTO work programme. The GATS agreement was successful in introducing the 'movement of natural persons' as a legitimate subject for trade negotiations, but the continuing negotiations with respect to this 'mode of supply' appear to be headed for rather modest results, not providing much more access than that contained in the GATS schedules. The implied parallelism of the treatment of the movement of labour and capital in the GATS agreement was seen as improving the negotiating position of developing countries in negotiations under its framework. However, there would seem to be initiatives aimed at short-circuiting this balance through negotiation of a Code on Investment which would apply to both goods and services and undermine the bargaining position of developing countries achieved in the GATS. This would seem to call for a counter initiative aimed at a multilateral instrument dealing with the movement of persons both in the goods and services sectors, in recognition that barriers to the movement of persons can indirectly restrict trading opportunities in both goods and services.

The concept of 'greater coherence in global economic policy-making' would of necessity have to extend beyond the WTO/IMF/World Bank cooperation foreseen in the Marrakesh Decision on this item and deal with a much broader range of issues and involve a wider participation of other international organisations. In addition to the immigration issue identified at Marrakesh, other examples of problems of coherence in the broader sense arose in the Uruguay Round. One example was the conflict between the internationally recognised principle that countries should develop and strengthen their national cultures, and the failure to include a 'cultural exception' in the GATS. Furthermore, the approach of the major developed countries to seek to incorporate principles based on national experiences into multilateral trade obligations could also be said to lack coherence as they ignore the historical process of development. In telecommunications, for example, private suppliers were instrumental in providing universal services in developed countries in return for receiving monopoly positions, and only later sought deregulation in order to be able to provide the more profitable value-added services which could be transmitted over the national network. In developing countries, however, universal service is far from being realised; thus pressures for liberalisation and cost-based services, as sought in the negotiations under GATS, could distort this process. The same observations apply to the TRIPs Agreement where many developed countries had abstained from applying patent or copyright protection in certain sectors until as recently as the 1980s.

Marginalisation

Since the latter stages of the Uruguay Round a debate has developed and intensified as to whether any country or group of countries could be said to have emerged as 'net losers' from the negotiations. While it is difficult to dispute the argument that all countries, especially the smaller and weaker ones, will gain from stronger multilateral disciplines, it is also evident that certain countries will incur important adjustment costs. These can include the higher cost of imported foodstuffs and of imported technology. Furthermore, as a result of the erosion of preferential margins, such as those under the Lomé Convention or the GSP, countries will be faced with greater competition in their traditional export markets. Some countries, which are primarily in the groups mentioned above, could be said to have 'lost', if only because the WTO Agreements do not deal with those issues of most crucial interest to them, such as the continuing decline in commodity prices, increased debt burdens, etc.

The preferential schemes were established to provide an additional competitive advantage to developing countries deemed to have a serious disadvantage in entering new markets and competing in international trade. The ability of the majority of the beneficiary countries under GSP and ACP schemes has not improved significantly. Thus, as the exigencies of multilateral tariff liberalisation require that preferential tariff margins be reduced, it would seem logical that other means be explored to compensate for the erosion of preferences, compensation in the sense of providing alternative measures of assistance to enable these countries to confront increased competition in world markets, and to prevent their being marginalised by the globalisation process.

At the national level increased import competition can often exacerbate the situation of those segments of the population already subsisting below the poverty level. In recognition that the benefits of freer trade are unequally distributed among different groups within the population, the governments of developed countries have spent large amounts on 'adjustment assistance' including subsidies and retraining. Most developing country governments do not have the funds for such purposes and an international effort is required in this respect. Special adjustment measures may be required to assist those countries which will face the most difficulty in adjusting to a more competitive situation, and the international community would seem to have a special responsibility to provide a sort of safety net to support those countries which will not be able to develop a competitive capacity in the foreseeable future.

Regionalism

The Multilateral Agreements of the WTO have considerably mitigated the discriminatory aspects of regional arrangements through the reduction and elimination of MFN tariffs and the adoption of disciplines at the multilateral level that exceeded the stringency of those of regional arrangements. However, regional arrangements have included provisions on subjects which were not on the Uruguay Round agenda, such as investment, labour rights and environment. The trade-distorting impact of regional agreements may not arise so much from margins of tariff preferences as from such additional provisions, as well as rules of origin, regional standards and regional information networks.

The Understanding on the Interpretation of Article XXIV of GATT was an attempt to come to grips with the problems created by the interface between regional agreements and the multilateral system, but it did not address the fact that regional agreements contain provisions dealing with a much wider range of policy measures than the 'tariffs or other regulations of commerce' addressed in GATT Article XXIV. Regional agreements in certain cases represent a response to the fact that the economic integration process had advanced to such an extent between the countries concerned that more detailed and extensive disciplines were required to govern their mutual trade and economic relations. Regional agreements have tested different formulations of rules in new areas. GSP schemes are also being used to introduce new links between trade and issues such as environmental protection, labour rights and action against the production of narcotic drugs.[12]

THE FRONTIERS OF THE TRADING SYSTEM

The Uruguay Round intensified and extended multilateral trade disciplines and increased their credibility. However, it is evident that the international trading system will be under continuous pressure to adapt to the forces of globalisation. The pressures for policy harmonisation, for greater coherence in multilateral disciplines and for a 'safety net' to protect the weakest trading partners are a logical result of the globalisation process and will continue to intensify. The international community is thus faced with the question of the extent to which these issues can be dealt with in multilateral trade agreements under the WTO umbrella, that is, to define the 'frontiers' of the multilateral trading system.

The Uruguay Round agenda was established in the early 1980s and responded to the preoccupations at that time. As indicated above, it extended the system of reciprocally negotiated multilateral trade rights and obligations to cover a wider range of policy measures which had not previously been considered as subjects for trade agreements, multilateral or otherwise. It must be admitted that there were pertinent arguments, which become more evident in retrospect, for considering the inclusion of services (i.e. investment, movement of persons, transportation, electronic data flows, etc.) and intellectual property within the trading system, such as the trade impact of policy measures in these areas, the desirability of applying GATT principles such as unconditional MFN treatment, and the greater facility in arriving at agreement when concessions in these areas could be part of an overall package. However, at the time, the addition of these items to the trade agenda could not be said to have been based on global consensus but rather on a process usually referred to as 'arm twisting'. It was made clear to those developing countries which resisted the inclusion of these items, that in the absence of new multilateral disciplines in these areas, the United States, in particular, was prepared to resort to trade restrictive measures in violation of its GATT obligations, to protect its interests. Furthermore, in the case of the TRIPs negotiations, the possibility that the international norms would be modified and incorporated into trade obligations was not foreseen in the Punta del Este Declaration but was introduced into the negotiating process at the Montreal Mid-Term Ministerial Meeting in 1988, and became one of the main factors contributing to the failure of that meeting to reach an overall agreement on all areas of the negotiation.

Regaining the initiative

Over the next few years, presumably by 1999 when the trade negotiating agenda built into the Uruguay Round agreements activates, decisions will have to be taken as to whether and which of the 'new and emerging issues' described above will be dealt with through an extension of the WTO system, that is through the negotiation of new multilateral agreements subject to the common dispute settlement mechanism, and the threat of possible trade sanctions or whether mechanisms other than trade agreements may be more appropriate for addressing the issues which will inevitably arise as the process of global economic integration proceeds and accelerates. The experience both of successes and failures of regional arrangements in integrating economies at different levels of development would seem to be particularly instructive in this respect. The current work of the OECD on these issues will also be of relevance.

The 'new and emerging issues' examined in the preceding paragraphs may represent a series of interrelated aspects of the general problem of the adaptation of the multilateral trading system to globalisation and trade liberalisation. To the extent that world trade and investment continues to increase as a result of trade liberalisation and improved multilateral disciplines it should lead to accelerated growth and development resulting in a greater capacity for developing countries to protect the environment and improve social conditions, and mitigate migratory pressures. In fact, the elimination of quantitative restrictions and reduction of tariff protection diminish the distortion of price signals and encourage economically sound use of human and environmental resources.

However, a serious danger arises from the potential political impact of the short-term adjustment strains which could provoke negative reactions from those elements of the populations of developed countries which consider themselves to be bearing an inordinate burden of the costs of the globalisation process. Globalisation appears to be leading to fundamental changes in the nature of work and in the rate of growth of incomes in industrialised countries and an increase in the inequality of incomes with unskilled labour being particularly penalised. It is also leading to an increase in the cost of government social programmes while simultaneously curbing the government's ability to generate revenues.[13]

If these are manifested in pressures for trade restrictive action they could present a serious threat to the system. The perception that unfair or anti-competitive practices are distorting trade and investment flows will exacerbate the risk that the pressures will find their way into policy decisions. There will be a need for the governments of developed countries to be seen to be doing something. The problem is how to avoid this 'something' taking the form of greater flexibility in the resort to trade measures against imports from developing countries.

An unequal distribution of the benefits of trade liberalisation and globalisation is also taking place among countries. The least developed and poorer countries may be faced with marginalisation if they are not able to develop a competitive capacity, or if the prices for their traditional export commodities continue to decline. In turn, their governments will be unable to assist those members of their own populations which may find their already precarious economic situation threatened by import competition. Preferential tariff margins may no longer provide a viable mechanism for assisting these countries to compete in world markets and more direct and positive measures by the international community would seem to be required. While lip service has been given to this concept for years, according to the pervasive ideology of the 1980s freer trade should benefit everyone, and the idea that multilateral trade liberalisation could create 'losers' was considered heresy. However, the experience with freeing trade in Europe has shown that policies involving massive transfers of resources are required to enable peripheral and disadvantaged regions to derive benefits from the process of trade liberalisation and economic integration. It has also shown that the freer movement of labour is a particularly important element in this process.

In this context it has been suggested that regional trade agreements can serve as useful laboratories for testing formulations of international rules for new trade-related policy areas.[14] The examination of the experience of regional agreements in successfully incorporating developing countries would provide insight for future approaches at the multilateral level, for example, the contrasting experience of Spain and Portugal in the EC and Mexico in NAFTA.

In light of the success of the Uruguay Round and the political significance given to the conversion of GATT into a World Trade Organization, it may seem surprising that the question would arise as to whether the multilateral trading system is equipped to deal with the challenges presented by globalisation and trade liberalisation. It is becoming more evident, however, that conflicting views are crystallising as to the appropriateness of the use of multilateral trade agreements to deal with the issues to which globalisation has given rise. On the one hand, some economists argue forcefully against any links between the multilateral trade obligations and what they view as social and moral issues such as labour rights and environmental protection, and even against the inclusion of competition policy within the 'umbrella' of the WTO, and some totally reject the idea of policy harmonisation. As noted above, developing countries concerned with the potential trade implications have tended to support this position. However, others who are equally opposed to protectionism, but perhaps more experienced in trade negotiations and closer to political realities, argue that trade agreements may be the appropriate mechanism for dealing with policy harmonisation issues. The question will have to be addressed as to whether the issues arising from globalisation and trade liberalisation, including the need to mitigate the tendencies to an unequal distribution of the benefits, can be adequately dealt with through multilateral trade agreements.

It may be more than a cliché to state that the adjustment to globalisation will require a global response involving not only the WTO and the Bretton Woods institutions, but the whole international system. While certain aspects of the issues identified for a possible new trade agenda could appropriately be dealt with through new trade obligations or the interpretation of existing ones and brought within the WTO umbrella, it is obvious that the whole gamut of the economic and social problems facing the world in the next century cannot be handled through a series of trade agreements enforced through the threat of trade sanctions, or through structural adjustment policies and low interest loans. It is also clear that the 'frontiers' of the multilateral trading system should be established through a process of consensus building, which takes account of the interdependence among the issues and does not merely reflect short-term responses to political pressures or relative bargaining strengths in establishing a negotiating package. It is also crucial that simplistic ideological approaches be abandoned in favour of a new pragmatism based on actual experiences, and serious analysis of current trends.

Many developing countries have increased their strength both as markets for exports and investment and as competitors in world markets with the industrialised countries. A large number of developing countries acceded to GATT during the Uruguay Round and became members of the WTO. China, the fourth largest trader, and Russia will probably become members in the near future. The character of the WTO will differ from GATT, and the familiar scenario of ministers and ambassadors from over one hundred countries waiting in the 'Salle des Pas Perdus', while the 'big two' negotiate the final conclusion may never recur in the future. The question is how to make this stronger position felt in international trade negotiations.

On the other hand, the future agenda should not be defined simply as an outcome of relative bargaining power, but also in recognition that failure to deal with the problems facing the weaker trading countries will have negative effects for all countries, particularly through environmental degradation.

In most of the issues proposed for the new agenda, the potential for conflicting North/South positions is evident. Those issues of particular importance to the 'North' are being examined in depth by the OECD. It would seem essential for the South to reform and streamline its coordination mechanisms and stimulate the sources of intellectual input at its disposal to address these issues, and that of the general position of developing countries in the context of globalisation and trade liberalisation as a matter of priority.

In confronting these challenges, developing countries will have to regain the initiative in the international trade debate. One test of their ability to do so will be UNCTAD IX which is scheduled to take place in mid-1996.

190

The scope of UNCTAD's mandates and the content of its current work programmes suggest that it can contribute in many ways towards a better understanding of the new issues on the international trade agenda in the context of the challenges of liberalisation and globalisation. Investment, trade and environment, erosion of preferences, poverty alleviation, competition policy, regionalism, monetary and financial policies, debt and commodity markets are already being examined by intergovernmental bodies according to their particular terms of reference. UNCTAD has been building up expertise in other areas, such as immigration policies and labour standards. However, it has unfortunately been under recent attack by those who have traditionally wished to deny the United Nations an independent voice on trade issues.

As defined in the Cartagena Commitment, UNCTAD's major role is that of policy analysis and consensus building, to provide constructive approaches, as well as viewpoints, and to generate political impulses which could also be considered by other institutions in accordance with their decision-making powers. UNCTAD IX would provide an opportunity for developing countries to ensure that such political impulses are aimed at providing direction in other international fora, especially the WTO, ensuring that the international framework which will have to be developed to confront the challenges posed by globalisation is consistent with their interests.

NOTES

1 For example, in UNCTAD resolution 159(VI), para. 14.
2 See Shiela Page and Michael Davenport (1994) *World Trade Reform: Do Developing Countries Gain or Lose?*, London: Overseas Development Institute.
3 See UNCTAD (1994) *Trade and Development Report*, UNCTAD/TDR/14: New York and Geneva, UNCTAD.
4 These positions evolved in meetings held in the permanent missions of developing countries at Geneva and in meetings held in the Geneva area and in various developing countries. Technical support from the UNCTAD/UNDP programme was often requested in this process.
5 See Paulo Barthel-Rosa (1994) 'El Nuevo Sistema Multilateral de Comercio', in Patricio Leiva (ed). *La Ronda Uruguay y el Desarrollo de América Latina*, Santiago de Chile: Alfabeta Impresores.
6 See UNCTAD (1994) 'The Outcome of the Uruguay Round: an Initial Assessment', *Supporting Papers to the Trade and Development Report, 1994*, UNCTAD/TDR/14 Supplement, New York: UNCTAD: 225–7.
7 Concluding Remarks by the Minister of Foreign Affairs of Uruguay, Chairman of TNC, Marrakesh, 15 April 1994, GATT document (MTN.TNC/MIN(94)6).
8 See Preparatory Committee Report to the WTO, doc. PC/R of 31.12.1994: 16.
9 See Diana Tussie (1994) 'The Policy Harmonization Debate: What Can Developing Countries Gain From Multilateral Trade Negotiations?' UNCTAD Review: New York and Geneva, UN.
10 See Steve Charnovitz (1994) 'The World Trade Organization and Social Issues', *Journal of World Trade*, Geneva.

11 See Michael Hart (1994) 'Coercion or Cooperation: Social Policy and Future Trade Negotiations', *Canada–United States Law Journal*, Vol. 20.

12 See Commission des communautés européennes (1994) COM (94) 212, final, Bruxelles. *Communication de la Commission au Conseil et au Parlement Européen.* Pour mieux intégrer les pays en développement dans le commerce mondial: Le rôle du SPG pendant la décennie 1995/2004.

13 See Michael Hart (1994) 'Coercion or Cooperation: Social Policy and Future Trade Negotiations', *Canada–United States Law Journal*, Vol. 20.

14 See Geza Feketekuty (1992) 'The New Trade Agenda', Occasional Papers No. 40, published by the Group of Thirty, Washington DC.

INDEX

ACP (African, Caribbean and Pacific) states: agricultural products 90; and European Union 53–4, 90–2, 100–1; Generalised System of Preferences 92–3; Lomé Convention; most favoured nation status 92; Multifibre Arrangement 96; non-EU markets 98; preference erosion 94–5; Uruguay Round 6–7, 82, 93–9; World Trade Organization 99–101
Adamy, W. 123
Africa: CITES 137; diversification 48; European Union 85; food prices 5; preference erosion 94–5; sub-Saharan 85, 86, 99–100; trade growth 27; Uruguay Round 82; *see also* ACP states
Agarwal, J. 93
agricultural products: ACP states 90; Central and Eastern Europe 159–62, 168; OECD 64, 66; tariffication 56, 85–6
agriculture: Aggregate Measurement of Support 40, 80, 161; developing countries 83–4; domestic support 40, 80; European Union 66; exports 95–6, 178; least developed countries 40, 41; market access 40; non-tariff barriers 39; protectionism 78; subsidies 40–1, 57, 161; tariffs 56, 78, 79, 85–6; Uruguay Road 77–81, 83–4; USA 67
agriculture, temperate 5, 77–8, 82–3, 85–6
America, North 24, 25, 26, 32; *see also* Canada; NAFTA; USA
anti-dumping 22, 43–4, 61, 76, 84, 98, 109, 115, 129
anti-subsidy measures 61
anti-surge devices 79

APEC Pacific Rim group 98
ASEAN Free Trade Area 24, 25
Asia: diversification 48–9; European Union 91–2; FDI 32; regionalism, 24–6; Uruguay Round 82

Baldwin, R.E. 20
Balladur, E. 120
banana dispute 99
Basel Convention 137
Benedickson, J. 140
Berne Convention 42, 117
Bhagwati, J. 25, 27
Blair House compromise 56–7
Borrmann, A. 24
Brand, D. 125
brand-names 62
Brander, J.A. 127

Cairns group 178
Canada, protectionism 56
car industry 55
Caribbean 6–7, 94–5; *see also* ACP states
Caribbean Basin Initiative 98, 121
CEEC: *see* Central and Eastern Europe
CEFTA countries 168
Central and Eastern Europe: agricultural goods 159–62, 168; Association Agreement 167–9; CMEA 10, 155, 157, 167; and European Union 10–11, 15, 165–71; and GATT 10–11, 157–65, 171 (n2); investment 170; market access 158–60; market protection 162–3; modernisation gap 169–70; and OECD 53–4, 165; tariffs 158–60, 163; trade changes 27, 156–7, 166; welfare gains 164; world trade 155–6, 163–5

193

telecommunications equipment 55
textiles and clothing 39–40, 48, 64,
 96; *see also* Multifibre Arrangement
Textiles Monitoring Body 75
Toepfer International 57
Tokyo Declaration 174
Tokyo Round: agriculture 40;
 developing countries 175; multilateral
 trade 37, 176; non-tariff barriers 1;
 public procurement 57–8; safeguards
 43; tariff reductions 20
trade: bilateral imbalance 18;
 creation/diversion 52–4; cross-border
 29–30; development-oriented 174–8;
 and environment 9, 50–1, 109–10,
 138–45, 149, 180; expansion 26, 28,
 29, 48; integration 28–9; international rules 49–50; principles 72,
 142–5; Uruguay Round 46–9, 95,
 109–10, 187–91
trade barriers 19–20, 37–8, 113, 126
trade liberalisation 42, 48, 63, 115,
 156–7, 169–70
trade marks 42
trade policy: changes 72, 135–6; political
 economy 20–1; review mechanism 46,
 106; social standards 120–3
trade sanctions 114 (n5), 116, 175
trade unions 117, 123–4, 127–8
trade-related aspects of intellectual
 property rights 42, 77; benefits 73,
 144; OECD 54; piracy 62; Uruguay
 Round 1, 42, 61, 77, 82, 183–4, 187;
 World Trade Organization 105, 146
trade-related investment measures 42–3;
 OECD 54, 59–60; Uruguay Round 1,
 42–3; World Trade Organization 105,
 110, 183
trading blocs 24, 26
Transatlantic Free Trade Area 27
transfer pricing 31
transforming countries: *see* Central and
 Eastern Europe
transnational corporations 29, 31, 182–3;
 see also multinational corporations
Triad 25, 28, 54, 55–8
TRIMS: *see* trade-related investment
 measures
TRIPs: *see* trade-related aspects of
 intellectual property rights

unemployment 2–3, 21, 34, 110, 120,
 126–7

unilateralism 3, 12
unions 117, 123–4, 127–8
United Nations 130; UN Commission
 on Sustainable Development 139, 147;
 UN Conference on Environment and
 Development 134; UNCTAD 139,
 174, 175–6, 190–1; UNCTAD (1994)
 28, 29, 30, 32, 55, 57–8, 59, 60, 61,
 126; UNEP 139
Uruguay Round 1, 17–18, 37–8, 49–51,
 61–4, 82–3, 178–87; ACP states 6–7,
 82, 93–9; agriculture 40–1, 77–81,
 77–81, 83–4; anti-dumping measures
 43–4; countervailing measures 44;
 customs unions 45–6; developing
 countries 71–2, 81–6, 147; dispute
 settlement 44–5; employment 68–9;
 environmental problems 138, 147;
 export subsidies 80–1; free trade
 areas 45–6; GATS 109; industrial
 goods 75–7; institutions 73–5; losers
 185–6; market access 39, 40, 176;
 most favoured nation status 61;
 multilateralism 18, 37, 72–3;
 negotiations 38–46; OECD 4, 52–4,
 63–8; services 41–2; subsidies 44, 109,
 144; tariff reductions 20; textiles and
 clothing 39–40; trade effects 46–9,
 95, 109–10, 187–91; TRIMs 1, 42–3;
 TRIPS 1, 42, 61, 77, 82, 183–4, 187;
 welfare effects 66, 164; World Trade
 Organization 46, 109
USA: agriculture 67; China 62;
 Department of Labor 125; and
 European Union 56–7; foreign
 labour standards 120–1; GATT
 violation 187; Generalised System of
 Preferences 121–2; Jones Act 107;
 Mexican tuna 143; price pressures 58;
 Trade and Competitiveness Act 121;
 wage inequality 127; working
 conditions 118

Versailles, Treaty of 114 (n4), 117
Visegrád countries: *see* Central and
 Eastern Europe
voluntary export restraints 22–3, 39, 43,
 53, 111, 175
voluntary import expansions 22

wages: developing countries 119;
 differentials 118–19; inequality 127,
 188; low 119; minimum 117;